A Spiritual Evolution is compelling, kind, humble and generous, as well as brilliant. It is beautiful. This book, (is) a brilliant expression of kindness and humble love... I have many friends who I want to give this to. Oh, just wait till you get to the Chapters on Justice and... do me one favor, even if you struggle, read at least through Chapter 4. After that, I dare you to quit.

Wm. Paul Young
best-selling author of several books
including *The Shack* and *Eve*

I think of John MacMurray and the growing company of men and women arising in the spirit and power of St Athanasius. The Incarnate image of the triune God – infinite love himself – has triumphed over every blasphemous image of the monster god... once and for all. I'm grateful for John MacMurray's pilgrimage to this revelation and for his commitment to leading us there.

The pastoral destination of John MacMurray's amazing journey and his fatherly theology (is) God is a loving father—not a legalistic judge, not an avenging warrior, not a childhood night terror... Jesus said that. And so too, have the best of his theologians—including St Anthony the Great and John MacMurray of Portland.

Brad Jersak, Ph.D.
best-selling author of several books,
including *A More Christlike God*

A Spiritual Evolution is a gift to anyone who seeks God. John MacMurray presents his theological autobiography with honesty and authenticity that overflows with light and life. Like an artist who slowly and methodically reveals a portrait of their subject, he paints a stunning picture of the Triune God revealed in Scripture in the face of Jesus Christ. With every verbal brush stroke he dismantles thoughts, attitudes, and behaviors that hinder our apprehension and experience of the Father, Son, and Spirit's life and love.

In Socratic style, MacMurray relentlessly and honestly pursues questions that matter. By pursuing answers through the cave to the other side, he removes our fear—restoring to us a God we can believe in and love with all our heart. I couldn't put it down until I saw the story to the end.

Geordie Ziegler, Ph.D.
Associate Pastor
Columbia Presbyterian Church
Vancouver, Washington

"I have been waiting for this book for years. The real story of one man's deliverance from the insanity of 'religion' into walking with the ever present—not absent and he left us a book—Jesus. If your heart longs to be alive and free, this book is a personal map. Beautiful!"

C. Baxter Kruger, Ph.D.
best-selling author of
The Shack Revisited, and *Patmos*
www.perichoresis.org

Nearly two hundred years ago John McCleod Campbell was deposed from the Church of Scotland's ministry for challenging the Calvinist orthodoxy that Christ died only for the elect--not for the world. Other preachers and teachers would follow Campbell, seeking to recover a more biblical account of the doctrines of election and atonement. Among these was George MacDonald, the novelist and writer claimed by C. S. Lewis as his primary theological mentor.

Two centuries is not an enormous stretch in terms of church history. Thus it is no surprise these issues have reemerged in the wake of a newly assertive Calvinistic orthodoxy. And once again voices from within the Reformed family have emerged to challenge the church to repentantly rethink any doctrinal formulations which have inadvertently created conceptual control over the truth of the gospel.

John MacMurray has written a theological memoir that describes a modern Pilgrim's Progress from within the Reformed tradition. It is of unusual honesty in that it combines a relentless intellectual wrestling joined to a deep respect for his readers. With self-effacing candor and wit, MacMurray untwists the distortions of mind and heart, which attach theology more to fear and control than to courage and freedom. Those privileged to have sat under his teaching will be delighted to find that his writing partakes of the same lively mixture of Philadelphia street smarts, unsentimental devotion to Christ, and the focused energy of a seminar conversation. The result is a fresh Trinitarian vision of human freedom, not as the pursuit of self-interest but as the freedom to be for the other.

Roger J. Newell, Ph.D.
Professor Emeritus of Religious Studies
George Fox University
Newberg, Oregon

A SPIRITUAL EVOLUTION

A SPIRITUAL EVOLUTION

Rediscovering The Greatest Story Ever Told

JOHN MACMURRAY

Foreword by Wm. Paul Young

A Spiritual Evolution
By John MacMurray

www.aspiritualevolution.com

Copyright © 2018 by John MacMurray

All rights reserved.

No part of this publication may be reproduced, stored in a retrieval system, or transmitted in any form or by any means—electronic, mechanical, photocopy, recording, or otherwise—without prior written permission of the author, except for brief quotations.

Published by Open Table Press
32370 SE Judd Road
Eagle Creek, Oregon 97022

ISBN 978-1-7323489-0-5

Unless otherwise indicated, Scripture quotations are taken from the HOLY BIBLE, NEW INTERNATIONAL VERSION (NIV). Copyright ©1973, 1978, 1984 International Bible Society. All rights reserved.

Cover and book design: Don Woodward / Ideawave / ideawave.com

Cover Illustration: Mitch Frey / mitchfreyillustration.com

DEDICATION

For my wife Terri
I see in you Their reflection,
for you grace all you touch
with love and compassion,
especially me.

*To journey without being changed
is to be a nomad.
To change without journeying
is to be a chameleon.
To journey and be transformed
by the journey
is to be a pilgrim.*

Mark Nepo

TABLE OF CONTENTS

Foreword — Wm. Paul Young 15

Introduction 23

1. Beginnings 33
2. I'm Right — You're Not 43
3. May I Have Another Slice of Humility, Please? 59
4. I Only Saw Two Persons in the Garden 71
5. Who Do You Know? 93
6. It's All About Relationship 111
7. I Love Justice 123
8. The Justice of Love 145
9. Relentless Love 165
10. The Father's Embrace 185
11. Into Darkness — The Healing of Our Souls 205
12. The Eclipse of Jesus 221
13. The Incarnation — The Beautiful Mystery 231
14. Jesus — The One and Only 243
15. This Pilgrim's Progress 271

Afterword — Brad Jersak 283

Acknowledgements 293

About the Author 299

FOREWORD

by Wm. Paul Young

She stands in front of me with her head bowed, carrying in her stooped posture the wounds of her life for any with eyes to see. I know she is the child of a mean drunk, largely abandoned, absent mother, no attachments, abused, and my friend. I know some of the holy ground of her story, where over time the fiery presence of love has been burning away whatever is not of love's kind. It is a grace-full and painful process, this burning of the false to uncover the true.

"Where is God?" we yell into what so often we perceive to be nothing more than an echo-chamber. The question better asked would be, "Where is her father, her mother, her grandparents, her community?" But no, instead we blame an ever-present God who refuses to stop our devastating choices and are furious that this God would dare relate to both abuser and abused with respect, and thereby allow innocents to suffer.

"What kind of God are you? Why do you so adamantly declare that because of the dignity of our creation you will let our choices stand? Oh God, if you don't stop him, who will? If you don't stop me, who will?"

We want a fist, or gun or cages to do within the heart of Human

Beings what only love can accomplish. Why? Because we don't trust that love is as powerful as the sword. Since we feel impotent to even change the brokenness within our own beings, we want a God who holds out a bloody sword to exact justice against the brokenness of others. If love will not protect me, at least I want someone to pay.

She stands in front of me with her head bowed, carrying in her stooped posture the wounds of her life for any with eyes to see.

"I want to tell you about the power of paradigms," she begins, her voice soft and present. "You were talking today about paradigms and I wanted to give you an illustration of their power from my own life."

For those of you not familiar with the term, and to put it simply, a paradigm is a way of looking at something; it is a pair of internal glasses through which you see and apprehend the world. John, in this book, describes them as "the grid of my existing beliefs" that judge what it is I see or hear. They are the eyes of the heart, mind and soul scratched, darkened and etched by pain, suffering and loss as well as partially wiped clearer by joy, wonder, love and relationship. We filter all our experience through these lenses, and then concretize our perceptions as truth. As a result, that which we believe to be true is as obstructed and clouded as the lens through which we see.

And paradigms are incredibly powerful. So powerful that they can obscure information that is right in front of us, but invisible because it is inconsistent with what is already assumed. I remember in college watching a film where the topic of paradigms was explored in science and psychology. In order to provide evidence about how powerfully paradigm shifts (changing how one sees) are resisted by the mind, the filmmaker engaged the audience itself. In one simple experiment, ten playing cards were flashed on the screen as you watched, each visible for 1/64 of a second; enough time your mind could register the card. Then, they repeated the sequence, same cards but slower: 1/32 of a second, again at 1/16 of a second, again at 1/8 and finally at ¼ of a second. Even then, as slow as it seemed, most of us watching were blind to the fact that the researchers had colored all the spades red and all the hearts black. When we reported the cards back, because of our card-playing paradigm, we saw black hearts as spades and red spades as hearts. It was a shock to realize that our minds had completely deceived us. Information, right in front of us, was invisible to us because we had assumptions (a paradigm) that would not allow us to see the truth. Our paradigm only allowed us to see what we already believed.

Why is this important? Because every human being sees the world, themselves and God through lenses that are crafted by genetics, experience (both painful and wonderful), by religion or its absence, by politics, by the anger and opinions of those around, by childhood trauma, by betrayal, by exposure, by social media, by the arts… and on and on and on.

The impact is profound! Perhaps I hear a rumor (gossip) about someone and I assume it is the truth. This now becomes part of my belief about that person, and everything they do will be run through this grid of how I see them. In addition, my paradigm of them will be reinforced by everything I see or imagine, by what others say and how they relate to that person. In fact, it is likely that I will now begin to add to the story, in order to reinforce the trustworthiness of my own paradigm. I see them at the market and they divert their eyes, proof that what I think of them must be true. And if anyone offers an alternative view, I simply won't be able to acknowledge it in any way other than that which I have already assumed and defended.

And this is not only true about others, but also about ourselves and God. We have a God-paradigm, and we will defend it sometimes to the death. For example, some folks have vociferously attacked the concepts of The Shack because it challenged a paradigm. Now, it is true that the concepts in the book might actually be wrong, but that is not the point. We experience emotional frustration and anger, along with cognitive dissonance where the mind seems to be in a conflict with the heart, or two ideas seems to be mutually exclusive but the newer one is more attractive. We find ourselves vilifying the other party, and if honest, somewhere inside of us we sense that something significant is being attacked and shaken.

If transformation is by the renewing of the mind, guess what? God, being love, must work with us to destroy our false paradigms, even those most precious, because they inhibit our freedom to love, to heal and to mature. And such a process is painful, arduous and confusing.

"I want to tell you about the power of paradigms," she begins, her voice soft and present. "You were talking today about them and I wanted to give you an illustration of their power from my own life."

"From my earliest memories as a little girl," she continues, "Maybe three years old, until I was a teenager, I would pray every night and ask God to change the color of my eyes to blue. You see, my dad was an alcoholic and almost every night when he got drunk he would turn into a fury and begin yelling at me, but there was one thing that hurt me the deepest, that I couldn't escape. He would say, "You are so ugly, even the color of your eyes are the color of cat sh*t!" So, every night before I went to sleep, I would pray, begging God, "Would you please change the color of my eyes to blue."

I am listening, shocked. I am right there with that little girl begging God to change the color of her eyes to blue.

"I thought," she paused, her head still bowed, looking at the ground, "That if God would only change the color of my eyes to blue, then my Dad would love me." She stopped, and looked up. "Paul, what are the color of my eyes?"

I am shocked again. I had never noticed before, but I was staring into two of the most beautiful blue eyes I have ever seen, and the question immediately crossed my mind, "God changed the color of your eyes to blue?"

"Paul," she smiles, "They were always this color, but I didn't know it until I was in my thirties."

Boom! That is the power of a paradigm. This precious woman was once a precious child who was lied to by someone from whom she wanted only love, and it instilled in her a 'color of your eyes paradigm'. For decades, even looking in a mirror, she couldn't see the truth.

In this book, a brilliant expression of kindness and humble love, John will present ideas that will challenge your paradigms. I invite you to relax and engage. There is much to be gained by such exploration, especially for those from my religious side of Christianity. This book will be deeply helpful. Oh, just wait till you get to the Chapters on Justice or the one on… Do me one favor, even if you struggle, read at least through Chapter four. After that, I dare you to quit.

One last note. How can I tell if I am only exchanging one paradigm for another equally invalid perspective? You won't, not in any absolute sense. Trust, not certainty, is the path. But here are a few ways to discern if you are moving in the right direction. Are you attracted to a new way of seeing or thinking, even if it makes you nervous? Can you see where your existing paradigm doesn't work? Do you trust the Holy Spirit to be your teacher? And finally, the one that helps me the most, "Is this new way of thinking and seeing, moving me in the direction of a greater authenticity and capacity to love; to love myself, my neighbor, the stranger and my enemy?" If it is, keep pressing into this part of the journey. God's love is bigger than your process.

My prayer is this – Please, dear God, heal our darkened eyes, so that we might see as you see, freeing us to love.

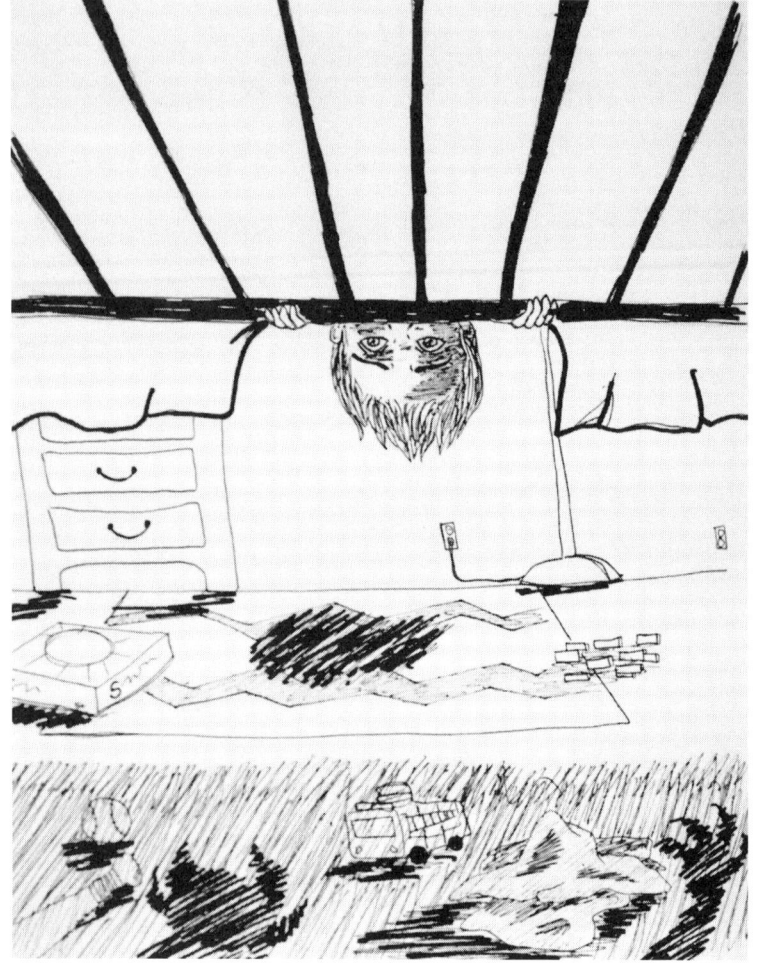

The Monster Under My Bed

by Elle MacMurray

INTRODUCTION

THE MONSTER UNDER MY BED

The darkness of my room embraced me like a good friend. Stillness and quiet offered their soothing touch inviting me to rest. It was the perfect place to sleep. But a whisper of movement stirred me. Was that a sound I heard? Still groggy, I wasn't sure. My eyes strained to see but failed to pierce the darkness. I held my breath, becoming perfectly still, listening even harder to detect the intruder. But the blackness only rewarded my effort with deafening silence. Frozen with fear, my heart pounded like an enormous tribal drum. Terrified it would reveal my presence; I squeezed my eyes shut, foolishly hoping that if I couldn't see anything, then *it* couldn't either. My five-year-old imagination, so often my gift, had become my enemy.

There was a monster under my bed. I knew it. I was sure of it.

Did I dare cry out to my parents? What if they didn't hear me? It most certainly would. Like a boa constrictor tightening its coils, fear gripped my throat and stole my voice. How could I get away? All I could think was: *This has to stop. This has to stop.*

In a burst of courage, I broke the stillness and in one desperate, chaotic movement, I tossed my blankets aside throwing myself over the edge of the bed. Hanging upside down, I glared into the darkness underneath my bed to confront my nemesis…

Forty years later, my anxiety is buried deep, a forgotten memory. I am a Bible teacher, and the truth is, I am vested in my identity. Much of my life has been an educational pursuit of Bible and theology. But after decades of time and effort in this discipline, my memories are awakened. I have discovered that, figuratively speaking; I am still that five-year-old boy afraid of the monster under his bed. It has been a long time coming, but I finally recognized my monster, and it is… God.

Well, it wasn't really God, but what's the difference when the eyes of my heart believed it was? He was the god of my imagination, the product of a story in which I found myself. This story was carefully crafted and shaped by a theology I had embraced to be true. Shame had been the companion of my fear for so long it was difficult to admit. I didn't feel safe, in part, because I was torn between love and threats. My spirit was being crushed. What could I do? Where could I turn? To the One I feared? That was an even scarier proposition. I needed a better narrative.

My friend, Ellen, is a beautiful, bright, and talented woman who, as a valuable member of a ministry team, has been helping others for over two decades. She has been happily married to Mark for almost the same amount of time. Of course, like other couples, their relationship has its ups and downs, but it is solid and it is good. If you sit with her four children for any length of time, you will hear them sing her praises, even if it is sandwiched between complaints about doing chores. And if you happen to visit them, as I have, you will be welcomed immediately. Not long after, you will see and feel the warmth and laughter of a home that is safe, because, above all, this family loves each other.

I do not write with exaggeration or hyperbole when I say Ellen is an amazing woman; she has my deepest respect and she is my friend.

Yet, all is not well in Ellen's soul.

Not long ago, Ellen, Mark, and I spent a rare evening talking on the porch. They had asked about some rumors they had heard. I shared with them how my spirituality was evolving, changing my mind and heart. They were intrigued with my journey, because both had worked with me in the past. As our conversation was ending, I concluded, "You guys, it's hard for me to articulate all this, but I keep thinking that God is better than I have ever imagined."

I looked over at Ellen, and it was obvious something was bothering her. I asked if she was okay, and she nodded, but her watery eyes betrayed her.

"Is there something you want to say?" I asked. She shook her head, gave her best smile, and held up a finger, signaling me to wait a minute. Her body shuddered gently as she attempted a deep breath, trying to maintain control. Then, with tears trickling down her cheeks, she mouthed the words, "Not now." I wanted to get up and hug her and tell her I understood, but for some reason, I didn't.

A few days later, I received an email from Ellen that eloquently explained her thoughts and feelings from our conversation. Here is part of it, which reveals the emotional pain that surfaced that evening.

> "I feel a little like the person who has read romance novels to escape a bad marriage or relationship and escapes for a while wishing that reality could be more like the story, only to end a book and have to gear up for the emptiness that follows and the shame in wishing for more. That is exactly how I would feel after reading books like *The Shack* or *Chronicles of Narnia*. Fighting with theology has been a process for some time."

I wish I had hugged her. I did understand. I think many of us do. Ellen needed a better narrative too.

Some of us insist our reality is better than the stories, even while we continue wearing a mask to cover the fear, pain, and doubt that spread like poison ivy across our souls. We maintain the "good

Christian life" – whatever *that* is – and remain in denial. Honesty only seems to make it worse, because, in moments of clarity when we realize the god we believe in is someone we cannot trust, we feel like we are in free fall. And that's just too scary to admit. Or, just as bad, we stuff our struggle down into some isolated chamber of our soul and press on, only to eventually crash and burn – no longer able to maintain the lie that God is good. Sadly, there are times when our turmoil of honesty sparks nothing more than a feeble attempt at posturing for credibility for a religious peer group. But aren't we just deluding ourselves?

Some change their expectations of God to match their reality. But their inner worlds aren't that strong or good, so they live out the remainder of their lives in frustration, sadness, or despair.

Far too many have become cynical because of their religious experience. Many blame the church as hypocritical or irrelevant, but I believe the problem is far more serious than that. The mass exodus of the disillusioned is so rampant it almost seems pandemic, but it reveals just how deep their frustration goes. They may still believe God exists, but they are angry. They say, along with Riddick in the movie *Pitch Black*, "Oh I believe… I just hate the [@#$%>*]." So, they chuck God overboard like Jonah, believing God is the problem.

And then there are those who just stop believing.

In my late twenties, I took a job teaching at a small, struggling Bible College. Many who attended were older, having decided to study the Bible formally after finishing university. For some, that had been so long ago it was another lifetime. This brought an unusual degree of maturity to our little campus. It was a great time in my life. (It was the closest I ever came in a teaching job to wearing shorts, a Hawaiian shirt, and flip-flops to work.) Even now, a smile crosses my face, and warmth embraces my heart as I remember the people and events of those days. They were good times.

Since the school was a small community, I got to know many of the students fairly well. Many became good friends. One, in particular, (I'll call him Bob), became a close friend. Our friendship extended far beyond our time at school. We had some great laughs, but we also shared some profound moments together. Many of them were in the context of learning and practicing our "Christianity."

But as time moved on, so did we. Our drift apart was probably a combination of things; living on opposite sides of the country certainly didn't help. There was no fault involved. It just happened.

Today, I'm not sure whether Bob would call himself an agnostic or an atheist; I have never asked him. And it doesn't really matter, because I have no desire to find a category for him. I do know he doesn't want to have much to do with the idea of God anymore. Maybe his reality didn't match the expectations he had learned in my class as to what to believe about God. I don't know. Whatever his reasons, he decided to jettison God and adopt a new narrative to make better sense of life.

I have no condemnation for him. None. He believes his life is better; and I have no doubt that in many ways it is, or he wouldn't have made the change. I also know that he believes this improvement in his life is due primarily to his journey *away* from belief. I don't agree entirely with that thinking, but I applaud him for getting up from his seat at the religious table. I also miss him.

Modern technology has eliminated geographical boundaries and shrunk our world, allowing us to easily connect with friends from the past. Not long ago, Bob posted something online. I responded in a personal message. Here's part of what I wrote –

> It's been way too long since we had any meaningful conversation... I apologize for that. I am a friend from the past, maybe a past with which you want to create as much distance as pos-

sible, but nevertheless, still a friend. I have no illusions that our friendship is current or good, but I'd like it to be. I never asked you how, what, and why you've changed, I just knew you had.

I want you to know I applaud your rejection of the god we used to worship. And I apologize for my part in teaching you of that god. I too, have left that table and walked away. Like you, I do not believe he exists. But I have not dismissed god per say. I discovered a better God. I found him to be different and far better than the one you and I rejected. But I'm tired of losing friends. And I don't want to walk out of the room. I'd like to think it's still possible to be together regardless of our differences.

I would like to talk (not debate or argue) with you about this. Mostly, I'd just like to listen. Not because there is some religious urgency, but because I agree with you that our lives are brief so all we do matters. But more importantly, you matter. And you matter to me.

So, would you tell me your story? I don't know if you have ever wanted to. Maybe you were worried I wouldn't listen or that I would argue or that I would treat you like a 'project' to get you back in the fold or maybe you just didn't want to bother. I don't know.

But if you'd be willing, I'd love to listen. I would love to hear.

Your friend,

John

Some of you might feel sorry for Bob, or even Ellen, as though their lives are somehow worse off or that God disapproves of their choices. Don't. They are on a journey, just like every one of us, and they have demonstrated a courage and an honesty that most of us need desperately.

I am grateful for Ellen and Bob's integrity and I am honored to call them friends. I also resonate with them. For I have tested the god of my theology and found him to be an anemic caricature – an imposter really – sitting at the religious table. So, I too have now excused myself from that table, because I have rejected the god seated there. Yet, I still believe.

I suspect Bob and Ellen's struggle is common to us all. Many of us have been, or maybe still are, enslaved to a religious environment that values conformity; so we scarcely whisper our doubts and fears. If we dare to speak of them, it is only in secret – with mumbled voices while cloaked in the darkness of some basement room so we can't be identified. But our courage is growing, and our whispers are finding a stronger voice. We've heard rumors of a better narrative – one that tells of a God who is better than we ever dared to dream.

I am grateful you are considering reading this book. Books being what they are, a one-sided monologue, I realize that what I am really asking you to do is listen. Listen to a story, my story. It's the story of a process of change that has transpired over several decades: a *spiritual evolution*, if you will. It is a journey that is intensely personal, brutally honest, and deeply spiritual. There were times when I felt like I was betraying a heritage or had become a traitor to the truth. Change is a difficult struggle for anyone, let alone a man approaching a half-century of "seeing" God from only one perspective. But I began to read and listen, study and think; and I asked questions… lots and lots of questions.

I remember when I gave myself permission to question the narrative that had shaped so much of my identity and rethink the story I had embraced.

I remember when those questions revealed how troubling my view of God really was and how deep the fear and doubts went that were slowly strangling my soul.

I remember when I first realized I might be wrong – a bit scary considering I had invested my entire life in a story that said believing the right information was what would save me forever.

I remember beginning to gradually believe differently – though I wouldn't dare come out and say it.

I remember when I finally admitted to myself that my beliefs were changing and evolving, and I was going to follow this wherever it led, because I was experiencing a relationship with God that was different – and better.

I remember when I discovered the courage to begin to teach differently. A few friends were honest enough to ask what was changing in me. But then I heard murmurs: "Heresy." "He doesn't believe the Bible anymore."… And invitations to teach began to disappear.

I remember how many who said they were my friends walked away, never once talking with me to hear what I was wrestling through. I guess they just assumed that the gossip they heard was really true.

And I remember the hurt.

But I also remember those, like Ellen, who lit up when I shared what was happening in my life and my experience of God. They shared a similar struggle.

You may be thinking, as I did, "John, aren't you just exchanging one view of God for another? Isn't it just a matter of time before you discover he's just a different version of the same monster?"

Maybe. But I don't think so, because I no longer live in fear of this God. The bait and switch is gone.

It's not that I found some secret narrative that no one else knows about. And I'm certainly not trying to reinvent a god who pleases my imagination and makes me feel better. I think my evolution is more that I'm *rediscovering* a story – one that has been around for a *very* long time. In fact, I'm learning again that it *really* is the greatest story ever told.

For the record, I'm not your adversary. I have no agenda to change your opinions or your beliefs. There is nothing hidden in my pocket or up my sleeve. I only wish to tell you of my journey and the questions I faced along the way:

Questions that set me free from the chains of religious dogmatism.

Questions that began to create *assurance*, not doubt.

Questions that banished my fears of a god that I discovered impossible to trust.

Thankfully, I am still changing because my journey still continues. Just because I've chronicled some of it in a book doesn't mean it's over. And it certainly doesn't mean I think I've found all the answers. I haven't. But my love and trust in Jesus is growing deeper and stronger. And this is a *good* thing.

This book is my invitation to you, the reader. Imagine us sitting at a table, where every person is treated with dignity, because you matter. The table is open – and you belong here. I invite you to join me in this journey of spiritual evolution. My hope is that along the way you will discover that, far from being the monster of your spiritual nightmare – God is better than you can imagine.

CHAPTER 1

BEGINNINGS

To err is human… but it can be overdone.
— Seen on a church sign

Imagine listening to your iPod and each playlist represents a season of your life. But suddenly it's not your playlist; it's someone else's, and then they hit shuffle. Where I grew up, that was called junior high.

My routines each day certainly seemed normal, but I had no idea where my life was headed. I thought I did, but the truth was, I was clueless. Maybe adolescence in the middle-class suburbs of America should be renamed "ignorant bliss."

High school wasn't much different. Confusion was a muzzled puppy, tagging alongside me through the school's corridors. For some, that can produce a deep discontent that leads to some desperate behavior. Not me. Nope. For me, it was more like a pimple. Most of the time, I was oblivious to its existence, until the mirror revealed it on my face. Though it was always embarrassing in public, it was really just a temporary annoyance or irritation. I don't mean that I didn't have my share of frustrations or struggles; I did. But I tended to avoid conversations about important topics like "purpose" or "finding meaning in life," because they caused even *more* confusion. I was too self-absorbed. The way I dealt with life was to act like I wasn't confused. But my act didn't last.

Some people turn to religion for help with their confusion, because it promises freedom. But it doesn't deliver. Instead, it offers dogma – and that's a sleight-of-hand move. Dogma may appear like freedom, because it provides answers, and answers create the illusion that we are not confused. Whether the answers are true or not is another matter. That seems far more like a formula than freedom.

Regardless, I never turned to religion, because I didn't need to. It was already being shoved down my throat. What I knew of God was attached to a Christian church, which seemed like a club organized for the singular purpose of making teenagers' lives miserable. Well, at least it made my life miserable. It had a massive rulebook and always interrupted my weekend plans. And besides all that, it was boring. So, for me, God-talk triggered a resentment waiting to ambush me at every emotional corner. God was someone to be avoided, not someone I should seek, a distant deity to be kept at arm's length.

My life mirrored what Pete Townshend called a "teenage wasteland." Though I had no idea what narcissism or hedonism meant, they were rapidly becoming words that described my lifestyle. Avoid responsibility, do what I want, party with the popular—just have fun. If you had asked me, "How do you think God feels about you?", I probably would've answered, "I don't think he likes me very much." I had this ominous feeling of *disapproval* – that God wasn't very happy with how I lived.

My father had a lot to do with that. Dad was strict and found fault in most everything and everyone. Maybe that's why he appeared to be unhappy more often than not. He had a quick unpredictable temper; and it seemed his anger was always there, lurking just beneath the surface. Though he was never abusive, he flirted right to the edge of it. He justified this behavior by hiding behind the idea that a father's authority was the final word of the house, which really meant *his* view was always the *right* view. A misguided sense of responsibility may have fueled that in him, but I don't think that was the real issue. I think most of it was just a masquerade for control.

One Saturday my dad decided he needed to remind me who was in charge in our home. He had made it clear that he didn't like my long hair, so that morning as I trudged down the stairs, it was no surprise to hear his greeting from behind the newspaper, "Get a haircut."

"Good morning to you too," I mumbled.

His face appeared from behind the paper. "I mean it. Get a haircut, or you can move out."

I stopped, a bit taken back by the threat of his bark.

"No hippies live here," he growled as he buried his face behind the paper again. I knew it wasn't a request.

I know it seems like a trivial thing in today's world, but for some reason, hair length was important back then. Kinda dumb, huh? At the time, I was in eleventh grade, barely sixteen. I'm not sure I was even shaving yet.

As I pled my case, he raised his hand to stop me. "You don't make the rules in this house. The Bible says, obey your parents."

I hate the Bible, I thought.

The ultimatum continued. "When you have your own home, you can grow your hair down to the ground, for all I care. But as long as you live here, you do what I say."

I didn't think he'd actually kick me out on the streets, but for some reason, I decided to stand my ground. I don't know why I chose it as the hill on which I would die. Maybe it was my rebelliousness, or maybe I just woke up in a grumpy mood. Whatever. But I do know I wanted some independence, and so began a battle of wills.

"I'm almost seventeen, dammit. I think I should be able to grow my hair as long as I want!" That was my feeble attempt at being a defiant smartass.

I'm not sure if it was the "dammit" or my defiant tone, but at that point, my dad got seriously angry. "You want independence? I'll give you independence! If you don't cut your hair, you need to leave, and I mean now!"

So, I went upstairs and packed a bag, each shirt and sock thrown in with increasing force as my frustration boiled over. Obsessed with the unfairness of it all, I stood at the door, ready to leave, having no idea where I'd go. My mom was crying – pleading with both of us – telling my dad he couldn't let me leave and me that I had nowhere to go. "Just cut your hair; it'll grow back," she begged.

Well, my dad won that battle. No surprise there. I'm kind of glad, though. I mean, how could I have explained that I became homeless at age sixteen, because I wouldn't cut my hair? Who would believe me?

I got a haircut that day, but it was, as Pink Floyd sang, "another brick in the wall" between my dad and me. It confirmed my dad's place firmly at the bottom of my list of people I didn't like. And he dragged God down there with him.

I didn't like being bullied. What teenager does? Using God as his enforcer or like a trump card to justify his view of reality only poured gas on the sparks of my rebellion toward anything to do with God.

My view of God, which was already on the ropes, took another hit because of the relational distance between my dad and me. He was an aloof man who kept even his friends at arm's length. Rarely was he emotionally transparent, except when he got angry. "Intimate" was the last word I would've used to describe our relationship. Some would say my dad was "old school." No matter. For whatever reason, only my dad and God know, he struggled with expressing love. When he tried to show it, which was rare, it was usually through gifts. It was as if he thought an external gift could replace a relationship of love between father and son.[1]

And then there were my friends. My three best friends were agnostic. Though they accepted the fact that my family was religious, I can't say I got a whole lot of encouragement from them to believe in God. They mostly just blew it off or made fun of it.

My larger circle of friends, like most of the kids in my high school, were far more interested in parties than theology and I definitely hung out with the party crowd. So, finding a place where I could fit in and be accepted was about as close as I came to a serious discussion of anything remotely spiritual.

In the end; my experiences with my friends, family, and church all left me skeptical and apathetic toward God. Disinterested at best. I don't remember being angry with God, and I don't think I had anything against God; I just thought he was someone I'd rather avoid. My distorted view of God only strengthened my resolve to run from him. I was kind of like a hamster, continuously running in his little wheel, unable to break free from my ever-turning, yet never-changing perspective.

The summer before my senior year, my wheel stopped abruptly and unexpectedly. I never saw it coming. It wasn't an earth-shattering tragedy, but it was life changing nonetheless. It was a major turning point in my life and it came from the least likely of places—I met a man named Rick, the new youth pastor at church.

For a long time, I couldn't stand Rick, and I didn't bother hiding my feelings about him either. I thought he was another Christian

---

[1] You may be thinking, "Whoa! MacMurray has serious father issues!" Hmm . . . and who doesn't? Now that I'm a parent, I know my children will have issues with me. It's unavoidable. I'm a fallen, twisted man. My hope is to minimize any damage I've caused and shorten their list of issues. I try to humbly ask forgiveness from my children whenever I wrong them. For the record, I loved my dad, and he and I reconciled. He lived with my family in our home for almost seven years; ever since I evacuated him the day before Hurricane Katrina hit the Gulf Coast. Papa Mac had cancer and forgot who I was on many days. He was two weeks shy of ninety-two when he passed into the embrace of the Father, Son, and Spirit.

do-gooder – all show to keep his membership at "Club Church" in good standing. He seemed phony to me, yet he treated me with kindness, respect, and love. Ironically, that was a huge part of why I thought he was fake. It was hard to believe he was for real.

That summer I went to a Christian youth camp in Florida with about a thousand other kids. No kidding. It was gigantic! On the first night of camp, a few friends and I planned to party, going off to smoke some weed. We were wasting no time in the "Sunshine State." But when I went to retrieve my stash, it was gone. As I was talking with my friends about what could possibly have happened, a couple of camp security guards entered our room and politely asked (required really) us to follow them to their offices in the basement. They weren't smiling. This was definitely not good. I wondered if they were going to cuff us.

You may or may not be aware of the social and spiritual climate of that time, for it was the early seventies. Those of us who grew up then might remember…

I was in a Christian camp, in the South, where Bible reading came before breakfast. It was the epicenter of all who would be conservatively religious. These kind folks equated smoking pot with the worst kinds of evil – from the "free sex" immorality of the hippies to the deranged and murderous behavior of Charles Manson. Pretty much every social ill that plagued our world was blamed on the people who sold and used marijuana. (Okay, that may be a bit of exaggeration, but not much.)

My uniformed friends escorted us through a maze of hallways, old painted pipes following us along the low ceilings, like snakes just above our heads. We shuffled farther and farther down endless stairs, each step leading us deeper into purgatory, until we finally arrived at "the Office."

It was a dimly lit room, like something out of an early 1920s cops-and-robbers movie. The walls were bare, except for a Bible verse framed next to a large wooden desk. It read, "Do not be deceived. God is not mocked. Whatever a man sows, that will he also reap." I could see what appeared to be a dungeon in the back.

As I sat there waiting, fear crawled from my stomach around my back, up my spine and neck and into my throat. When the chief of security, a man who had more in common with a Mack truck than a human being, entered the room, I was a wreck. After what seemed like hours of interrogation, I pleaded with them, "Please, please, whatever you do, do not tell our youth leader." All I could think of was Rick squealing to my dad and me being grounded for my entire senior year. My yearbook picture would be a mug shot, probably lifted from the local police station, me in stripes holding a card with a series of numbers on it, a pathetic look on my face. They made no promises.

A couple of days later, while everyone was going to lunch, Rick called three of us into a side room. I assumed he wanted to talk about how we were enjoying camp.

We filed into the room, and he got right to the point. "I'm the one who took your drugs." His tone wasn't angry; it sounded almost apologetic. He had the look of someone who was very uncomfortable, as if he was in pain.

We froze – like deer caught in headlights. It was like I was in a cartoon, and all I could imagine was a tombstone at the end of a pile of dirt engraved with, "Here lies John – RIP." My life was over.

At first, I was mad. *Who the hell does this guy think he is butting into my life like this? I really don't like this guy.* But then I kicked into self-preservation mode, my mind racing to come up with some kind of lie that could save me from my dad's wrath. Rick sat quietly and watched me squirm, my facial expression changing from anger to panic.

"John, I have known for almost a year now that you smoke pot, and I've never told a soul. I know you don't like me – I've heard things – word gets around, you know? But I've been praying for you, hoping you would end your destructive choices. So, I took your stash, hoping you'd listen to some of what's going on and come to know that Jesus really cares about you. I do too."

He knew? How did he know? Who could have told him? Oh my gosh – he can read my mind! As I slowly began to recover from the initial shock another shock wave crashed into my mind… *he knew and he hadn't said a word.* I couldn't figure this guy out. But I knew right then that all my assumptions and judgments of him had been dead wrong. I had been blindsided by love… and it was beautiful.

In the months that followed, I hounded Rick like a mosquito goes after blood on a hot humid summer day in the swamps of Louisiana. Rick suffered hundreds of conversations and millions of questions and he listened with the patience of a saint. Over time, I started believing the whole Jesus/Bible thing was true. His Jesus was different. He was no longer the distant, disapproving deity of my dad or the boring rules-loving god of my church.

As my perception of Jesus started to shift, I began to experience joy. Like pouring sugar into a steaming cup of Northwest coffee, sweetness flooded my soul.

My heart knew it. My head did too. Wanting to know truth began to matter to me. I wanted everyone to know what I had discovered.

However, a strange thing happened as I grew in my discovery. I'm not sure when or how it began but I slowly lost the joy that had arrived with my encounter with Jesus. It was almost as if I woke up one day and "truth" had become more like a set of propositions than a relationship with a person. I think part of the reason for that slow drifting was that, unlike relationships – which can be messy and constantly changing – propositions are more concrete and can be analyzed and studied, resulting in what seems like certainty. This fit right into the habits and ruts that I had been living in previously.

But I have since discovered there is a lot of illusion that passes for certainty. What I think I was really chasing was *assurance*.

Additionally, when we regard truth only in the abstract, it allows us to think of it as a set of ideas or dogma that needs to be defended. To imagine there is a battle, an "us and them" gave purpose to my studies, even to my life. I was determined to be on the front lines, leading the charge!

As a result, it seemed like the more I learned about the Bible, the more exclusive and prejudiced my Jesus became. I thought that was a *good* thing – at least the exclusivity part. Truth is exclusive by its very nature, right?

Differences were emphasized between those who believe Jesus and those who don't, and that emphasis became my focus. Ever so slowly, my joy of the truth was replaced with arrogance over my perceived possession of the truth. That "us and them" that I imagined? They weren't just some fanatical types, who persecuted anyone who believed in God; it was anyone who didn't see Jesus the way I did.

My best friends became those who perceived the truth as much like me as possible. Within our youth group, cliques developed based on different opinions as well as the kind of shoes people wore.

Subconsciously, I thought the way to measure success in my spiritual life was to have answers to every question. Well, at least the really important ones. After all, don't answers help eliminate confusion? They do, but I had gone far beyond simply finding answers, I had become obsessed with being *right*. So much so, that I equated my "rightness" as proof of my spiritual growth.

For me, doctrinal certainty was the same as spiritual maturity.

Maybe this period of my life was just the normal immaturity of a high schooler. Or it may have been just plain stupidity. I have no doubt that, to some degree, both of those things were true. But when you're perceived as a spiritual leader with a master's degree nearly twenty-five years after high school and you're still obsessed with being right? What's my excuse then? It's not just immaturity or stupidity anymore. Maybe, I was the one who was the monster.

Today, I have come to think that dogmatism is really just profound doubt masquerading as certainty. What began with purity and joy deteriorated into a quest to be right - assuming that would place me alongside the One who is always right. What could be wrong with that?

Just this – My love of the truth became a love of ideas, not love of a *person*.

CHAPTER

2

I'M RIGHT, YOU'RE NOT

What we know is a drop.
What we don't know is an ocean.

— Sir Isaac Newton

As a young follower of Jesus, I began to learn the Bible and, implicitly, a way of interpreting it. I never really questioned this because of the excitement and joy of my newfound faith. This interpretive "lens" became like glasses (that I rarely took off) through which I saw God, others, myself – *everything*. This is not unusual. Everybody constructs a world-view, a way of seeing life. What I was building wasn't bad; there was a lot of good in it too. No one's way of seeing and understanding is *all* bad, neither is it *all* good. However, the longer I wore these glasses the more my attitude became unhealthy. There was a very dark side beginning to emerge. I found that the more I learned, the more the gospel became about being right instead of being the good news of Jesus's love for the human race.

Bible College only reinforced this – big time. Seminary gave it an air of respectability and intelligence, but it also drove the wedge deeper into my heart.

I had a list of questions that I assumed would grow shorter as my knowledge grew greater. Not so. The list grew longer. A *lot* longer.

Meanwhile, my desire to teach also grew. I figured all I needed to do was learn some basic communication skills and then I would be able to teach. Sure enough, opportunities began to come my way, and I began to influence others. Now they could catch my cold too.

| I Confess | As my knowledge of information grew, so did my arrogance. |

I needed someone to keep me from running in the circle of the same perceptions over and over again – someone that would set me free of my hamster's wheel. Maybe I just needed someone to break the cage.

Isn't it odd that our good nature has been so bent and gnarled that we can take information – even information that is good and true – and turn it into an advantage that gives us superiority over others? You've heard it before: knowledge is power. Sadly, when it should bring life, it often brings death instead. Saint Paul warned a group of people about this: "Knowledge puffs up, but love builds up."[2]

I wonder if they listened to his advice. I didn't.

On the other hand, knowing a person doesn't seem to have the same effect as simply knowing information. Instead of arrogance, it usually leads us toward love and humility.

Have you ever met someone who didn't have any educational degrees but knew Jesus well? I have. His name was Amos. He was a retired farmer with Pennsylvania Dutch roots. He was a loving, humble man, always serving those in need. Quick to listen yet slow to speak, he was always ready with a word of kindness or encouragement.

---

2 I Corinthians 8:1

One day we were in a leadership meeting, and a passionate debate was taking place – more like an argument. Voices were raised, dire threats were made, and tempers boiled over. After everyone else had finished voicing their opinions, Amos was the guy in the room who spoke calmly, humbly and lovingly. He offered a piece of wisdom that hadn't occurred to anyone in all of our bluster. We were embarrassed, maybe even a bit ashamed. Thankfully, we took his advice.

Amos was Jesus staring me right in the face.

| I Confess | Subconsciously, I thought of myself as better than Amos. |

Though I respected Amos and he made an impression on me, I paid little attention. After all, he was just a simple man, not really a teacher. So, I continued my quest to be right, which I thought would secure my status as an authority and validate my success as a teacher.

I have a sense that I'm not unique in this regard, that I'm not alone. This saddens me deeply. I've wondered if maybe we aren't all running in the same hamster's cage together. As long as I looked around me, everything seemed okay. Every once in a while, someone broke out of the cage. "Hey, there goes Rick and Amos. Wonder where they're going?"

Have you ever been to a class that began by pointing out what is different or unique about Christianity? I taught those. I'm embarrassed to tell you how many conversations I began by emphasizing what is different and *superior* about what I believe from what others believe. Too many.

There were times my lectures weren't really about finding truth because I assumed I already possessed the truth. That's a bit strange, isn't it? As if the truth is a thing, a commodity that one can possess, right? And if I dug a little deeper into why I taught I found that there were times my motivation to teach was simply a means to feel better about myself.

Why? Why would I teach with such shallow motives? It went something like this: I became convinced that my beliefs were unique and therefore true, so it seemed obvious to me that my beliefs were better than other beliefs. This thinking is so flawed I am amazed I ever bought into it. But I know why I did. Like I said, it made me feel better about myself.

First, since when does unique equal true? Second, to feel better about myself, I crossed a line from "my beliefs are better" to "I am better." So, the way I was able to feel better about myself was to establish in my mind that I was superior to others. Ugh! Third, the entire enterprise was based on the assumption that my interpretation of the information was accurate. I could go on, but I hope you get my point.

Here's the rub: I trust Jesus, and I believe he is the truth, so I think to believe him is better than not believing him. But it morphed into *I am* better than you are. I'm "in," and you're not.

If you sensed that attitude in someone, how would you respond? Would you even like that person?

Here's an idea: what if, when we are engaged in conversations on spiritual matters, we ask people what they think and then treat their thoughts and answers with dignity and respect by listening to them, because we actually value their thoughts, whether they agree with us or not? Doesn't that sound like a conversation you'd like to have with someone who you know disagrees with you?

Call me crazy, but I think if I'm less argumentative, I'll have fewer arguments. Isn't that a good thing?

Do you think God agrees with your opinion of him most of the time?

Some of the time?

Ever?

When God disagrees with us, does he dehumanize us by no longer treating us with the dignity and value he gave us when he created us? Does God stop loving us when he disagrees with us? Does God have an insatiable desire to prove to every person in creation that he is right, and we are wrong? Or does God just send everyone to hell if they disagree with him?

Let that sit awhile…

What if God had designed life so that every time we thought incorrectly, something would happen that embarrassed us but proved he was right? For example, what if we gained an ounce of weight every time we were wrong? Oh man… I'd be the size of ten humpback whales – literally. Or what if every time we were wrong, a buzzer sounded, alerting people to our stupidity, and a small purple cloud magically appeared over our heads, like in the cartoons, that said, "Wrong!"

Aren't you glad you're not God? But my problem – and it is a problem – is that, many times, *I want to be.*

Have you ever thought about all the denominations in Christianity and the hundreds of variations within each denomination? Study them. I would suggest that many of the "distinctions" you find are over issues that have more than one legitimate interpretation. And by "legitimate" I mean an actual, valid meaning.

What does it say about us if there are issues that can be legitimately understood in several different ways yet our opinions of them so divide us that we find it impossible to get along? Is our disagreement really over the truth or merely our perception of it?

How important is it for us, as a community, to be right?

How important is it for *you* to be right?

When a pastor of notoriety was interviewed by *USA Today* regarding his opinion on the popular novel, *The Shack*, he said, "If you haven't read *The Shack*, don't!" Then he went off sermonizing on its evils. Is this about "defending the truth" or who is right?

When another notable pastor/author tweeted a three-word epitaph about the author of *Love Wins*, was he "defending the truth" or merely pointing out who he thought was right?

Incidentally, less than two weeks after the promotional video for *Love Wins* was released, a devastating tsunami struck the west coast of Japan, causing unimaginable suffering, pain, and loss to tens of thousands of people. Yet, students at a local Christian university (many preparing for careers in ministry) were arguing vehemently over the book *far more* than voicing any concern or prayers for the survivors of the tsunami, even though the book had yet to be released.

By the way, where did we get this idea that truth needs to be defended anyway?

Sadly, I am no better.

I confess	**I wanted to be right to win the admiration of others.**

Often, when asked what I thought about a book, my reply would be, "I really like the book, *but...*"

Why did I have to throw the "but" in there? Though I may have agreed with some of the ideas in a particular book, I felt compelled to state where I disagreed, because I wanted whoever was listening to think I knew at least as much as the author did, probably more. If I blew out his light, maybe my light would appear brighter.

Hmm… because I believed I was right, I had to let people know the author was wrong? Really?

If being right wasn't so important to me, when people asked my opinion of a book, I could simply say, "I really liked the book" and leave it at that. No "buts." I wonder if we realize that the only book that we will ever agree with 100 percent is the one we write. And even that will change in a few years.

I have asked myself why I felt and acted this way. Here's what I came up with: it strengthened my perception of being a man of authority. If I could convince you the author was wrong, then, by default, you would think I was smarter than the author.

If I was smarter, then I was a better authority.

If I was a better authority, I would have more influence and power.

If I had influence and power, I would be perceived as a leader.

If I was a leader, I would believe I was successful.

If I believed I was successful, I could feel good about myself.

If I felt good about myself, I would be happy.

And I would continue the cycle as long as I could – to remain happy.

Truth had little to do with *any* of this.

I Confess | **I was becoming like my dad.**

I have had my fair share of arguments, maybe more, with people I love and with those I barely know. I've influenced others to do the same. And, like my dad, the card I pulled most often was the "God card."

I also became an expert at finding fault in others. If there was a "Zen master level" at being judgmental, I was practically there. The truth is, most of the time, I cared more about being right than I cared about people.

As an observation, not a judgment, pastors and teachers in the hierarchy of celebrity found within the Christian subculture are especially adept at subtly turning the good news of Jesus into the gospel of "I'm right" or "I'm better" and if you agree with me, together we are better than them. Few will discuss this, and even fewer will admit to it. But it's there, rooted deep in our blindness. Have you listened to the way many pastors "preach" to their congregations?

You may be thinking, "That sounds really judgmental." I assure you, it's not.

I know, because I'm guilty. I'm a teacher.

Why does this surprise us? It shouldn't. My job was at risk, and so was my identity.

It was like the "I like the book, but…" thing. The "but" was there, because it allowed me the illusion of influence and control. It inflated my ego and self-worth by helping me feel like people still needed me. They needed my expertise to help them navigate the murky waters of God's revelation. In my arrogance, I equated my opinion of the truth *as the truth*.

Is it any wonder that I (like so many others in leadership in churches and Christian organizations) struggled and complained so often of being under appreciated? Why is it that we think we have failed when someone stops attending our church, class, or meeting?

This isn't just a pastor or teacher thing. We all do this. How often do we fight or argue with others in a desperate attempt to cling to our self-perceived identity? Husbands and wives do it. Children and parents do it. Employers and employees do it. Teachers and students do it. It seems it's our *modus operandi*.

People imitated my lead as a teacher. The problem is, my lead was only as good as it followed Jesus's lead. Let's just say my leadership wasn't as good as I thought it was.

The other day I happened to be out by the road in front of my house when a car started slowing down as it approached my driveway. I didn't recognize the car so I was a bit curious as to who it might be. When the van finally reached me, and the passenger window came down I was delighted to see the smiling faces of an old friend and his wife. Before they were married, Mark and Lisa had both been regulars at a bible study I taught for college-age people. Even though we live only a short drive from each other, we haven't been very good at staying in touch. Our lack of communication isn't intentional on their part or mine. It's just life. But seeing them again made me miss them.

We reminisced a bit and I brought up all the years we had met in our home. Mark mentioned that he had recently run into another student from the community that met in our home and they too had taken a stroll down memory lane. He proceeded to tell me how they remembered with fondness the nights when someone would venture a viewpoint that didn't see scripture or God through my glasses and how they loved the way I would "rip them to shreds". He was quick to add I always did it with patience and kindness, but they thoroughly enjoyed how I would dismantle people's opinions. I immediately apologized for my former behavior, but he waved me off interrupting my apology graciously explaining that he wasn't trying to find fault with me – on the contrary, he was complimenting me.

We talked a bit more and promised to connect with each other soon, agreeing it had been far too long since our last conversation. But when he drove away all I could think was, *Oh God, this is how I am remembered by those I taught – an expert at dismantling others' opinions to prove I was right!*

What was that I was saying about the way I used to lead?

I Confess	I wanted influence and enjoyed the esteem of others. Like my dad, I liked the illusion of control more than taking the risk of authentic relationship.

I had heard the sirens' song, and their voices seduced me to the dark side of influence – lust for control. Rarely was I aware of my distorted thinking. It's not like I was an arrogant SOB, but ignorance does not absolve me. Far too often my leadership was more about my own hidden agendas than Jesus's love and truth.

But candidly, it doesn't matter whether I was aware of this or not. What I knew for sure was that being right was *extremely* important to me; so much so, I was willing to sacrifice relationships to maintain my "rightness."

However, being right wasn't the real end game for me. The pot of gold at the end of my rainbow was control. But control is an illusion. It creates the impression that I am the master of my destiny.

So, I clung to being right like it was my life preserver – because it was. I defended my "rightness" with tenacity and passion, because I thought my life, *not the truth*, depended on it.

The real problem was that my identity and self-worth were connected far more to being right and being perceived as an expert in the Bible than Jesus's relationship with me.

My disease was often self-inflicted. However, I bought into a subculture that bowed to an invisible hierarchy as the evidence of success, providing the perfect environment for the cancer to grow. I mean, if everyone around you is playing football, why would you quote the rules of basketball?

It seems to be the norm among us religious types that we become so focused on being right that the only time we won't debate, argue or rail with rhetoric is when we are serving someone less fortunate.

They need our help, so we treat them with kindness, a listening ear, and a compassionate heart.

We can argue with them later when they've gotten better...

I Confess	There were times I would have rather been right than help my neighbor.

I hijacked authentic relationship. In my hypocrisy, my compassion could be as thin as the paper on which this book is printed. Many times, I only acted with compassion, because I had an agenda. By impressing others with how I seemed to act like Jesus, my so-called philanthropy gave me "props" by making me look good in the eyes of others. This inflated my illusion of success. Real compassion and love of the other for the other's sake was only a speck in my heart.

Add to this the intoxicating belief that I was one of the "good guys" doing God's will, and it all became heady, delusional stuff. Disagree with me about something that matters to me? Watch our "relationship" come crashing down with the speed of a tornado ripping through a trailer park. And if reconciliation were ever going to happen, it would require an apology on *your* part.

The excuses I used to justify my lack of compassion were pathetic. But the motives of our hearts are exposed when someone comes to us in need who has absolutely nothing to offer in return that could promote our agenda or enhance our status. Maybe this is one of many reasons Jesus encourages us to help the poor.

Is it possible to be a person of conviction and passion for truth yet live with love and humility? I believe it is. I haven't met a lot of people like this, but I've met a few. Enough to know it's possible. It's hard, no doubt. It's the razor's edge.

Jesus is a person of conviction and passion. He is also the epitome of love and humility.[3] He doesn't just have a passion for the truth; he *is* the truth.

Imagine for a moment Jesus teaching the Scriptures; the One who claimed to be the Word teaching the written word. As you listen, he is interrupted. People begin quarreling with Jesus. They tell him he's wrong, that he's not teaching Scripture correctly. Publicly embarrassing this rogue rabbi is not enough for them to elevate their imagined status among the crowd. They go far beyond the label of heresy; they accuse him of being demon possessed.[4]

The irony is nearly unimaginable. Arrogance is at a crescendo. They are arguing with the One who inspired their scriptures and accusing him of not knowing what he's talking about. They claim to know the scriptures better than he does. He is wrong, and they are right.[5]

So many times, I've struggled with stories like this in the gospel narratives. How could these people be so blind? I mean, if Jesus is the eternal Creator, then he is speaking the words he gave them. That is certainly the view of the gospel narrators.

Who are these people?

They are the religious leaders of their community seeking to follow the one true God, the God of their ancestors – Abraham, Moses, and David. They call on others to do the same. They are not some fringe cult that drinks Kool-Aid. They are the leaders and teachers of their faith. They are in *love* with their scriptures, memorizing huge chunks regularly and teaching it faithfully day after day, week after

---

3   Matthew 11:28-30.
4   This story is found in Matthew 12:1-42.
5   How does Jesus respond to this scathing accusation? Does the narrative read, "From that time on Jesus went throughout the countryside defending his interpretation of the Scriptures, proving everyone else wrong"? Interestingly, Matthew chooses to quote Isaiah 42:1-4. It sheds light on Jesus's response, particularly in Matthew 12:19, "He will not quarrel or cry out"

week. They see themselves as defenders of the truth. They are the moral pillars in their neighborhoods who pursue morality with a zeal that would make us *very* uncomfortable. They are very conservative both morally and doctrinally and even politically.[6] They are the gatekeepers… they are the Pharisees.

I Confess | I was a Pharisee.

The thoughts above described me. I studied and memorized scripture. I wanted to follow the one true God. And yet, I stood in my self-righteousness, enslaved to my pride and the performance-oriented thinking that fueled it, ready to fight or argue with any who disagreed with my view of Jesus, *including Jesus.*

I had to repent many, many times. I still do. Again, I wonder if I'm alone in this. Could it be that we modern religious types in the West are rapidly becoming, maybe already are, the new Pharisees?

When will I learn to love without an agenda?

When will I learn to love simply for the other's sake?

Maybe we should take our cues from Jesus and join him in a walk of discovery of what it means to participate in his very life and truth. The life and truth of God.

Jesus's truth is incarnational, not ideological.

The scriptures tell us of the eternal Son who came in the flesh to include us in his relationship with his Father. This required a stooping down on God's part, unparalleled in the history of religion. A stooping down to reach us in the darkness in which we live and rescue us from our own self-destruction. This humility was the stunning revelation that God loves us *for our sake.*

---

[6] Observe John's take on their collusion with the current administration, particularly in their plot to kill Jesus, in John 12.

God did not come to us in flesh to prove he was right.

Maybe the reason we think it's so important to get all the right answers is because we see life as one gigantic test, and God is the great teacher in the sky keeping the final grade book. It's pass or fail. Deep in our hearts, we're scared to death that we will fail the ultimate exam.

My friend, Paul often says, "John, in the end, truth is not a perfectly balanced organized set of beliefs. Nor is it a list of doctrines and creeds that you check off whenever you agree. Truth is a person. His name is Jesus."

I am not saying I don't believe in propositions; I do. Besides, that would be silly. It would be impossible to have a meaningful conversation without propositions. For the record, Jesus stated many propositions according to the narrators of the gospels. Here's one: "I am the way, the truth, and the life…"[7]

Did you see that? Truth is a person.

Every one of us is travelling through this thing called life. And for each of us, our awareness of what is true and good is also at different points along the way. Sure, there are millions of side roads, detours, turnouts, and points of interest that draw our attention, but we are all on the same journey.

For too long I have embraced the gospel of "I am right!" And if you don't agree with me, "You are wrong!" Too long I've lived in arrogance disguised as a lover and defender of abstract truth.

I no longer want to live there.

---

[7] John 14:6

Today, I want to be able to embrace anyone with the love the triune God has for everyone. A love that takes into account right and wrong but also sees beyond it to relationship, a love that goes beyond our wildest imagination, even when we're wrong.

I want to bear witness to his relentless love, not my ability to win an argument.

CHAPTER 3

MAY I HAVE ANOTHER SLICE OF HUMILITY, PLEASE?

> *Humility is the "snow leopard" of virtues;*
> *actual sightings are rare indeed.*
>
> — Anonymous

I assume that if you're reading this, you have decided to stick with me, even after my confession about my descent into the abyss of the "I'm right, you're not" way of thinking and my hopeful, ongoing ascent back to sanity. So, I'm gonna go out on a limb here… I've probably raised a few questions, yes? Kind of like mosquito bites on your religious skin that itch like crazy. And if you're like me, it's not just a few bites; your entire body is covered. Here are a few that occurred to me.

"John, do you believe that what you believe is true?"

Absolutely. If I didn't, I hope I'd believe differently. Why would I continue believing what I know or think is a lie?

"So then, what's the difference between believing that what you believe is the truth and believing that you are always right? And if there is a difference, how do you keep the one from morphing into the other?" Good questions. Probably a lot of parts to an answer, and I'm not sure what they all are, but I think I've stumbled onto a couple ideas. Namely, humility and teach-ability, cousins in the virtue family, if you will.

I would suggest that these qualities are not only necessary to discern but more importantly, they are crucial to the learning process making it *transformative* rather than merely an accumulation of data. In my opinion, these are forgotten virtues. Few people talk about them. Probably even fewer aspire to them. I can't remember the last time I heard a preacher speak on either topic. I would propose that everything we think, feel, and believe needs to be wrapped in the clothes of humility. I might even go so far as to state this is some sort of truism for me. I don't see how we can ever escape the vice-like grip of arrogance without a healthy portion of humility.

Some of the most meaningful times I've ever experienced were when I spoke with close friends, and we shared our dreams, shared what we really want our lives to be. Here's something I've never heard anyone share in those conversations: "I dream that my life will someday be marked with humility." It is a remarkable thing that someone would dream of being virtuous, but even among the virtues, it seems no one wants to be known for humility.

I remember being in a particular class my last semester of college. I can recall the room where I was sitting, even who was teaching, but I have no idea what was being said (if only we teachers knew). Anyway, for some reason, and I haven't a clue as to what it was, maybe boredom, I recall having a conversation with God in my head during class. And this part I remember like it was yesterday – I asked God to make me a humble man. I said that because "man" is my gender and "humble" is what I thought I should be but knew I wasn't.

I also recall that immediately after offering my short prayer, a question bolted into my consciousness: "Why do you want to be humble?" And in a moment of unguarded honesty, I silently replied, "So others will know that I'm humble."

I was sitting in one of those desk chairs – the ones where the desk part flips up from the side. Simultaneously, my body slumped down and forward, my elbows crashed on the desk as my face fell into my hands, and I thought, *"Oh God, I am so messed up."*

It was a teachable moment.

| I Confess | The "false" me is not humble and never will be. |

You don't have to do brain surgery on me to see if you can find humility hiding in there somewhere. You can dig around all you want. You won't find it. It just doesn't exist in the false me. But the real me is humble. And I actually want to be; I really do. My prayer those many years ago was genuine. It's just that the minute you think you have it, you don't.

After many decades, I'm beginning to live out of the truth of my being, but many times it feels like I'm climbing Everest: I'm only a half day out of base camp and I've already lost my Sherpa. But I know the head Sherpa. Her name is *Ruach*.[8] Her name means, "wind," "breath," or "Spirit." She helps many a clueless climber.

For me, humility has been as elusive as a jackrabbit, and I feel like I'm trying to catch it with two broken legs. So, before we go and try that, maybe we should ask, "What is humility anyway?"

Defining humility isn't easy either – at least not to me. Here's Webster's definition: "the quality or state of not thinking you are better than other people." This helps a bit by explaining what humble people *don't* think, but what do humble people actually think?

We call it a virtue, so we all agree it's a good thing. But that doesn't define it either. Clearly, it's a mindset more than an action. It's a way of perceiving ourselves and reality. Yet, we can only see humility when people act. That helps. At least we have a category for it, but still no definition.

Beyond this, most definitions fizzle. They may list a bunch of words, but all they're really doing is attempting to describe it. For-

---

8   Ruach is an English equivalent of the Hebrew word rûah. The vast majority of times it is used in the Old Testament it appears as feminine.

tunately, the descriptions are usually pretty good. So, for what it's worth, here's my attempt:

Humility is kind. When we see people act in humility, kindness is present too.

Humility is tender and compassionate. It is sensitive. It genuinely cares for the needs of others.

Humility gives preference to others. Its love of others is equal to its love of self. It is not self-centered or self-seeking.

Humility is level headed. It is not conceited. It doesn't think more highly of itself than it should.

Humility doesn't brag. It is content to be silent. When it must speak, it does so with deeds and truth.

Humility doesn't seek or crave attention, status, or fame. It doesn't need the praise of people to feel secure or validated. It doesn't want to be "somebody." It already knows it is.

Humility doesn't lust for control; it trusts the One who is in control.

Humility neither listens to nor believes the whisper, "I am not…" It is secure in who it is and comfortable inside it's own skin.

Humility is willing to serve without reward. The good it does in service is reward enough.

Humility isn't independent, and it does not live in isolation. By its very nature, it needs others to be manifest.

As I thought about this, it dawned on me that humility looks an awful lot like love; so much so, I'd say it's an expression of it. It also occurred to me that there is a core idea behind and throughout my description.

I think humility is a virtue born out of coming to terms with who I really am. In other words, it's an identity issue. And my identity is primarily an issue of who I am, not what I do. When I begin to understand what true significance, value, and worth are and where I find them, then, it seems, I am on the road called "humility."

I am coming to the realization that my worth and my value were given to me, along with every other human being who has ever lived, when God created me. My accomplishments, my knowledge, my virtues or my beliefs do not increase my value as a person, as though they are assets to be added to the ledger of my worthiness.

In most cultures, sports are not the venue where we normally see humility. Quick: give me your top five athletes who are humble… go! They don't come bursting on the scene, do they? This is particularly true of professional athletes, and even more so in the West, where huge sums of money are at stake. But every once in a while, we get a peek at it. In athletics, it's called "selflessness" or "class."

I remember watching game four of the 2014 NBA Finals, the San Antonio Spurs vs. the Miami Heat. I don't usually watch the NBA; I've lost interest. Not in the game itself, but in the way it's played. I prefer college hoops. But alas, it too seems to be disintegrating into the same game. No surprise; many of the players are playing with the hope they can get in that other game – the NBA. I digress.

I like watching the Spurs. They play together. Unselfishly. As a *team*. So, I was watching the game, and San Antonio put up a shot. Then, from out of nowhere, Kawhi Leonard, who, at age twenty-two, would become the championship series MVP, came flying down the lane, grabbed the ball about two feet above the rim, and slammed it down with both hands, all in one graceful motion. In the classic words of Chris Farley in the movie *Tommy Boy*, it… was… awesome! Those of you that saw it and remember it know I'm not exaggerating. It was truly an extraordinary play. Had they been at home in San Antonio in front of their fans, it would have been madness and bedlam.

But it's what happened *after* that impressed me even more. Leonard landed, turned, and ran back on defense.

No shirt grabbing or chest pounding.

No standing under the basket like a frozen statue screaming until he ran out of breath.

No "in yo face" intimidating stare down of his opponents. Leonard just turned and ran back to play defense. How cool is that? I *loved* it. I can't say that's humility exactly, because I don't know the young man. But in the heat of competition, it was awfully close.

Here's my point: humility will not allow me the illusion that I am superior to others because of my achievements, abilities, knowledge, or beliefs. It resists the temptation to think or behave in a way that conveys any notion of that. I can't be condescending and humble at the same time. They are mutually exclusive.

I realize this kind of thinking flies in the face of our utilitarian culture – which it seems, the church has adopted, embraced and promoted. Well, at least I did. And in my experience, it seems many others have as well. But this is a revolution in thinking of which I'd like to be a part.

My value and worth as a person do not come from what I do or how much I know. It comes from who I am, by virtue of being human. God's breath of life infused every one of us with value and worth. This is why everyone I meet is worth knowing, and everyone has value to offer my life. Their value is often not realized by them and hence not offered, but it is there all the same. No matter our race, gender, education, or socio-economic achievements, our worth and value are intrinsic to what it means to be human, because the Father, Son, and Spirit gave this to us when they spoke us into existence and crafted us in their likeness.

Not only am I discovering that my beliefs add nothing to my worth as a human; neither do my contributions or performance, whether good or bad. I believe in Jesus, but this does not add one bit of value to me as a person. Not a thing. My value does not increase because I believe something, nor does it decrease if I don't.

However, a large number of religious types think we are worth more to God if we have the correct beliefs and/or behave in the right way. I know. I used to think that way. Consequently, I taught with that perspective.

That said, practically speaking, knowledge and experience do, in fact, add value to life situations.

Say you are in a serious car accident. You need immediate medical attention. The first two people to arrive on the scene are a professional pianist and a registered nurse. Clearly, the nurse's training, knowledge, and skills are far more valuable to you at that moment. Unless you *really* want to hear a Brahms concerto played on the hood of your car. Sort of obvious, right?

But what isn't quite as obvious is this: as far as our identities are concerned, the nurse and the pianist are equally valuable. Neither is better than the other. Both were given value by a Creator who loves them deeply. And the proof of that is this: they are human, and they are here. *They exist.*

I am also beginning to understand that humility never acts out of self-love, self-worship, or selfish ambition, no matter how you "Christianize" it or dress it up with whatever religion you choose. That's a bastardization of truth any way you slice it.

I've always known that I am not God. It's not rocket science. Only God is always right all the time. Yet, at many times and in many ways, I have acted as though my knowledge made me God-like. I was convinced God agreed with me, which made my opinions unquestionably right. This, in part, may explain the sickness and malaise we call the human condition.

I am growing to learn that my beliefs are just that: *beliefs*. I may believe something to be true, but that's just it – I *believe* it to be true. Is there room for arrogance when confronted by wonder and mystery? Humility, it would seem, slams the door on arrogance, because it recognizes we need each other.

Are there not issues and questions of God that will never be answered by the observable, verifiable, scientific method? Don't we all address these things with faith? (even though there are mountains of evidence, stacked higher than the Himalayas, upon which the claims of Jesus stand) So, whatever answers or understanding I may think I have, they ultimately need to be grounded in God's character, which is good. And the revelation that "God is good" is Jesus.

It seems that what really matters are not my beliefs but who I know. Life is in a person, not the accuracy of my beliefs. It is him that I trust.

"But," I used to protest, "how can you say that? Literally hundreds of scriptures proclaim that belief/faith are necessary for eternal life!"

I know, I know. The gospels claim Jesus said this repeatedly. Hold that question, okay? It's a good one, and it deserves consideration. We'll get to it when we discuss relationship.

I've often wondered: What was it about Jesus that drew people to him? What did they see? What did they experience? Here's what I think might be at least a part of it —

Since Jesus knew exactly who he was and who his Father was, he had no identity crisis. He never lived out of a false sense of himself. As a result, his very nature was humble allowing him to stoop beneath us to lift us up to a place of dignity and worth – a place we find hard to believe of ourselves. He treated us with self-giving, other-centered love and compassion. So, when people encountered him – his words, his tone of voice, the compassion they saw in his eyes – their souls felt their worth. This is still true today.

I studied under and, on a couple of occasions, had the privilege to teach with Dr. John Sailhamer, a brilliant professor who received his PhD in Semitic languages from UCLA. He has since passed through death's vale into the embrace of the Father, Son, and Spirit, but he is still considered by many to have been one of the world's top scholars in Old Testament studies.

John had just finished a week-long intensive, 8:00 to 5:00 every day, and I was taking him to the airport. I thought it had been a terrific class. My mind and heart were full. We had discussed some deep issues, and the conversations had often been long and academic by necessity. But he brought a joy, a real enthusiasm for his craft. He always had time for any student or any question. His demeanor never changed no matter how vigorously we disagreed. Always kind, always gracious, he was clearly comfortable in his skin.

I don't remember exactly what we were talking about in the car; probably something that had come up in class. However, I do remember there being a long silence, and then he spoke with a soft, steady voice that revealed a man of conviction, a man who had given his life, almost fifty years, to research, study, and teaching. He spoke with a tone that I knew was serious.

"I hope I've expressed God's words well," he said quietly. "I find new things all the time. Things that tell me I've been wrong. *I have so much to learn.*"

I looked over at him, and he was gazing out the windshield with the look of someone deep in thought. He turned and smiled at me. "I really do."

I experienced real humility in the presence of Dr. Sailhamer.

It was Jesus staring me right in the face again.

So, let's return to our original question from the beginning of this chapter. I believe genuine humility is crucial to preventing my beliefs from devolving into the "I'm right, you're not" mentality. But I think there is another part to this answer, and that is…

Teach-ability

Being teachable is linked somehow with humility. Maybe it's one of the ways that humility expresses itself in our lives.

How does one become teachable? Where does it start?

Being willing to listen?

Having a thirst to know, an inquisitiveness to ask?

Being willing to do the work of reading and studying?

I think the starting point for being teachable is the admission that my ideas or beliefs may be wrong. It doesn't matter how wrong, whether it's just a tweak to my viewpoint or major surgery. If I think I'm right with such a passionate zeal that I can't even consider the possibility that I'm wrong, then what reason would there be to change? It seems obvious that I am only willing to change *if* I believe there is the possibility that I may be wrong.

I Confess	**I thought I was teachable, but I wasn't, not really.**

I believed I was teachable, because I was willing to listen to others whose views and beliefs were different from mine. Being willing to listen is a good thing, but for me, it was mostly just a ruse.

The truth was, I would listen, but I had no interest in *hearing*. I would listen with my mind shut. Primarily because I didn't believe "they" had anything to offer. My mind was either made up, or I assumed I knew more than they did. I endeavored to be compassionate and have a teachable spirit, but arrogance was the idol to which I bowed.

Sometimes, I would listen *and* hear, but it was only so I could construct better arguments to defend my view or attack theirs. I would listen, quietly searching for a crack in their beliefs, where I could find leverage to convert them to mine. For Pete's sake, we had classes that trained us to do this! We were also taught that we should do this politely. God knows, we didn't want to offend those we tried to dismantle with our arguments. That wouldn't be Christian!

Interestingly, in the instances mentioned above, I always sensed my attitude wasn't quite right – even in my blindness. Though I rarely acknowledged this to God – or anyone else – I finally realized that I wasn't very teachable. That awareness was a glimmer of hope that my self-deception hadn't completely overrun my sanity.

However, there were also rare times when I really wanted to be teachable, conversations when I tried to listen and hear without an agenda or when I tried to learn without trying to manipulate the outcome. Those were my *best* times. I have found many sincere and genuine people in this place. But those attempts were fatally flawed too, because they fell short of transforming my view and, thus, my life.

When I was presented with a different idea or belief, I would typically examine or evaluate that idea through the grid of my existing beliefs. By that I mean my beliefs would be the judge of the truthfulness of what I had been given. If I agreed with the idea, I'd add it to my matrix. If I didn't agree, then the learning process stopped.

When I did this, I thought I was being teachable. I wasn't. What I was really doing was comparing ideas or beliefs with my own. So, though I learned, I only learned things that reinforced my existing beliefs. Consequently, my ideas and beliefs became even more entrenched, because the entire process only confirmed the viewpoint I already held.

What if genuine teachability looks a bit more like the following? First, I acknowledge the possibility my current beliefs may be wrong. This creates freedom and space to be willing to listen. Then I leave all my agendas back home in the bathroom. I already have a device that was designed to get rid of that crap. Then instead of just critiquing a different view, I give that view permission to critique me. This involves examining and evaluating my existing way of seeing life through a lens I may not be used to wearing - not unlike trying on a new pair of glasses to discover if I can actually see better.

At first, especially if we're talking about a wholesale change, this may seem a bit more than we can handle, almost like a betrayal of what we've been taught. If that's the case, it will be scary – or at least a bit unnerving. But it is only then that our ideas or beliefs can transform us.

This is not as easy to do as it may sound. In fact, it's very hard. But I'm convinced it's worth it. If we hope to grow beyond our upbringing, culture, and prejudices, then we must be teachable and engage these conversations with humility. It's essential. I hope you will find this attitude and perspective in the pages that follow, for that was the spirit in which this book was written.

So, here's the question: am I willing to swim in what may be, for me, new and maybe even uncharted waters, to see if it brings healing and refreshment to my soul?

In the pages that follow, I explore where smarter and wiser people hesitate to go. I jump headlong into some profoundly deep pools: the nature of God, justice, the Incarnation, and so on. I don't do this because I believe I'm some sort of guru who has found hidden truth that no one else has heard. Nor do I think I have some new insight to offer the world. On the contrary, I've discovered that the narrative I'm suggesting has been around for a long time. I'd like to think I'm someone who's interested in *recovering* some things we might have forgotten. I have no desire to agitate a hornet's nest. This just happens to be where my journey has taken me. My guess is that if you're still reading, your journey resembles mine.

God knows, I don't know it all. But, thank God, now I realize it too.

I'm learning, and I'm growing, and I'm finding that I'm more in love with Jesus than ever before. And I'm also discovering that he's better than I ever thought he was… and those are the *best* things.

CHAPTER 4

I ONLY SAW TWO PERSONS IN THE GARDEN

We want to share with you the love and joy and freedom and light that we already know within ourselves.

— Papa in The Shack

If I were to ask you to list the most significant influences in your life, you could probably name several pretty quickly. For some it might be music. Others might cite a book or piece of literature. Some would take a broader approach and point to culture or their life at home, school, or work. Many would make it more of a "who" question. They would identify parents, husbands/wives, friends, teachers, great personalities in history, and so forth. There isn't a "correct" answer to this question. How could there be? It's a personal question.

I think by now you are aware that our perception of God is pretty high on my list. The narrative you and I learned about God – whatever it is – has shaped what we believe him to be like. If I'm right, then our concept of God is foundational for the construction of our worldview. I know it was for me. In fact, much of this book is my story of how some ideas, both precious and sacred to me, affected the quality of my "house." Some were good, others bad. Good foundation, good home. Bad foundation, and I call *Allstate* and hope their hands are as good as they promise.

One Sunday I was teaching a class in a church that I had attended for over twenty-nine years. About 150 or so people were in the room, many of them I knew. I was curious about something, so I started our time together with a question.

"How many of you have been attending this church for at least five years?"

Almost every hand went up.

"Please, keep your hands up. How many have attended for at least ten years?"

A few hands went down.

"Fifteen years?"

More hands dropped.

"Twenty?"

About half the room still had their hands up.

Finally, I asked, "How many have been here since the beginning, since the first time you met as a church?" As I recall, about fifteen hands were still waving in the air.

I don't remember if I said anything at that point, and I'm not sure exactly what I thought, but I remember being impressed. Not only because of how long they had attended, (thirty-three years) but also because they had seen it all. They had been involved throughout the entire history of the church – and they were still there.

"Here's my question," I continued. "Regardless of how long you've been around here, when was the last time you heard in a sermon, Bible study, home group, or whatever, a presentation on the subject of the Trinity?"

The room was quiet as they thought. I waited a bit. Silence. Then someone muttered, "Can't remember ever hearing any." A bunch of heads nodded in agreement. Others were still thinking.

I was taken back. I didn't think their experience would be unanimous.

There I was, standing in front of a room of good folks. They treated each other with dignity and respect. Jesus was their Lord. They believed and studied the Bible. They were committed to what many would consider a good church. Yet, no one could remember a single message about the Trinity. Thirty-three years worth of messages, lessons, and Bible studies. Not even one… *ever*?

For me, it confirmed a growing suspicion.

"Wow!" I exclaimed, breaking the silence. "This is a bit surprising, isn't it? No one can recall this subject ever being taught? Now before you get too far ahead of me, don't read into what I'm saying," I cautioned. "I didn't ask the question to embarrass the staff or condemn the pastors and teachers. I'd never do that. Heck, I'm one of the teachers!" We all laughed. "But really, what do you think this means, besides the obvious fact that we have clearly ignored the subject?"

My words hung in the air like a Portland fog. I waited again. More silence.

"Maybe," I offered finally, "we haven't talked about it, because we're afraid. Or maybe we don't think we can ever understand it, because the Trinity doesn't make sense to us, and we feel foolish for believing it every time we try to talk about it. Or maybe it means we don't think it's that important to talk about. At the very least, it means something in our thinking is terribly out of balance."

I Confess	**I had completely ignored the Trinity.**

All three possibilities I suggested above were true of me. Somewhere along my journey, I adopted the idea that the Trinity is not something easily comprehended. And this is true, right? But I took that to the extreme. If I couldn't understand it, why bother thinking or talking about it? So, I didn't.

It also didn't make sense to me. How does 1+1+1=1? But I had seven years of university and graduate studies in Bible and theology;

I should know this! Embarrassed, I felt a bit foolish when I tried to explain it, because I thought I should but knew I couldn't.

Interestingly, I don't remember ever having a prolonged discussion about the Trinity during all those years of education. Oh, it was mentioned and defended, but that was about the extent of it. Consequently, an implicit learning was taking place as I subconsciously observed the absence of conversation about the Trinity. Later, as I began to teach, I imitated this approach to the subject with my students. I rarely, if ever, mentioned it. More importantly, the net effect for me was, though I genuinely believed the Trinity was true, that belief had little influence on my theology or me.

I do not say this to blame my teachers or my school. Ultimately, the responsibility lies squarely with me. However, in my experience in the American Protestant church, it seems we have banished the subject of the Trinity to somewhere in the back of the closet between the book, *What Do Earthworms Eat?* and the movie, *Watching Moss Grow: The Apocalypse*. At least I did.[9] Thankfully, that is changing, and the conversation is growing.

Here's the weird thing: as "Christians," we believe that understanding God as Trinity is essential to what it means to be a Christian. It is and has been considered orthodoxy for the majority of Church history. This is true across denominational boundaries. C.S. Lewis thought the Trinity was so essential to the Christian faith that he included a discussion on the subject in his book, *Mere Christianity*. By "mere" he meant basic, foundational, essential.

So, for all my talk about orthodoxy or what is "mere" Christianity, why did I never schedule a single hour in twenty-nine years to teach about a subject supposedly so core to my faith and so essential

---

9   I encourage you to pick up a copy of a systematic theology written by an American scholar in the last fifty to seventy-five years. At what point in their systematic presentation do they place a discussion of the Trinity? I think you might be surprised at how unimportant many deem this discussion to be. Thankfully, this is changing.

to what we understand God's being and nature to be?

My question lingers even now. What do you think it means?

I can't answer for the leadership back then, and I don't want to try. But I wonder if there isn't an incredible disconnect for many of us, larger than we care to admit, between what we say we believe and what we actually believe. It's not as far-fetched as we might think. This scenario continues even today.[10]

So, though I won't answer for others, I *can* answer for me.

| I Confess | When I thought of Adam walking in the garden with God, I always visualized Adam and another person. It never occurred to me that it might have been Adam with three other persons. |

The main reason I never taught on the Trinity was because I rarely thought about the Trinity. Quite frankly, I didn't think it was that important. I figured, "I don't think about this a whole lot, and I seem to be doing okay, so how important could it be?" Ugh! I really did have a "caveman" attitude.

Obviously, God as Trinity was *not* the starting point in my thinking about God. And yet, in an ironic twist, I would have summarized my life's message as a pursuit of knowing God, even though I rarely, if ever, thought of God as the relationship of Father, Son, and Spirit. Confusing, huh?

Little did I know my foundation was in such bad shape that my "house" of theological ideas was about to implode. Where was that Allstate number anyway?

---

10   The experience of my church is not unique. Unfortunately, it is more common than we might think. I have since told this story many times around the country, and, as a result, many have told me of similar experiences.

For me, the Trinity was a theological construct that I acknowledged in my head as true, but I lived from my heart as though it wasn't. Jesus aside, the god I worshipped, prayed to, and spoke of was far more like Aristotle's "Unmoved Mover," a self-centered, non-communal deity. A being who has been alone in isolation from all eternity. He was a deity who, in his perfection, thought only the best thoughts. These, of course, were necessarily of himself, for who is better than God? And no matter how I tried to "theologize" that god, he was flat-out narcissistic.

Relating to God as the community of Father, Son, and Spirit had about as much effect on me as drinking a diet soda once a month will help me lose weight. Or walking fifty feet to the mailbox will prevent me from having a heart attack. I had a wee bit of cognitive dissonance.

At best, I envisioned some hybrid likeness of God. Like I said, it never occurred to me there might be four persons in the Garden.

So, who was the God I was attempting to know and, in turn, encouraging others to know?

| I Confess | There was a disconnect between what I believed and the way I lived. |

Suppose I told you I intellectually agree that God exists as a Triune being, but then I teach and act like God is an individual. Wouldn't that make you question the genuineness of my belief? I think it would. It's kind of like being a practical atheist. That is, someone who genuinely believes God exists but lives like he or she doesn't. The person's intellectual assent has no influence on his or her life.

Practically speaking, I was non-Trinitarian. This is far closer to heresy than orthodoxy; no small thing for a Bible teacher of the Christian faith. I certainly never thought I was flirting with heresy.

The hypocrisy of my belief never occurred to me. If you had called me a heretic, I might have looked at you like you had brain damage. Quite possibly, I might have called you an idiot – with love, of course – and never spoken to you again.

What difference does it make if I believe God is a triune being? I am beginning to learn that it makes all the difference in the world!

If theology is the study of God, then the question of *who* God is must be our first question, the starting point of our discussion.

Maybe you've never thought about God's nature or essence, but if you did, where do you think you'd start? Maybe a better way to ask is this: what do you think is the deepest truth of God's being? If you were to peel back the layers of all that he does, what would be the source of his actions—the reservoir, so to speak, from which his thoughts, feelings, and actions flow?

Over the past several years, I often ask this question at the beginning of a meeting in which I've been invited to speak. I know; there's not much entertainment value in that, and I would venture it's not the best first impression to make with a bunch of young people. Problem is, I really *do* think it's the best place to start when having a conversation with someone who wants to know God.

Typically, I'll write people's responses on the board. Different words, usually describing God's character, are lobbed into the discussion. By the time we're done, our list looks like a course on the attributes of God.

But as I list each character trait on the board, I press the question further. "But is there something behind that, something deeper, even more essential?" This, I think, is an important question, for no matter which attribute we pick, it is nothing more than a description of a person. And that which is deeper than the character trait of a person is *the person*.

I would share what I believed for most of my life was the answer: God is the sum total of all his attributes in perfect balance. But that doesn't really change the problem. Are you the sum total of all your characteristics, or are you more? And here's a bit of a curve: God is not just one person but *three*.

What I was suggesting to my students is that the deepest truth about the essence of God's being is that he exists as a *relationship* of three persons. Consequently, this should be the starting point of how we think of God and the foundation for how we engage in any and all conversations about him.

So then, I offer this to begin our discussion of the question, "Who is God?": God is a being who exists as three persons in communion.[11] God does not possess relationship as a quality of his character. Relationship is not a thing God does; it is *who God is*.

He is a triune being. That is his essence. His being is indivisible. The Father, Son, and Spirit think, feel, and act as one. They are inseparable. In fact, this oneness is so much their reality it is said that they are *in* one another. Yet, they exist as three distinct persons in the one being without losing themselves or being absorbed into each other.

If the relationship of the Father, Son, and Spirit is not the fundamental truth of God's nature, then what is? What is "behind" the back of the Father, Son, and Spirit? Who is the "god" who is really God?

Let's consider the alternative: if God's essence is *not* relationship, then relationship is foreign to his nature. He only takes on a relational mode of existence when he creates other persons. Relationship becomes an add-on, something added to his deeper, truer self. This would mean there was a time when God existed alone in isolation, because there was no other to which he could relate.

---

11 *"The Christian God is not an Absolute Individual in isolation, but a community of persons in selfless, abiding communion."* Kallistos Ware, The Orthodox Way, rev. ed. (Crestwood: St. Vladimir's Seminary Press, 1998), 28.

Further, if there was a time when God was alone then it follows logically that the deepest motive of God is to serve God's self. All he thinks, feels and does is for himself – his self-interest. For before he creates, there is no 'other' to love, care for, or relate to. So then, he is actually a God of self-centered love and self-glorification. We call a person like this a narcissist. And if this is God, then we are so screwed.

What we are back to is Aristotle's unknowable deity, the absolute individual in isolation, and we have *no idea* who that god really is. We are left clueless. We are left with a god we do not know, so we make one up, spawned out of the confusion of our minds.

This was the monster under my bed.

And here's the thing: as long as I lived thinking of God as a monster, I had no assurance. If God was first and foremost a lover of himself, then how could I ever really trust him? I would always doubt, way down deep, stuffed in the bottom of my soul, wondering, "Is he really good?" Sometimes, I felt like I was juggling chainsaws while on fire, strapped with dynamite, trembling over a pit of starving alligators, balancing on a thread and saying, "I hope he loves me…"

Have you ever had a friend who only loved you because you gave him or her things – a one-sided relationship – and as long as life was unfolding as your "friend" imagined it should, the relationship was great? But if life ever got really tough and everything went squirrely or, God forbid, your friend blamed you for his or her difficulties, did you have any idea how the person would treat you?

What kind of relationship exists when one of the persons lives in fear of the other?

Can you ever really trust someone like that? Ultimately, you know such a person will only look out for him or herself.

Ever have a friend like that?
Try having a god like that. Try trusting a god like that.
You may already have. I *know* I did.

In my journey, it was my theological studies that fueled my fallen imagination. No matter how much religious vocabulary I used to make God look good, he wasn't. Is it any wonder fear lurked in the shadows of my soul? For if God is not good, then there is no safe place to be found anywhere in this life or the next.

Some, no doubt, would respond with, "Isn't it normal to feel like that regarding God?

I would suggest (adamantly) that, no, it isn't normal to live in fear.

But I would argue with myself, convincing myself God wasn't like that because of Jesus. That is so true, but we'll get to that later...

I confess	The God of my imagination had replaced Jesus as the revelation of God.

How far had my imagination fallen? The catch-22 for me was that it was my mess, the false me, if you will, that was twisting my theological education.

Though I never intended to read my theology into Scripture, the truth was, I did. I defined words like "justice," "holiness," "glory," and so on by infusing human versions of these words into their meaning, and then I projected them onto my vision of a solitary God. This was problematic for several reasons.

- Even our best definitions are not as good as God. He is better.
- I thought of his attributes as descriptions of an *individual*, not descriptions of a relationship of three persons. I rarely, if ever, thought about what their relationship was like.
- These descriptions were more like abstract ideas than descriptions rooted in relationship. For example, what would God's grace

look like if it were defined as a characteristic found within the relationship of the Father, Son, and Spirit? No matter how we think about grace, our best shot at knowing what it actually is requires that we try and understand it as a description of how these three persons relate.

Consequently, I ended up seeing God two different ways. First, through a lens seeing him as someone who seemed to care more for himself than anything or anyone else and, second, as someone who loved me enough to die for me. This caused no small amount of tension and confusion.

For example, it seems to make sense, at least to me, that whatever God cares for originates in what he is essentially like. I mentioned previously that I didn't think relationship was essential to God's being. However, I *did think* moral perfection was essential to his being. So, within God's being, morality (the essential) trumped relationship (the non-essential). Practically speaking, this meant morality was more important to God than those whom he had created. To personalize it, he cared more about my behavior than he cared about me.

As I got older, I became increasingly aware of how often I stumbled morally. I believed God loved me, but when I applied this view of God to my failures, I was *certain* he didn't like me. I assumed he was constantly disappointed with me, because I so rarely got it right.

And, though some told me this was not true, my inner conflict made that difficult to believe. And what Bible teacher is going to admit that?

My thinking led to far more than tension. I became a frustrated, insecure, performance-driven leader who convinced others of my version of a "holy" god. And I had the theology and texts to prove my point.

I took pride in my "high view of God," teaching with passion that his purpose in creating everything was for those he created to glorify and honor him above all things, so his greatness would be displayed throughout eternity to everyone, everywhere. I taught that he made all things to bring himself happiness and that his dreams and designs for creation were for his pleasure.[12] His goal in creating was to be praised by all he had made. For some reason, he wanted someone else, besides himself, to see and speak how great he is.

Sharing his life of loving communion wasn't his purpose for creation. Putting it on display and having us all gawk from a distance at how beautiful he is was the goal. If we happened to get the "crumbs of his goodness from the table," that was only a gracious by-product of creation, not its purpose. That's like saying the purpose in studying is to pass a test; if you happen to learn something along the way, great.

What this amounted to was me perceiving creation as the plan of a being who resides somewhere "up there" spinning out clever ideas that make him look good. Then again, if God is really like that, then God has objectified humanity. In other words, we are merely objects to be used for some grand, self-fulfilling design; not persons who are loved with an overflowing and everlasting love.

This god – *my* god – was a self-inflated, egocentric deity. Add omnipotence, and you have a monster more terrifying than any sci-fi movie has ever imagined.

But God isn't like that, is he?

I remember buying my son, Chris, his first bike. After teaching him the basic idea of how to ride, we put the training wheels on and let him practice. After a week or so of riding every day around our driveway, he got the courage to try riding without the help of the

---

12 *"God has done all things, from creation to consummation, for the preservation and display of his glory." John Piper, Desiring God: Meditations of a Christian Hedonist, 1st ed., (Multnomah Press, 1986), 33.*

extra wheels. My wife and I were pretty excited. I held the bike as he climbed on, his oversized helmet sliding off to one side. We gave him some final instructions and asked, "Are you ready?" He gave us a thumbs-up, we gave him the countdown, and then the big push.

"Lift off!" I announced.

"Start peddling!" his mom encouraged.

I ran right behind him with my arms extended on either side as he wobbled for about thirty or forty feet, ready to catch him if he fell. Then, all of a sudden… he got it. He found that sweet spot with his balance, and he was off.

We started whooping like crazy Green Bay Packers fans. After circling our driveway, he rolled up to us and hit the brakes. From beneath his crooked helmet beamed the largest, most contagious grin ever to grace a little boy's face. Undiluted joy was written from ear to ear. Terri and I looked at each other and saw the same grin on our faces. "Way to go, Superman!" Terri exclaimed as high fives were profusely exchanged.

What if, when the laughter and congratulations subsided, I had turned to Chris and offered this imaginary advice since it was obviously a teaching moment…

> "Chris, your mom and I love you. I hope that teaching you how to ride this bike we gave you shows that. But our love for you is not the main reason why we did this. We want you to ride this bike throughout the neighborhood to tell everyone this story of our goodness to you. Let everyone know how awesome we are for loving you, for blessing you with this bike and teaching you how to ride. We want you to ride for our glory.

After all we have done for you, it is the least you can do for us, okay, son?"[13]

Eerie right? Actually, it's sick, twisted, and more than a bit narcissistic on my part, yes? Yet, I heard and verbalized this kind of thinking for the first forty years of my life. Ugh!

The truth is, we gave Chris the bike simply because we love him – period. It was a gift. We participated with him in his discovery of joy and celebrated the new confidence from his accomplishment. *This was our glory.* We didn't need to offer any "spiritual" advice. And we certainly didn't need to burden him with some guilt-motivated sense of responsibility to do something for God. Is this not a far better narrative of God's purpose in creation? In our hearts, we *know* it is.

Yet, I presented the story of creation as if God made it all so everyone would acknowledge his greatness. When we disobeyed, God's purpose took a nosedive into free fall, because in our broken condition, we weren't about to acknowledge anybody's greatness other than our own. This obviously offended God and brought him displeasure. And apparently, there was a rule in play that specified the penalty for our disobedience in displeasing him was eternal death. If that isn't scary enough, consider this: God created the rules and established the penalty knowing this outcome… *and he created anyway.*

Since most of humanity are not followers of Jesus, this narrative suggests that God creates knowing most of his creation will experience eternal death. Why would he do that? How does this scenario fulfill what I previously believed was God's goal in the first place? Far more will spend eternity hating him than singing his praises.

---

13 *Sharing in our children's discoveries and accomplishments is the joy and glory of any good parent whether we are teaching them to drive a car, clean a bathtub, or swing a golf club. Dr. Baxter Kruger deserves credit as the one who made this connection for me between these moments and our view of God when he told of his son learning to ride his bike. I share a similar experience.*

Believe it or not, the narrative gets even worse.

Some believe he not only knew the outcome, he chose or ordained it. They teach he elected some for heaven and so gave them the ability to respond to his love. But this would mean he also chose not to give others that same ability to respond.

So, if God's purpose in creation was his pleasure, and the net result of his plan was that most of his creation would experience eternal death, based on this version, what pleases God most? Humanity's eternal life or eternal death?

Do you realize what this says about the nature of the God we are supposed to worship?

What if this is God's plan, and he *didn't* choose the outcome? Where does that leave us?

Is the eternal death and suffering of most of the people who have ever lived simply collateral damage for the Father, Son, and Spirit?

Is the majority of the human race just acceptable losses in God's design for creation?

Do either of these options sound like a plan birthed out of a relationship of three persons who are totally and completely in love with each other? Does this purpose seem like a design that flows out of their divine oneness?

My confusion of who God is was like a cyclone in my mind. But you know what the worst of it was? The cyclone never even "pinged" my radar. I was totally blind. I wonder if my radar was even on.

It was like I was back in the hamster's cage, and I had no idea I was there. The cyclone finally hit the radar while I was reading and studying the gospel of John. But it was a slow, incremental process. It took years.

Some time ago, a friend who was working on a book asked me to research the life of Jesus portrayed in John's narrative. I was happy to do this, because John's story had always intrigued me. I had already done a lot of study, and it had become one of my favorite gospels, particularly John 13–17. There were a lot of delays to the project, and it ended up taking about seven years to complete. But those years weren't wasted. For almost a decade, I studied and discovered things in John that changed everything for me.

During those years, I was a guest teacher for an adult class at church. Once a year I would dump my thoughts and questions about John's Gospel onto them to see if it made sense to anyone else besides me. A sensible precaution, since my wife had previously accused my sanity of being dubious on more than one occasion. I affectionately called them my "guinea pigs." They would give me feedback, which forced me to clarify my thoughts and study more. They were a gift. Over the years with them, my thoughts about God gradually changed, particularly about the Trinity.

I would explain my ongoing attempts to look at John's narrative compositionally. I discovered – that by noting what John selected and how he arranged his material – it seemed he went to great lengths to compose his story of Jesus in a way that answered the question, "How does God save us relationally?"

I observed that only John, of all the narrators of Jesus's life, starts his story with relationship. In John's beginning, before anything is created, God exists in relationship with the Word. This is a narrative bomb. Then John implies this relationship is intimate for the little word "with" implies "face to face". Later in the opening paragraphs, intimacy is no longer implied. John becomes explicit with his repeated phrase, "he is in the bosom of the Father" (KJV). Can he be any closer?

This intimacy has been true from before the beginning, because the Word is God too. And since the Word is also God, it follows they don't just exist in a relationship; their nature, as the being called God, is relationship!

Adding to the significance of these words is that John intentionally placed these as his *first* words of Jesus' story. In doing this, these ideas illuminate the entire narrative. The opening's function is to shape how we read the rest of the story. We are to see everything about Jesus through these glasses. Here's his opening paragraph –

"In the beginning was the Word,
and the Word was with God,
and the Word was God.
He was with God in the beginning."[14]

For John, Jesus's story starts not with his birth or even with the creation but with his existence in relationship with his Father from the beginning. This is how John would have us think of Jesus.

I'm acutely aware how hard it is to get our minds around all this "stuff" about the Trinity – a being who is relationship. We have nothing in our physical world or in our experience that is similar. God is completely unique, one of a kind. There is no other like him. This is the meaning of the word "holy." Far from being a moral or legal description of God, holiness refers primarily to his utter uniqueness. He is *different*, which is the root word from which we get "holy."

But do not let the difficulty discourage you, as it did me, from thinking, studying, and meditating on the stunning and staggering beauty of God's nature. I think it may be the single greatest thought ever to engage the mind and heart of a human being.

So then, what is the relationship of the Father, Son, and Spirit like? Here's one of the best descriptions I've ever read of the Trinity:

> The Trinity means that; strictly speaking, God is not alone. Within the being of God there is relationship – three persons

---

14 John 1:1,2

united in mutual love and communion without loss of personal distinctness. The relationship of the Father, Son, and Spirit is a rich and unclouded fellowship that is so deep and true, so open and close, and fired by such pure love, that we are driven with historic Christianity to say they are one. Anything less than "one" betrays the very closeness of their relationship. Yet the Father does not become the Son or Spirit and the Son and Spirit do not become one another or the Father. This is a relationship of oneness, yet not absorption. This is a relationship of thorough going communion in mutual self-giving love, in which the Father, Son, and Spirit have such a profound freedom to know and be known that they share all things together without losing themselves in enmeshment.[15]

Are they not altogether beautiful? They have set a fire ablaze within my soul. My heart and mind have been captured, reshaped, and impassioned with beauty, wonder, and love.

In the Triune God...

There is no manipulation, vindictiveness, or hypocrisy...

No competition for power, status, or respect...

No hiding, pouting, or misunderstanding...

No envy, covetousness, or jealousy...

No selfishness or self-seeking glory...

No arguing, bitterness, or contempt.

There is no darkness in his nature, and his nature is relationship.

Jesus does not pick up his ball and go home because he doesn't like the way the Father and Spirit are playing.

The Father doesn't become angry because his Son and the Spirit brought their filthy, ugly, and sick friend home.

The Spirit doesn't slip into deep depression because the Father and Son get all the attention.

---

15 Dr. C. Baxter Kruger, *Across All Worlds: Jesus Inside Our Darkness* (Jackson, Mississippi: Perichoresis Press, 2007), 31.

They have been and always are kind, honest, compassionate, open, loyal, and humble with each other.

They have always and will forever take pleasure in each other, deeply care for each other, affirming and serving one another without expectations.

The truth is, they are head over heels, "out of their minds" in love with each other! They *adore* each other. Their love is passionate and pure beyond anything we can imagine. They willingly and freely live out their relationship together with a deep, profound, and mysterious love for the other. They have always been this way, and there is never a moment, nor will there ever be a moment, when they are not.

They are *all* this and a thousand other, better words we would invent to describe them. And whatever the best ideas of these words might mean, these words are infinitely better in them, because the words find their truest, fullest meaning in the three of them. They are the archetype.

The *best* of our relationships, as beautiful and fulfilling as they are capable of being, are merely the coos of newborn infants pointing to the staggering beauty of the love the Father, Son, and Spirit have and are in one another. "This relationship is a communion of love which God himself is in his being as God."[16]

They are the one God. A being who, in the essence of his nature, is a community in loving communion. There is nothing that has been created that wasn't formed from their shared life. *All creation* finds its source in their relationship. They are the reservoir from which creation finds its existence and purpose. And they are eternally connected to you, me, to all of it. If they weren't, we would no longer exist.

Does that not make a difference in us? Does their relationship not encourage us to trust? It does for me. The God I knew before was

---

16 T.F. Torrance, *The Mediation of Christ*, American ed. (Wm. B. Eerdmans, Grand Rapids, MI 1984) 74.

a mere shadow of the God I'm beginning to know now. The beauty of their relationship has changed me dramatically. And it is not just because I have different information. Nor is it because I have come to believe differently, though that is part of the relational process. It is because I have experienced relationship with them in ways I can neither prove nor explain.

Trust, not mental agreement with an idea, is at the core of this relationship.

I needed to rethink everything. I needed to think of God's purpose in creation in light of their shared communion. Whatever that purpose may be, it cannot be contrary or inconsistent with their shared life.

Is creation an act in which they simply made their life available to us, so we could taste its goodness?

Was creation's purpose an example of how relationships should be - which we are supposed to imitate?

Was creation's purpose to put their relationship on a pedestal so we can all admire their pure glory?

No, no, no. It must be *infinitely* better than that.

It is the Father, Son, and Spirit who create. Creation, *you and me and all that has ever been made*, are birthed out of their relationship.

Every thought…

Every idea…

Every dream…

Every act…

Everything is birthed out of who they are.

What if their purpose in creation was an act of amazing and extravagant love?

What if their goal in creating was that their creation would participate and live in their communion?

What if God's greatest pleasure is sharing what the Trinity is and has? Could *this* be his glory?

Could it be that the Father, Son, and Spirit create humanity for the purpose of including us in their circle of life and love, so we can live in the joy they have experienced age upon age upon age?

If so, then Creation should be seen as a gift not only to us but also to each of the persons of the Trinity.

Imagine the moment they breathed life into everything. Imagine their delight when they saw themselves mirrored in the first of humankind fashioned in their image and likeness.

My son thinks of it like this: their shared life is like beautifully choreographed movement between the three of them. It is the great eternal dance. And every one of us is included, right smack in the middle of it. There are no hoops to jump through to be in. Everyone is included; no exceptions.

The Incarnation has made it so.

This is the declaration of the gospel. This is the good news.

But the human race has turned away and neither sees or hears the beauty we are in. Many of us have spent our entire lives with headphones on, captivated by the white noise of lies we have believed, ignorant of the astonishing love that awaits us. But somehow love breaks through and we hear the music and see the beauty of their dance, feeling, for even the briefest of moments, what CS Lewis called "the weight of their glory". And so, with the joy and exuberance of young lovers at their own wedding reception, we take off our headphones, grab the hands of the Father, Son, and Spirit, and dance *with them*. This is the response of love and trust to their invitation to freely participate with them.

As a professional photographer for most of my life, I have sought places that display the incredible beauty found in nature. I have hiked in deserts, mountains, and forests through any weather you can imagine all over our wonderful world. I have seen some amazingly beautiful things – mountains that took my breath away, sunsets that brought me to tears, vistas that left me muttering, "Oh my God, Oh my God, OH MY GOD!" I have witnessed color, form, and light merge at the perfect moment to create dazzling displays of beauty and wonder. So, it is with no small conviction and experience that I say this…

The Father, Son, and Spirit are more majestic than a thousand snowcapped mountains robed in the fires of a sunset.

They are more brilliant than the brightest sun on the clearest day.

They are more mesmerizing than the endless power of the ocean crashing on rocky cliffs in rainbow light.

They are more beautiful than anything imagined or created.

The relationship of the Father, Son, and Spirit is the most beautiful wonder in existence.

And they are manifesting their relationship everywhere, including in you and me!

It is in that circle of unending and overflowing love where every single human being finds belonging.

As I am learning to think of God first and only in this way – that this is the unchanging nature of his being, that every word he speaks and every act he does, that it is *this* God who speaks and acts – I am beginning to know him truer and better. This brings life to me, eternal life, and that makes all the difference in the world.

CHAPTER 5

WHO DO YOU KNOW?

"I'm looking for a bridge I can't burn down."

– Jon Foreman

The other day, I had one of those rare moments of leisure, kind of like a "coffee moment" for someone who doesn't drink coffee. I contemplated what I should do with this strange gift. My silent prayer was answered when my eye caught the remote. (Don't judge me.) About a minute into surfing for God knows what, I happened to scroll past ESPN. It wasn't Bugs Bunny, but my thumb hit the brakes anyway. And that is where my guilty pleasure became really good.

The ESPN host and three retired athletes-turned-TV-analysts were watching a segment about Mark Keys, a disabled man who uses his time to handwrite letters to people asking them the following question: "What was your best day?"

Some of those who answered were professional athletes from the National Football League. Four players were featured in the piece: Chuck Bednarik, Eric Dickerson, Bruce Arians, and Walter Payton.

All their answers were moving, but most notable to me were Dickerson and Payton, two of the greatest running backs who have ever played football. "There have been many (great days), and most of them did not involve sports," Dickerson said. What he chose to share as his greatest day was really more like a string of days. He spoke of the long conversations he enjoyed with his dad before his passing. Their discussions were mostly about God. Eric recalled his father's dream: that his son would grow to know the God of whom they spoke. Extraordinary. I would liked to have known Eric Dickerson's dad.

Walter Payton responded to Mark's letter years ago, before he died of cancer in 1999. His son, Jarrett Payton, had never read his father's answer. He didn't even know it existed. ESPN filmed Jarrett reading his father's letter for the first time. The elder Payton wrote that his greatest moment was sharing his induction into the football hall of fame in Canton, Ohio, with his son. His induction was a great honor, but what made it his greatest day was *sharing it with his son*. Jarrett sat there, stunned. He was at a loss for words. Visibly moved, he barely kept his composure and told the ESPN crew how this news was "breathtaking."

Tears welled up in my eyes. But it didn't end there.

The host of the show then asked the three former players what was their greatest moment. All three talked about relationships, not accomplishments. The third gentleman responded without hesitation, "the births of my four children." Then, in a moment of unrehearsed transparency, the ESPN host spoke of his daughter, who was born with a learning disability and had been told she'd never make it through school. But she *had* finished high school and had graduated with honors. The greatest day of his life was when she received her acceptance into university.

His love and pride for his daughter choked his words, so that his sentence trailed off, unfinished. Silence was the only voice in the studio. One of the analysts laid his hand on the host's shoulder as he wept openly, trying desperately to rein in his emotions. A rare thing to see on TV, let alone ESPN. Kudos to them for keeping it on the air.

Who can deny the power of relationships? Think about it; everything you think, feel, and know – good or bad – everything you are is because you are connected in some way to someone.

Ah, but "relationship" is a double-edged sword. It can be the sweetest, most beautiful experience your soul will ever savor, or it can be the foulest, most twisted, repulsive hell you can imagine. It can be the vehicle that brings joy, laughter, fulfillment, and – best of all – love, or it can be the conduit through which bitterness, jealousy, and hatred fill and ultimately consume you.

Some would have us believe that strength of character is measured by how little we need others. The more independent we are, the stronger we are. That's garbage. That may look good in movies or commercials, but try and live isolated from any relationship, and you'll find that it's hell. We crumble into madness like an empty plastic Pepsi bottle implodes when exposed to pressure.

I would guess that every one of us has, at one time or another, knowingly exposed ourselves to the risk of relationship, because the hope that it will bring fulfillment outweighs the fear that it won't. So, we dare, are compelled even, to connect to others. Timidly or boldly, it makes no difference; we long to engage in knowing the other while simultaneously revealing ourselves so that we are known by the other.

Why take this risk? Why endure the pain of our souls being ripped apart by rejection or allow ourselves to suffer the devastating wounds of treachery and betrayal? Could it be that we are relational creatures by nature, and so we intuitively know that relationship is life to us and isolation is the death of us?

It seems that what we humans really care about is not a what; it's a *who*.

In order to flesh this out a bit we need to take a brief journey back to our beginnings…

In a familiar and elegant account, we learn in Genesis that we did not give life to ourselves. No human ever willed himself or herself into existence. The biblical explanation for our existence is that the Father, Son, and Spirit, created life out of his life. He is the Author, the Source of life. All life finds its origin in God. Consider for a moment the majesty and beauty of the Father, Son, and Spirit speaking creation into being and imagine their sheer delight in fashioning us. Humbling, isn't it?

We also learn that the first humans (Adam and Eve) lived in a communion of love with each other and God, not because they did something right or believed the right things, but because they were relationally connected to God, the Source of life. And this relationship was good. It was intimate. They were "face to face" with him. They *knew* God.

The love between the Father, Son, and Spirit is not coerced. Neither is their love for creation. Their love is freely given by choice. Created in "their image," we were "wired" with the ability to choose, so we could participate in their love in the same way they do. And in order for that love be real to us, God provided us a choice, an instruction that could be followed, ignored, or disobeyed. With the gift of being endowed with his image came a warning: if Adam and Eve disobeyed, the inevitable consequence of that choice would be their death.

So, when our first parents grasped for independence, their turning away to autonomy disconnected them relationally from God, who was the Source of their life. Alienated from all they had known and estranged from the One whose love gave them life, the consequence, *not the punishment*, was their death. Kind of like when you pull the plug on your computer; it "dies," and so, too, when Adam and Eve sinned, they died.

In the past, what I mistakenly read into that story was that Adam and Eve died because their Creator was so furious with their disloyalty that he punished them. That is, God intentionally inflicted a penalty on them because they failed to keep the rule he set up. And this penalty, he decided, would be death.

But it seems if there is a punishment to be found in this story, it is *not* their death. Death is the consequence of trying to live independently from Life. The "punishment" was their banishment from paradise. And yet, if you think about it, this was for their good as well as the good of everyone who followed. Though it is clearly a penalty, Adam and Eve's exile seems more like a gift of mercy, an opportunity for restoration.[17] For if the Father were to let Adam and Eve continue eating from the Tree of Life while being relationally alienated from him, each other, and themselves, it would be tantamount to him abandoning his beloved creation to never ending darkness. Eden would no longer be paradise. It would be a living hell.

The fall was a turning away from the Three-in-One who gave them their identity telling them who they actually were. This turning was not only a rejection of their Creator, it was a also a rejection of their humanity, which was fashioned in the likeness of God. At a fundamental level, this was a relational catastrophe. Alienated from everyone they knew, they hid in the bushes, terrified. In grasping to know the good and evil, they wound up knowing nothing. Not God, themselves, or each other. This walking away was a relational divorce from the One who had lovingly guided them into all that was good. This was an act of independence.

But when you declare independence from the Source of Life, where do you go now to find it?

---

17 I believe St. Paul has a similar thought in Romans 11:32, "God has bound up all to disobedience so that he might show mercy to all." Paul seems to be implying that God's consigning of the entire human race to disobedience is, in fact, an incredible demonstration of God's mercy upon us all. Without that, humanity would never give up its futile attempt to "live" independently of relationship with him, which is eternal death.

Well, it seems we (the human race) have gone just about everywhere and looked at just about everything. We've been at it for so long that I'm not sure we remember what we're looking for. Donald Miller cleverly highlighted this thought in his book entitled *Searching for God Knows What?*

Assuming I understand correctly what a relationship is, then, for relationship to exist, it requires at least two beings. In the Bible's story, one of them, God, already has eternal life. He is life. When Adam and Eve fell, God did not die relationally or in any other way. But Adam and Eve did. And we did *in or through* them, vicariously.

Furthermore, God already knows us. Not just everything about us but intimately knows us. He calls us friend, brother/sister, son/daughter. Are these not terms whose definitions reveal intimacy in relationship? And God's relationship with us is good. Not that he approves of everything we do. Obviously. But he is not alienated from us. He does not need to be reconciled to us; we need to be reconciled to him. He never walked away from us. Even when we brought death into the mix, he never changed his mind about us. It is the human race that is fallen, not God.

What we left in the garden was a relationship. What we lost was life.

But early in the story we learn something astonishing about our Father, the Creator. God doesn't stay in Eden waiting for us to come back. God goes with us. He takes on our problem and makes it his own. He wants to rescue us from alienation and death. Several questions surface immediately:

Why would he want to rescue us? How will he do it? How can he do it?

Even more, I think this narrative also offers a viewpoint that clarifies what humanity's problem actually is.

It is not that we are living the wrong way. That's just a symptom. It is not that we believe the wrong things or don't believe enough of the right things. That's just blindness. It, too, is a symptom.

It is not that we love the wrong person or thing. This is closer to the truth, but it's still a symptom.

Our problem is this: *we don't know God.*

Our hearts have been captured, our minds deceived, and our lives destroyed. We live a blind, broken, and twisted existence. In our brokenness of not knowing the most wonderful Being of all, we have looked, even searched, for a god to replace him. And we have found millions. I would suggest that all, including my religious version, are the product of our fallen imaginations.

So, if knowing God is life…

and we don't know him…

Then true life can only be found in a *re-turning* to him, in the reconciliation of our relationship.

If this is true, then the following words, spoken by Jesus and penned by John, are some of the most important words we could ever hear. They are rather simple, but they are a *bomb*.

"Now this is eternal life: that they might know you, the only true God, and Jesus Christ, whom you have sent."[18]

This statement has become one of the most meaningful I have ever read because I realized that all of my study and thinking about God, Scripture, and eternal life needed to be reworked from a relational framework. That thought had never occurred to me.

It seems this would be just a natural extension of the implications of thinking of God as Father, Son, and Spirit. Yet, this was a total reshaping of my thoughts, a paradigm shift on a grand scale.

---

18 John 17:3

Have you ever thought about what eternal life is? I mean, have you ever tried to define it? In my circles, most equated it with "being saved." Presumption is our culture.

Set that aside for a moment.

Usually, what I came up with was pretty straightforward. Eternal life is to live forever. You know, life without end. Well, of the hundreds of times in Scripture where the phrase "eternal life" is used, the quote above is where it comes the closest to a definition. If there's a better one, I don't know it.

Whatever we might understand eternal life to be, John, the narrator, wants us to think of it in *relational* terms. Forget duration of time or quality of life for a moment and think with John of eternal life relationally. John hears Jesus say that eternal life is found in knowing *someone*.

You may be thinking, "Of course, this is nothing new. I've heard that all my life." Well, I have too – probably said it a thousand times.

So, if eternal life is a relationship with God, why do we reduce it to formulas?

Why do we talk about it like it's a pre-packaged, ready-to-sell life insurance policy?

Why do we treat it as a thing?

Why do we systematize it into doctrines?

Have you ever wondered why Jesus revealed his Father to us with stories? Why would God choose the literary form of story? Why not bullet points, like we memorize in school or hear in sermons? Why not an outline of all the truth that we need to know, so we can be sure we pass the test and get in?

Part of the answer may be that stories invite us into the truth in a way propositions can't. They invite us relationally. They help us "see" truth by putting flesh on it, for truth is ultimately a person.

I Confess	I taught that if I believed certain things *about* Jesus, then I had a relationship *with* Jesus.

For years, I understood and presented a relationship with Jesus as equal to a codified set of beliefs. I would take these very stories that beckon to us relationally and organize them into a list of principles to apply or systematize them into a set of beliefs to follow. Unfortunately, I have sat in classes and listened to sermons that encouraged and taught me to do this. Regrettably, I taught similar classes.

For me, the phrase "believing in Jesus" had come to mean believing information about him. Belief was only a cognitive exercise (i.e., the acknowledgment that what Jesus claimed to be and do was a true fact). This meant that eternal life was acquired educationally, not relationally. Is it any wonder why having the correct information was so important to me?

But it also explained the ease with which I became distracted and my repeated efforts through my good behavior to gain a deep and abiding assurance. Most of the time, in books that I read or sermons I heard, the reason for this vacillating in my life was blamed on my lack of faith. I just wasn't committed enough. I wonder, how many of us have bought into this "salvation through education" thinking?

But what if Jesus's idea of believing is more relational? What if believing is more about trusting a person than believing things about them? In his prayer, Jesus understands eternal life as knowing his Father, not just information about him. Knowing information or even having the correct belief system, as good as both of these things might seem to us, is not the same thing as being in relationship.

I realize that information can help lead us into relationship, but it's never to be confused with relationship. Information was never the goal. It's hard to imagine God creating us for the purpose of winning *Jeopardy*.

Knowing God is being in relationship with him. Eternal life *is* the relationship. If you are in relationship with God, then you have eternal life.

Why then do you suppose we place such value and emphasis on information instead of relationship? Some will protest, "Our church is about relationships!" That may be. But what is the activity in which most churches engage? Is it not Bible study? What activity consumes the vast majority of most church gatherings? Is it not sermons? Why do you think we do this? Could it be that we think eternal life is an educational experience instead of a relational experience?

I do not say this casually, simply trying to find fault with our current state of affairs. I have spent most of my life studying and teaching the Scriptures. As I said earlier, I was vested in this identity. But if believing in Jesus is the way to eternal life, and we understand "believe" as the confession that his claims and deeds are factually true, then having a good education about the Jesus story would be the most important task of any human being on the planet. Right? So it was for me.

Let me ask you this: if I know George Washington was the first president of the United States, does that mean I know him? What if I studied every piece of information available about George Washington and became an authority on all things "Washington"? Would I know him then? I may feel like I know him, but the truth is I never even met him. So, no matter what I know about him, it isn't the same as knowing him.

Isn't this also true when it comes to knowing Jesus? Why, then, did I think that learning all I could about Jesus from the Bible and history would be the same as knowing him? Moreover, if that is true, if that is the only way we get to know him, how much do we need to know/believe before we have eternal life? And how will we ever know when we know/believe enough?

It seemed everything had to make sense for me to feel safe with him. I think at least part of this came from believing I had to know as much about God as I could in order to experience relationship with him. And I didn't know how much. Who does? I was trapped in my own theology.

On dozens of occasions I have heard Dr. C. Baxter Kruger state, "Revelation is about the personal self-disclosure of God."

If this is true (and I think it is) that the revelation of God means the unveiling of God himself – not just the transmission of accurate truths or information about God – then doesn't it follow that our reception of that revelation would require an encounter, not with information or ideas, but ultimately, with *God in person*? Just like with George Washington, to know God I need to actually *meet* God and experience life with him.

Have you ever met someone who had a real personal encounter with Jesus, and they knew almost nothing about the Bible or the theology of salvation? I have.

One of them is a young man named Jason. His story is quite remarkable, amazing even. Several years ago he attempted suicide. That night he had an experience that was as real for him as his marriage or the birth of his three children since. He will tell you he met Jesus that night. Though he didn't know much about Jesus, and even less about the Bible, his life radically changed. And it has remained changed ever since. He loves his family, has more humility and love in his little toe than I have in my entire being, and will do anything for anyone he can help. He is still in love with Jesus – not his experience. Today, I am honored to call Jason my friend.

I Confess | **I had little respect for people like Jason.**

In my arrogant rationalism, I would have dismissed Jason and others like him. I viewed their stories in a condescending way, as emotional sensationalism, at best, and encounters with the demonic, at worst.

"It doesn't square with the Bible; they're probably not even a Christian," I would judge.

But people like Jason know Jesus. It is Jesus they worship. It is Jesus, not some idol, that Jason loves.

In my imagined spiritual superiority, I would critique how some would slaughter an interpretation of a text and justify my theory of how someone gains eternal life. "They don't know the Bible. They don't know what they're talking about," I would piously protest.

But these people had a joy and a love that, when set next to me, revealed my spirit for what it was, a quagmire of arrogance and condemnation. So, I knew the Bible better, but they knew Jesus better. Which is life?

Is it possible to believe wrong things about someone yet have a relationship with them?

Absolutely. I do it all the time with God, my wife, with just about everybody. My knowledge is neither complete nor always correct. So, if a person knows Jesus but doesn't know much theology or doesn't handle biblical interpretation very well or believes things that you or I would consider wacky, weird, or just plain wrong, can they possess eternal life? *Yes, they can.*

To be clear, I am not suggesting that you can believe anything you want and have a relationship with Jesus. If someone doesn't believe any of Jesus's claims, why would they even want a relationship with him? If they believe he is still dead, why would they want a relationship with a dead guy from two thousand years ago?

It's worth repeating: eternal life is knowing God. Eternal life is a relationship with a being who is personal.

"But," I reasoned, "don't we acquire eternal life by believing specific information about him, and only then it becomes a relationship?"

Can we enter a relationship in a non-relational way? *Possibly...*

Does doing things for God mean you have a relationship with him? Maybe, but not necessarily.

Does believing God did things for you, even dying on a cross, mean you have relationship? Maybe.

Can you have a relationship with an event? We may experience an event – it may even contribute to the development of a relationship – but the event, or your experience of it, *isn't* a relationship. At least not a personal relationship.

If I present eternal life as something you can acquire non-relationally, that is, by believing about the event of the cross, am I not misleading and ultimately inconsistent with Jesus's definition of eternal life? Am I not teaching people to have a relationship with an inanimate thing?

Should I teach or trust in the cross as though the event is greater than the One who died on it?

| **I Confess** | **I had a twisted view of the cross.** |

I encouraged people to believe in what Jesus did as more important than who he is. Not only did I inadvertently separate the person from his actions, I emphasized what Jesus did over and above who Jesus is. Salvation was found in what people believed about his death on a cross, not in the person who hung on it. To say (which I often did) that the relationship became personal when I believed he died for me would not do. All I had done was believe an additional piece of information.

I do not say this to minimize the event of the cross, which is a significant part of our salvation, but rather to focus our attention on the Savior, by and with whom we are brought into relationship. That is, brought into his life, the eternal life he shares with the Father and the Spirit.

If you chafe at my words, I know *exactly* how you feel. These questions rocked the core of what I believed and taught about eternal life. This was a crisis of no small proportion. But if I take Jesus's definition seriously, which I'm convinced we should do, I believe that no matter who was involved or why the event occurred, we don't have a relationship with a thing or an event; it's with a person.

As George MacDonald so beautifully inquired, "If the woman who touched the hem of His garment had trusted in the garment and not in him who wore it, would she have been healed?"[19]

When I first saw a young woman named Terri, who later became my wife, it was from a distance. As I studied her, she looked about 5' 4", had a slim, attractive figure and was really cute. She had brown hair, gorgeous blue eyes, and her smile was radiant. But what I really noticed was her tan! It was early June in Portland, and we hadn't seen the sun since September. *Where'd she get that killer tan?* I wondered. Within an hour, I had a boatload of information about her, though I still had never met her. Had I begun to know her? Nope. I had only begun to gather information about her. Knowing her would require talking with her. What did she love? What made her laugh? How

---

19 George MacDonald, *Creation in Christ: Unspoken Sermons* (Vancouver, BC: Regent College Publishing, 2004) 98.

did she handle stress or conflict? What moved her? These questions, and hundreds like them, were not answered because I was given information, no matter how good or clear or correct that information was. Neither were they answered simply because I believed the information. Answers to such questions come when life is shared and experienced together in communion.

Even though these questions are important, relationship is far more than simply finding answers. If having answers to all my questions about her was all there was, then I would have reduced relationship to just a task to be accomplished. Though our relationships may feel like that at times, they certainly aren't. Relationship may, at times, be initiated with shared information. But as I said previously, they are never to be confused as the same thing. Doesn't my relationship with Terri develop as I experience her in the midst of all the currents of life? Being with her, participating in the same experiences, communicating with honesty, this is the stuff of relationship.

Our first road trip (of many) as a family was a two-week adventure from Portland to Palm Springs and then over to Los Angeles. Our return journey on Hwy 101 took us up the entire coast of California and Oregon. We explored Big Sur, Monterey Peninsula, Santa Cruz, San Francisco, Redwood National Park, and the wonderful beauty of the Oregon coastline.

It was a delightfully stress-free trip – a rarity, let me assure you. The highlight for me was a side trip we did from Palm Springs to the Grand Canyon. The national park has long been, and still is, one of my favorite places on earth. No one in our little tribe had ever seen it but me. I was so eager for them to see it; I was giddy, like a kid going on his or her first date. I wanted to show it off so much you would have thought the Grand Canyon was my own personal creation, like I was the one who made it.

When we finally got to our hotel, we were a bit rushed, if I remember correctly. We threw our stuff in the room and we were immediately out the door again. I was beginning to panic because I knew we were running out of time. I had been meticulous in planning our trip so that we could arrive at the canyon in time to see the sunset. As a photographer, I love the last hour of the day, when Nature rolls back the curtain and reveals the staggering glory of her beauty. Admittedly, the show begins with the sunrise, but it is the late afternoon when her spectacular display begins its final and most impressive act of the day. As the sun descends, it moves like the tender touch of a departing lover across the lips of his beloved, its rays reaching out like gentle fingers to caress the face of the massive walls. The ancient rocks blush, revealing shades and hints of color that redefine our sense of *grand*. I remember my first experience of Nature's enchanted golden hour at the canyon, where the magnificent embrace of her beauty first touched me. Ever since, I had dreamed of sharing in my family's first experience at the park, hoping they would see and feel the same magic I had almost twenty years earlier.

If you've ever visited the Grand Canyon, you know that when you reach one of the many vista points along the way and pull into the turnout to park your car, you still can't see the canyon. Kind of weird for something so big, don't you think? When we got to a turnout, I was frantic with anticipation.

But when we hopped out of the car, my kids questioned my sanity, because they couldn't see anything. Regardless, I yelled, "Let's go!" Seriously, this was it – a special moment, a life memory for the MacMurray clan! We were about to see the Grand Canyon, one of the most awesome natural wonders on the planet, and I desperately wanted them to love it as much as I did.

We scrambled over to the edge, and the vista exploded into our view. "Oooh… Ahhh!" my family exclaimed. I couldn't contain my joy and pride, not that I wanted to, as I stood at the edge of breathtaking beauty surrounded by those I cherished most in this world. I had this ridiculous grin beaming across my entire face as I savored the moment. *Oh, this is good*, I thought. I had reached parental nirvana.

After about ten minutes or so, my childlike smile still lingering across the aged lines of my face, the children became restless. Even a bit bored. "Dad, can we go get some ice cream?" My heart sank a little bit.

"But it's just getting good," I pleaded. "It changes right before your eyes as the sun goes down. It just keeps getting more and more beautiful…" My words trailed off as I saw a couple of them look at their mom, hoping she'd plead their cause and get them some ice cream.

My smile vanished and my joy evaporated, leaving me listless like a boneless chicken teetering at the edge of a chasm of disappointment that wasn't so grand. Elle, our middle daughter, has always had the most sophisticated relational radar in our family. So when she saw her dad deflate like an emotional balloon, it pinged her like the sun pings a rooster.

She shuffled over to me, looked up, and, in the cutest voice, with the most innocent expression, offered words of *life*. "I'll stay with you, Dad, if you want to take some pictures." She stood next to me grinning – Jesus smiling at me through this precious third grader.

My heart nearly melted. A cherub had descended to rescue me from the burden of disappointment that threatened to destroy any dreams of beauty shared with my family. Spasms of emotion gripped me. Pride, admiration, love, gratefulness, and a dozen other emotions flooded my soul as I gazed with wonder at this little angelic messenger. The rings of Saturn would have been too small a gift for my Elle.

This was *sacrifice*, an extraordinary gift of love. For if there was anyone in the MacMurray house who loved ice cream, it was Elle. And I *knew* it. I knew what she was giving up to be with me. My eyes became misty, but all I could sputter was, "Thank you, Elbow!" My face beamed once again with irrepressible joy.

So, on that fine August day, Terri rescued two of our children from their father's obsession with the perfect family vacation, and I came to know, in a wonderful and stunning way, a little more of what sacrificial, other-centered love looks and feels like from my extraordinary eight-year-old. I experienced the grace of heaven, a bit of the circle of the self-giving relationship of love that God *is* through my relationship with my remarkable daughter.

I experienced *life* that day through a relationship with a person, not just because I attained more information.

CHAPTER 6

IT'S ALL ABOUT RELATIONSHIP

"For too long the contract-God of Western jurisprudence has dominated our concepts of God. We need to recover a biblical understanding of the Triune God..."

— J.B. Torrance

Ever since I can remember, I have heard that eternal life is a relationship with Jesus Christ. I grew up in the shadow of organizations that recited this phrase in every piece of literature they passed out. I can't remember a time when I didn't believe and teach it to be so.

Yet, there was also a time when, had you suggested that eternal life was a relationship in process, I would have feared the good news of eternal life was being poisoned and compromised. Astonishing, huh? Though I held to the belief that eternal life was a relationship, *I treated it like a transaction.* That's like saying I love ice cream but throw up every time I eat it. Such is the seesaw of my soul. My behavior exposed a paradigm that I had bought into for years, a perception that was foggy at best, bankrupt at worst, one that obviously revealed my lack of clear thinking.

As a younger man I parroted what I had been taught and presented eternal life as a transactional formula. God offers eternal life. Since he paid for it (at the expense of his Son) it's free. The only currency I need is to believe it. Accept his gift and I get to ride the glory train.

In this view, someone could theoretically take the gift and yet dislike or even walk away from the God who gave it to them.

Interesting. I can get eternal life but continue to live independently of the Source of Life? Is that possible? How then would this change us from Adam? How does this reconcile a fallen race? How is this salvation?

To be blunt, the real problem with this view is: transactions *don't require relationship.*

Maybe you're like me, having thought of eternal life as a thing you possess instead of a person you know. Indeed, the Scriptures declare eternal life is a gift. This is true. But this is precisely where I missed it.

The gift is not a thing; it's a *person*. It is Jesus. He gives us himself. Eternal life is not a commodity he gives to us as though it's separate from him.

God's love is self-giving. So, when God loves us he gives us himself… the gift is him.

Jesus isn't the path to eternal life, and eternal life isn't the path to get to know Jesus. Eternal life is in him, because he is life, and there is no other. Knowing him is eternal life.

I Confess	A transactional formula had a certain appeal to me.

It gave me a framework to use as a way of knowing who was "in" and who wasn't. Now, I could easily divide the "ins" from the "outs." All I had to do was ask a series of simple questions to find out what a person believed. Had the transaction taken place? Had they accepted the gift?

But saying that eternal life is a relationship… oh, that was unnerving. How do you measure a relationship? How could I ever tell who was "in"? That was far too vague for me.

Wait a second, why did I need to know who was "in"? Why was that so damn important to me?

It had never occurred to me that it is possible to believe someone and yet never know or love them. On the other hand, can a person really love someone and *not* trust them?

I shudder at the legacy I may have left to the next generation – that eternity hangs in the balance of a god who merely wants a transaction completed. One of the greatest ironies (maybe "tragedies" is the better word here) of the current American evangelical version of Christianity is that we have made a claim so bold and so amazing, yet we have treated it like anything but a relationship and taught others to do the same.

This "transactional" framework for eternal life also made sense to me, because I thought God's problem with me was primarily a legal or moral one. So, most of my thinking was focused on the questions of how God cleans us up morally and saves us legally. Though these are legitimate concerns, they aren't the primary or essential questions. Morality or the Law is not our first or greatest problem.

The question that is begging (screaming) to be asked is, "If God is to rescue us, how does he do it *relationally*?" I never heard this question, nor did I ever ask it.

I have to admit, another reason I liked this idea was because it was simple, quick, and convenient. And having swallowed the cultural Kool-Aid that says these qualities are preferred as better ways of living, it was easy to adopt them into my view of eternal life.

Magic wands, answers with the flick of a switch, solutions with the ease of a remote… what better news could there be than eternal life is just a transaction?

But aren't relationships the opposite of this? Don't they take time? And because of the fall, aren't they terribly messy?

Maybe the real reason I liked the idea of eternal life being a transaction was because I didn't want God to get too involved with my mess. Save me, sure, but mess with my mess? Maybe I *liked* my mess. So, the only time I really wanted relationship with God was when I needed his help. You know, when the mess overwhelmed me and became too much.

| I Confess | I tried to market God's gift of eternal life. |

The result of my thinking like this? It became easy to believe salvation was something to get and make sure I had rather than someone to know, walk with, and love. Teaching eternal life this way subconsciously led me to present Jesus as an item I was trying to sell. The goal was to "make the sale." Get someone to buy what I was saying and complete the transaction. There were times when I found myself trying to market God, so I could sell a relationship. Wait, how do you sell an actual relationship? Isn't that kind of absurd?

But I can be creative. Downward spirals are easy.

Step 1 – Put the relationship in some killer packaging. Think about the coolest religious event you've ever heard of – a rocking band, laser light show, movie theater seats, state-of-the-art sound system, an off-Broadway drama, and a guest appearance by Brad Pitt. Well, maybe not him, but Tim Tebow at least! Then include a speech by the funniest, most engaging speaker you can imagine, telling you Jesus can make your life better. He can make you a better you.

Step 2 – Turn it into a formula that's easy to do. Come up with three or four steps to success. One step, if you're a really good communicator. Less is better.

Step 3 – Guarantee it with a better life. Pull the God card and use yourself as an example, albeit humbly.

Interestingly, this paradigm, which I thought was great, allowed me to quantify the relationship by tracking the number of "sales." (We say conversions or baptisms in "Christianese.") As a result, I measured my ministry to determine my success. And success is what I wanted. It validated my work. It validated me.

Why would I try and measure the success of a relationship with quantifiable data?

What if I did this with my marriage?

I kissed my wife three times today.

I only asked her to have sex with me 87 times this week, down from last week's 124 times.

I even put the toilet seat down three out of five times today!

Seriously, I fear my personal agendas, success not the least of these, influenced my understanding of something as fundamental as eternal life. Treating eternal life as a transaction, as a thing, a commodity, contributed significantly to my dementia.

| I Confess | I was torn between intimacy and transaction. |

What if we really did take our cues about relationship from this strictly transactional view? Where would that leave us in our marriages? Our parenting? Our friendships? Our relationships would be hell on earth. Sadly, many are.

Yet, in an almost instinctive way, we *don't* think of these relationships as a deal we've entered. A good parent or spouse would never view their relationships as a transaction or even a series of them. Why do you suppose that is? And why then, do you suppose we *do* believe that relationship with God is a transaction?

Here was my attempt at an answer: the transaction is only what begins the relationship.

Really? Had I ever begun a relationship with anyone in this way? You know, one that led to intimacy? I have filled out applications for employment that resemble this thinking. I have entered contracts like this. But I've never begun a relationship like this. And even if it could happen, it seems this would be the exception to the rule.

I had a best friend growing up named Robby. You know what made our relationship a relationship? I can tell you for sure, it wasn't because we made some kind of deal or entered into some kind of childlike contract. It was simply that we liked each other. Enjoyed being around each other. Did things together. The more time we spent together, the stronger our relationship became. In fact, we made a "blood brother deal" after we realized we had a relationship that we didn't want to lose!

How did the idea of relationship get turned on its head?

How is it I can make something so non-religious, religious?

Consider this – transactions are static. In contrast, relationships are dynamic. Therefore, the movement of the relationship, in whatever direction, is a *process*. My friend, Paul, says it's an incremental process. To think of eternal life as a transaction is to doom the relationship to never growing or developing as it should. Why? Because the only relational process would be in the agreement itself. Once the transaction is complete, the process is over.

It seems John makes this point repeatedly throughout his narrative. I would even suggest it's a theme of sorts. One of many examples is the story of the royal official in chapter four.

An official walked over a day's journey to implore Jesus to go home with him, so Jesus could heal his son. Sounds like faith to me. He believed Jesus was able to heal others and he acted on that belief.

Jesus responded that he wouldn't go home with him, but his son would be healed anyway. The man "took Jesus at his word" (NIV) and began his journey home. Sounds like trust again.

On his way there one of his servants met him telling him the news that his son was healed. The man inquired as to when this actually happened. When the servant answered, the man realized it was the exact time when Jesus said his son would be healed. John tells us, "then he believed."

What? This man showed faith twice already in the story. What do you mean, "*then* he believed?"

I think John's strategy here is to show that trust, which is at the core of what a relationship is, is a dynamic process. His story is an illustration of eternal life's relational dynamic. Trust develops. Relationships grow. And they never have to end. Relationships and trust don't reach a saturation point. They can always grow stronger and deeper. When will we come to the end of knowing, loving, and trusting a Being who has no end?

On the other hand, if this had been a transaction, John would have told us this man had faith, and the miracle happened. That's it. No process. Nothing dynamic. God said he'd do it, the man believed, and that was it. Why would he need God now? In fact, relationship wouldn't have occurred to him.

| I Confess | Entering a contract with God held more promise than a relationship with him. |

Oh, how little I thought of him and his commitment to me. For most of my life, I described eternal life more like a working contract than a relationship. And more often than not, the description of my contract with God ended up being a set of ideas and beliefs that just happened to be my beliefs. I would ask others to enter this contract, as though the relationship was actually with me or the organization I was involved with. Another idea that was incredibly convenient; I know.

Here's a sample of the contract. The contract is initiated by a transaction with God. For God's part, he said he would give me this thing called eternal life (which means, in most people's minds, I get to go to heaven). Jesus's death would pay for it. The deal was offered to everyone and was free. For our part, we needed to accept this contract by believing in what Jesus did for us on the cross. That's it. Done deal. Once I accepted the terms of the contract and the transaction was complete, then eternal life would be my possession. Then I could begin a relationship with him.

But think about it for a moment. In this scenario, the relationship is distinct from eternal life. In Jesus's definition, *relationship is eternal life.*

Many years ago a friend of mine, let's call him Kyle, came to me for advice. After the initial shock that he wanted advice from me, I asked him what it was about.

"My relationship with Julie is better than ever. I think I want to marry her."

I looked up. "Think?"

"Yeah," he said slowly. "I'm just not sure." He paused, "How'd you know you wanted to marry Terri?"

"Let's not go there," I replied. "I was an idiot. It took me years to answer that question. So, I'm not quite sure why you're asking me. I think I stumbled and bumbled my way in that entire relationship thing. Nearly blew it, to be honest."

"But you guys are good together," Kyle said. "Your marriage seems healthy. You must've done something right."

"Thank you." I grinned. "But if that's true, then I think that's due more to Terri than me. I mean it; you should talk to her"

Kyle sat silently for a bit. Then he looked at me with the kind of look a two-year-old daughter might give her father. A look that's full of hope, and her eyes, they get really big, you know? Yet there's a hint of desperation just behind them. It's a little pathetic but in a very lovable way. Very effective too.

"Look," he said, "I was just hoping you might have some advice."

What do you think I said? If I had answered Kyle the way I used to describe the way to eternal life, I would've said something like this: "What do you believe about Julie? If you believe she is your one true soul mate, then you should marry her. Because, Kyle, just think, she'll help you straighten up your finances, help you think of others beside yourself, help you with cooking, cuz God knows all you eat are hot pockets. You're probably one of the horniest people I know. Being married to Julie will relieve that sexual tension you're always carrying around. You won't be lonely anymore. But most of all, you'll just smell better."

What do you think of that answer? It would have been true at every point. Suppose Kyle got married based on my hypothetical answer. Would his marriage have been a relationship? In the broadest possible sense of the term, maybe. And that's a big maybe. But their marriage would have been strictly utilitarian and pragmatic. It would simply be a contract with a social partner instead of a business partner.

Don't contracts exist to give some sense of security to both parties that each will fulfill their part of the transaction? That each will do as they say? This social contract would outline ways that Kyle and Julie could help each other. For what end? Wouldn't the marriage exist for what they could get from each other, not what they could give to each other? Though their behavior might benefit each other because of what they agreed to do, that result would simply be "positive fallout." The truth is, their marriage would have been based exclusively in self-love, which is narcissism. Can we really call this a relationship? Even a bad one? At the very least, it is not relationship in the sense Jesus meant when he said eternal life was "knowing his Father."

So, though my answer would have been true, it would've been ridiculous. A bit funny, perhaps, but still ridiculous. Why? Because marriage isn't a contract; it's a covenant. And we know, in the deepest part of our hearts, that the marriage covenant is about love. A love that wants to, and eventually will, share and give all that we are to the other. The only place a covenant relationship can flourish and experience the intimacy we all long for and need is in the crucible of love. Utilitarian may work but only temporarily. Only an other-centered love will last.

And isn't the love we long for a self-giving love? Who wants to be married to someone whose love is only for himself or herself?

I Confess	My god liked intimacy, but he only gave it to those who met the terms of the contract.

For years I thought relationship with God was a working contract. God's the boss; I'm the employee. Or maybe it was a political contract. God's the king; I'm the servant. Or maybe it was a teaching contract. God's the professor; I'm the student.

My problem was; I could be an employee and never know the boss.

I could be a servant and never know the king.

I could be a student and never know the professor.

My understanding of knowing God, as Jesus meant it, was, shall we say, a wee bit off.

But probably the most important thought to consider in this conversation is this: If eternal life is just a transaction or contract, what does this say about God himself? Wouldn't it say that he doesn't care about relationship? Instead, what he *really* cares about is whether his terms of the contract are met? And these terms – are they not usually presented in quotas of legal righteousness and moral holiness – described in laws and rules? Does God love his rules more than he loves us?

Isn't this exactly what we believe about God? In honest moments, I realized that, for me, it was. Why else would I say that completing a transaction and accepting the terms of his contract decide eternal life?

So, what do you think the Father of your soul wants with you? A transaction or a relationship? A contract or a covenant? If he wants relationship, then does he want something temporary or one that lasts? Utilitarian and distant or personal and intimate?

What if the relationship, at least the way God understands the idea, isn't a transaction or contract?

What if God wants an intimate relationship?

What if God is a self-giving, loving Father and what he really wants is *us*.

What if our relationship with God looks like the relationship between the Father, Son, and Spirit?

What if they not just invite but also include us in their relationship? That is, the very life and love they have experienced forever?

What if this is eternal life? Then the good news is better news than I ever dared to dream.

And the implications... oh my gosh... they're staggering! *Everything* must be thought through relationally.

It seems to me that, for our part, relationship exists with God, especially the kind Jesus talks about, where I trust them, because I know them. Trusting someone enables us to see ourselves like the one we are trusting sees us. And in a circular way, my knowledge of God - being a dynamic, relational knowledge - grows as I experience my trust reassured, because he never betrays my trust.

When I was around four or five, my father was swimming and playing with my older brother, having what appeared to be an absolute blast. I was standing on the side, wanting to be in the pool but afraid to get in. I never asked him, but I'm pretty sure my dad saw the look of longing on my face. Standing in water that was deeper than I was tall, he walked over to the side of the pool and opened his arms, beckoning me to jump in and join him. Even at that young age, my mind reasoned it was foolish. I hesitated. I was scared. But I knew my father. And the power of *his relationship with me*, knowing him as my father, freed me to trust and overcome my fear. And so I jumped.

I think relationship that is eternal life looks a lot more like *that*.

CHAPTER 7

I LOVE JUSTICE

> *"The weak can never forgive,
> forgiveness is the attribute of the strong."*
>
> — Gandhi

Several years ago, personality tests were all the craze. At school and work, in restaurants, and at parties, they were the buzz. People asked what my "letters" were, and I would shuffle my feet silently, never knowing how to answer. Their question sounded like code, a mysterious, secretive, "members only" code. I wanted in. It was embarrassing.

People would argue about which test was more accurate. But really, most worked essentially the same. Based on a series of questions, the test formed a generalized profile of a person's dominant personality traits.

Eventually, I took one of the tests – against my will, I might add. Here's what I learned. I was a "J," an off-the-charts "J." Justice was *very* important to me. (This was something I think I already knew.) Even as a child playing games, I would get more upset if I felt a game was unfair than I would about losing. I never liked losing, but I hated cheating, especially when I lost.

I am aware that your personality probably differs from mine. You may not be nearly as obsessive about justice as I am, but even so, I think we all want it. I would suggest it's universal. In the heart of every image-bearer is a knowledge that injustice deserves and cries out for an answer.

We hope for it, fight for it; many have given their lives for it. I think we love it. For we love when someone takes up the cause of victims and defends the powerless. We love justice, because it cradles a promise that all will be made right.

The concept of justice so permeates our lives it seems to dominate our stories in literature, cinema, music, and so on. So, it's no surprise when I say story has played a significant role in shaping my notion of justice.

Most often our stories involve the struggle of good versus evil. Hopefully, the story ends as good prevails and justice is fulfilled. The plot is familiar: the protagonist has been wronged, and a disaster looms on the horizon (the landscape is endangered, genocide threatens a race, or the universe will be destroyed). Evil threatens to rise up and destroy the good. Conflict is heightened, and tension mounts as the good navigates a labyrinth of fear and terror to escape destruction and exact justice. Usually, the story resolves with the punishment/destruction of the evil and the vindication of the good.

Since my J was off the charts, my favorite scenes in movies/TV were typically when the "bad guy gets it."

Walter White unleashes his final "solution" on the gang that murdered his brother-in-law in *Breaking Bad*.

Mark Walberg, in *The Departed*, waits for Matt Damon in his apartment and proceeds to execute him without trial.

Clint Eastwood, in *Unforgiven*, finds courage in his whiskey bottle and confronts Gene Hackman with his shotgun and blows him across the room.

Andy Garcia, in *The Untouchables*, slides across the floor of a train station and catches a falling baby carriage, baby inside, tumbling down the stairs. While balancing the carriage with his leg, he aims his pistol at the gangster, who is holding the key witness in the

Al Capone trial at gunpoint.

"Got him?" Kevin Costner asks.

"Yup," Garcia replies,

"Take him," Costner orders.

And with that, Garcia promptly puts a bullet between the gangster's eyes.

I quietly pumped my fist and whispered, "Yes!" The cheers in the movie theater during such films confirm our mutual love of what we call justice.

I think the reason we see the good guys as good isn't because they are morally better than most; they aren't. We perceive them as good, because they exact punishment on the villains.

But then along comes *Les Miserables*. The beauty this story offers is a different form of justice juxtaposed to the one with which we are all too familiar. It moves us, stirs within us the hope of a hint of grace and mercy in justice. Can justice be better? Somehow, *we know* she is better. We catch a glimpse of this justice, and she is beautiful. Strangely, she also looks familiar. We want to know her, because, through seeing her, we begin to realize the justice we have known is an imposter of hatred and revenge.

My desire for justice is not confined only to the make-believe worlds of theater and cinema; it extends to my experiences of everyday life on our planet.

In a world overwhelmed with suffering, which we inflict on each other – a parent abusing his or her children, terrorists slaughtering innocents, slavery spawned out of our prejudice or sexual perversions, the blatant aggression and militarism of tyranny, the oppression of the weak by the powerful and the poor by the rich, all of this grinding us into the dust – I want justice.

Far closer to my heart, when someone takes advantage of and/or hurts my wife and children, I want justice. In fact, whenever someone does something I consider unfair or immoral, whether to me or to others, I want justice. Don't we all?

Naturally, justice is also fundamental to our concept of God, regardless of what religion we follow. For it seems our hope that all will be made right only holds promise if there is a Someone untainted by our corruption who has the power and wisdom to make it so.

But is his justice the same as ours?

Maybe his justice gives existence to the idea of justice in our minds and hearts. It is because he is just that justice runs so deeply through our veins.

I mentioned earlier that the way I have chosen to earn a living is as a nature photographer. I grew up with film, so I have a darkroom. I still use it – old school, I know.

Have you ever been in a darkroom? It's so dark, you can't even see the outline of your hand. Your senses struggle with spatial relationships. If it's completely quiet and you are still, you feel almost disembodied, because you see nothing, just blackness. Those who have experienced this kind of darkness know exactly what I mean.

Imagine being in this darkroom for a very long time. At some point, you realize there is someone in the room with you. You don't know how he or she got in there; the person is just there. For whatever reason, he or she decides to open the door, just a crack. A single beam of light pours in. Like a cramp, your body cringes, and you bury your face to shield your eyes. It hurts. You don't want the light. You scream at your mysterious companion to close the door. Maybe they do, and maybe they don't. But if they keep it open, ever so gradually, your body begins to relax. Your eyes water and blink uncontrollably, still wincing from the pain. But as they slowly adjust, you bask in the clarity and warmth the light provides, and gladness, joy's cousin, greets you. In time, you yearn for more, so you open the door further. As you step into the light, joy joins her cousin, and what you feel is *relief*, a bit like freedom, freedom from darkness.

This was not unlike my long, difficult journey from what I had called "justice" to the justice belonging to the Father, Son, and Spirit. This struggle with the concept of justice was at the root of my fear of darkness and the monster veiled within it. But when this caricature of God died, I became fully alive, free to live in the embrace of the fresh, sunlit air, no longer enslaved to my fear of the monster under my bed.

There is struggle in this journey, and there is pain. But there is gladness and joy too. His justice is fierce; it is fire. But he is better than we can imagine. I believe that freedom and trust grow from understanding and submitting to the goodness of his justice.

In the summer of 2010, my sister came to stay with my dad while I took my wife and three children on a short-term mission trip to the small country of Slovenia. My father was eighty-nine at the time and had been living with us for about six years. We really couldn't leave him by himself due to his age, his cancer, and the onset of dementia, which was becoming more pronounced.

Unknown to us, during our absence, my sister secretly began maneuvering to gain control of our father's estate. Upon our return, she acted as though our relationship was completely normal. We didn't have a clue. Why would we?

We discovered her clandestine mission and how deep it went ten days after she left, when I received a phone call from the attorney she had retained. He informed us of her "grave concern" that we were financially abusing my dad by taking advantage of his dementia and stealing his money. Yet, she had deceived us and falsely accused and slandered us to her lawyer. This was a betrayal of the deepest kind.

We were stunned. Blindsided. Hurt. My dad had lived in our home for almost seven years, and we never took anything. She left without a word. No questions and no correspondence. Who does stuff like this?

We figured we must have done *something* that caused her to take such drastic measures. But we couldn't think of anything that would warrant her betrayal. Despite numerous calls, texts, and emails seeking any kind of explanation to this madness, my sister refused to answer. It got so bad that my wife, who doesn't have an enemy in the world, became physically ill for three days.

About a month later we received a letter from her attorney informing us that he had filed a petition on her behalf for control of Dad's finances. Again, after dozens of failed attempts just to ask why she was doing this, we received only silence. Consequently, we were forced to hire an attorney, because she insisted on going to court.

This ugliness went on for almost two years. And it got uglier.

My emotions became ragged. My anger, self-righteousness, and desire for "justice" nearly consumed me. As I descended into this vortex of a black hole, I happened to be reading George MacDonald's book, *Creation in Christ: Unspoken Sermons*. There were two sermons in particular that, after I first read them, I couldn't quite wrap my mind and emotions around. So, I read them over and over again. They were; "It Shall Not be Forgiven," MacDonald's discussion on forgiveness, and the sermon on "Justice."[20]

During these months, competing notions of justice warred for my soul. On the one hand, there was my sister's version, which had been the same as mine. To this day, as far as I know, my sister believes she did the righteous thing. I do not know what motivated her heart, but I know she believed she was justified in what she did. Sadly, she sacrificed her relationship with us and our children, who

---

20 I believe George MacDonald's sermon on justice is the best thing I've ever read on the subject. So, I freely admit my eternal debt and make no apology for borrowing heavily from his thoughts. The best I can do is pass along what I continue to glean from this treasure. See "Justice" in Creation in Christ: Unspoken Sermons (Regent College Publishing, Vancouver, BC: 2004).

are her last living blood relatives on earth, on the altar of her so-called justice.

On the other hand, there was MacDonald's version, which I believe comes much closer to the real thing in God, a notion of justice that sang to my soul but was gut-wrenching to live in because it beckoned me to not only let my revenge go, but also bid me to submit to the fire of his just love, which wanted to free me from *my* darkness.

The questions that surfaced during this difficult and painful time were no mere exercises in theology. Here are a few of them.
- Do I long for my version of justice or God's? Which version will shape the way I act?
- Do I succumb to my speculations re: her motive, thus condemning her without knowing her story, her heart?
- What does it mean to truly forgive? Will I cling to my self-righteousness instead of forgiving?
- Will God sacrifice his relationship with me or my sister to maintain his holiness and justice? *Does he need to?*
- Will relationship trump my desire for vindication?
- Will I lust for vengeance and retribution or pray for her deliverance from the evil that is consuming her?
- Is there any kind of punishment that can eliminate my sister's hate and replace it with love for me?
- How can I reconcile with someone who has no desire to reconcile?
- How can I respond to self-righteous superiority that only accuses, never answers; only blames, never apologizes?
- What is justice to someone who believes I am to be despised as her worst enemy?

While wrestling with what I read and knowing it to be better than what I currently thought, and simultaneously finding no power to quench my thirst for revenge in my circumstances, the struggle was *agony*. The knot in my stomach was so often my companion I thought I had an ulcer.

I can't tell you how many times, late at night, I was on my knees beside my wife in bed, reading excerpts from these two sermons. Many times, tears would well up in my eyes. Sometimes they were painful because of the blackness being revealed in my heart or because of what I thought forgiveness and justice were. Or because of what horrible things I had thought and said about the Father. Or because I didn't want to let my version of justice go. I was in love with this movie version, because it allowed me to keep my lust for vengeance.

But other times – oh, there were other times – my tears were exquisite because of the sheer beauty of a God who was better than all my learning had ever taught me. Or because of the joy that change was happening ever so gradually in my heart. Or because I was overwhelmed with the reality of a Being who, *for love's sake*, will not let anyone get away with anything. Instead, he will meet us in our darkness and destroy the sin in us and heal our broken souls that we might live in the freedom of God's love and goodness!

Today, as I write this, I smile when I think back on those weeks and months. Not that I'd ever want to do it again. No thank you. But I smile, because to think that God would take what I was reading and through the struggle of living it immediately invite me to meet him in a real personal encounter; this I now see as an act of relentless, eternal love.

I tell you this not to place myself in some sort of sanctimonious religious light but rather so that you will know that in sharing my story, this is not just an intellectual argument, exercise, or debate. A new understanding of God's justice has gripped me, and it won't let go.

My version of justice has been transformed, and so have I. The craving for my sister's punishment has faded, replaced with a passion for the destruction of the things in her that are destroying her. Now, *I want her freedom, not her punishment.*

I wish I could tell you all has been reconciled; it hasn't. But someday it will be. In me and my sister.

> **I Confess** | **In my former version of justice, if someone acted with evil or behaved immorally, what I really wanted was for them to be punished.**

I wanted them to suffer, to experience some kind of penalty: a fine, jail time, even death. It seemed to me this was fair. They deserved punishment because of their evil. I figured justice wasn't justice unless some type of punishment was involved. I wanted my sister to experience betrayal to the degree we had. If I couldn't have that, where was justice? Honestly, this says far more about me than it does about justice.

I live just thirty minutes outside of Portland, Oregon. Not far from where, as I write this, an enormous fire is raging. This fire happens to be in the Columbia River Gorge, a place I often photograph and have grown to love. It is one of the most beautiful and scenic areas in the United States. Consequently, I am deeply saddened by the destruction. And I am angry…

From what we have heard at this point, some teenagers shooting fireworks in an incredibly dry forest started the fire. Allegedly, an eyewitness admonished and warned them, which they subsequently laughed off, continuing with their momentary thrill.

The destruction engulfed over forty thousand acres of pristine land. Homes have been devastated, businesses lost, and commerce derailed. The I-84, a major interstate highway, was closed, along with the rail line connecting Portland with all points east. The ripples of economic impact will be felt for quite some time.

But, for our community here in the Northwest, it goes deeper than that. For many of us, we feel the carnage of the fire in the gorge personally. We have encountered beauty there, and we have been forever changed by it.

It's not surprising that this has instigated a lot of conversation about justice and punishment. Over the past few days I have observed that anger, almost visceral, has been the most common emotion for our community. And that anger has been aimed directly at the people responsible for the fire that now rages.

I think we should feel anger toward what they have done and even the alleged attitude with which they did it. How can we not? Something precious was stolen from us. It is a blow to our collective psyche.

Usually anger has a companion in tow – punishment. And many, many people, crying out for "justice," have called for the severe punishment of these young boys, to the point of suggesting that their parents be punished as well.

But is punishment justice? Is it even what these young men need?

Or is it what we need to satisfy some deep desire for them to feel the pain they have caused us?

Punishment would be warranted if it helped them learn the value of what they so carelessly destroyed. But punishing them because we feel anger toward them is petty, vindictive, and appeals to something in us that I don't think is very healthy. It is the resurrection of my former version of justice.

Punishment does not necessarily lead to learning responsibility. Nor will it bring the gorge back. It will not put out the fire. It will not change the attitude or behavior of the persons responsible. It will simply inflict suffering on the boys who did this. In our society, our justification for punishment is that we see it as an effective deterrent.

But the truth is, we don't know if it is. There is no guarantee that punishment deters anything.

Then *why punish?* Why do so many want to punish these young men?

We want to punish, because we see it as the means to justice. But punishment will bring justice about as much as spreading honey on my bread will make me a bee.

Should there be consequence to their actions? Yes, absolutely. Here are some possibilities.

- Have them sit and listen to those who lost their homes and all that was in them, going through the rubble and debris of what remains. Maybe this will help them feel the loss and pain they inadvertently caused.
- Have them help rebuild those homes.
- Have them help with the cleanup and with the inevitable mudslides and erosion that will occur.
- Have them help repair the roads and structures that have been destroyed or damaged.
- Have them help rebuild the trail system.
- Have them go to counseling.

Wouldn't this be more just than simply punishing these young men?

As I was writing this, a thought occurred to me. How amazing would it be if, in the months ahead, I met these young men who started all this as we worked side by side for the restoration of the gorge?

This debate raises an important question: how much evil must be committed to deserve my former version of justice? In the case of the gorge fire, it may seem obvious, but in most cases the answer isn't so easy.

For example, what about a lie? Ten lies? Becoming a habitual liar? In moments of honest clarity, I know I act with evil motive and intent, and I'm *certain* I don't want to face my former kind of justice. But this version gets worse. I took my idea of justice and threw it back into God. I defined his justice with my version of justice. In my view, God's justice was like mine, except purer and definitely more intense.

The brokenness in me that wanted this… I wonder how much of my concept of God's justice had been tainted and shaped by my version of justice?

In the spring of 2011, Osama Bin Laden was found and killed by a squad of Navy Seals. Immediately, it became the topic of all news media, social media, and general conversation in America. Many people rejoiced and even celebrated his death. I understand this. He scarred our country deeply by orchestrating the events of 9/11. Many, especially in religious circles, called the event "the justice of God."

For me, a US citizen, this was American justice. But was this *God's* justice? How do we know this? If Bin Laden's death was an act of God's justice, then isn't every death of every person an act of God's justice? Don't we *all* do evil? Should people be happy and rejoice when I die, because God exercised his justice by taking my life? If this is how I understand God's justice, then Osama Bin Laden was an instrument of God's justice when he killed thousands in his attack against America. Bin Laden certainly believed he was.

In my attempt to work this out, I turn immediately to comparison: "But I'm not as bad as he was!" That may be accurate, but this is the cry of the self-righteous. The truth is, it doesn't matter how much evil has stained my life or others, because *every one of us is both a victim and a victimizer*. I find it quite revealing that when I've had this kind of conversation about justice with Christian folk, rarely have I met those who see themselves as someone who oppresses or victimizes others. But to use a metaphor borrowed from C.S. Lewis novel *The Lion, the Witch, and the Wardrobe* – Turkish delight stains the fingers and smears the mouths of everyone.

And if I was right, that God's version was my version on divine steroids, then everything would unravel, and we would be ruined. Because, isn't hell God's ultimate punishment of evil... forever?

| I Confess | I thought that justice for a victim was synonymous with punishing the oppressor. |

In my version of justice, I was more interested in the evildoer being punished than the victim being healed. I rarely considered that justice included the healing of the victim. I'm not sure that ever crossed my mind. However, I *am* sure I *never* thought justice included the healing of the oppressor. In my mind, my sister didn't deserve healing; she deserved punishment. I believed justice was accomplished when the evildoer received the punishment he or she deserved. I think I understand the relationship between "deserve" and punishment, but what does the idea of deserving have to do with justice?

Having already assumed God's justice was like mine, this meant the goal of God's justice was realized in the punishment of the evildoer. God punished for the sake of punishment, because punishment is justice. I reasoned that God simply paid out what was due. In truth, my "justice" looked a lot more like vengeance. But I could justify that too. Doesn't Scripture say that God has vengeance?[21]

Not long ago, at the request of a friend, I watched a sermon on YouTube by a well-known Christian writer/pastor. He addressed the question, "Where do victims of evil find comfort?" His text was the passage from Romans to which I just referred. His primary point

---

21 *"Vengeance is mine says the Lord."* (Romans 12:19-21)

was that their greatest comfort comes from "Knowing that God will have vengeance. He will get them (the evildoers) in the end. His wrath will be far worse for them than any evil they have perpetrated on you."

Really? Never mind that someone else's suffering does nothing to nullify evil or bring about restoration. Never mind that the suffering of another never brings any comfort to the hurting victim. If he's right, what does this say about God's nature?

In this view, vengeance ups the ante in the game of justice. God doesn't simply punish evildoers according to what is due (my former view of justice); he increases the punishment beyond whatever evil people do.

How can this be? Is God really like this?

How do I understand this thing called vengeance, especially when it's attributed to God?

The text clearly tells us not to repay evil with more evil (12:17). Yet, it goes on to say we are to leave room for God's wrath; let him exact vengeance (12:19).

Have you ever felt like the Bible text is just playing a theological shell game with us? This paragraph always seemed to feel like that to me.

Does God have a double standard?

That which is evil for us, does it miraculously become good simply because God does it?

Was it God who established that evil deserves punishment and his justice will dispense it appropriately?

I adopted the response of others: the reason he tells us not to repay evil with evil, even though it deserves it, is because we can't pull it off without screwing up. And because he can, it is just for him to exact vengeance on his children for the evil they do.

In other words, retributive vengeance isn't evil in itself. It's *the way* vengeance is done that makes it evil. And since only God can do it perfectly, it's not evil when he exacts this kind of vengeance.

This used to work for me. First, because it absolves God from doing an evil thing. Second, it lets me off the hook – I was free to desire vengeance, because it wasn't evil. Third, I didn't have to figure out how to get it; God would do it for me. I could justify wanting my sister to pay for her betrayal, and God would make sure it happened.

Really? Is it possible that we believe things about God that are just not true?

I know I have. I still do. More often than I realize. Is it possible that God is better than this?

Maybe Paul meant something different. Did you notice how the text instructs us in how we should respond to evil? It tells us to "overcome evil with *good*" (v. 21). I believe this is how God avenges evil. In God's version of vengeance, he doesn't defeat evil by repaying us with more evil. He overcomes evil with good. Could it be that God destroys his enemies by making them his friends?

I Confess	I taught others God was indeed like this pastor's version.

There was a time when this pastor's statement made sense to me. It grieves me that I thought so little of God that I assumed his justice demanded vengeance and that he punished for punishment's sake. I wanted *so badly* for my sister to face *this* god. Honestly, I am horrified at the god in which I used to believe.

For all my talk of love, the twisted, ugly truth was this: I hid behind my version of his holiness as though it somehow explained and excused him in doing an evil thing. Though I would have denied it to my death, I actually believed in a god who needed to be appeased or placated. My god demanded not justice, not even vengeance, but *punitive retribution*.

And by retribution I meant vindictiveness, a kind of personalized cosmic karma. Not merely a passive karma that delivers natural consequences but God actively paying out what is due. And only punishment, the deliberate infliction of suffering, can do this and satisfy him. Cloaked in religious piety and language, I rationalized my lust for vengeance and called it justice, because, I reasoned, "I am becoming like him." Though in truth, it was far more like I was fashioning him to be like me.

I think this is called self-deception. Mine ran very deep.

Some may say that my portrayal of this view of God's justice – one that sees justice as primarily retributive, one that declares God's righteous demands need to be appeased – is both imbalanced and a misrepresentation.

That's possible, I'm certainly capable of misrepresentation and presenting information that is out of balance. Who isn't? But I don't think I'm too far off the mark because as I've stated several times already, I know this narrative – I taught this version of "God's justice" for decades. And if you were to talk to everyday folk who hear this theory week after week as I have, you would find many come away thinking God is cruel and "monster like." So then, at least from a pastoral viewpoint, this is no red herring or caricature.

As I have reflected on what I believed and taught, what could be worse than deliberately believing this? The only thing I can think of would be the joyful worship of *this* god, made after *my* likeness.

I did that too.

How did I get there? I think partly it was a result of interpreting the Scriptures through the lens of human hate, revenge, and resentment, not the way of God's justice.

I believe God is just and exercises justice, both passively and actively. I believe he has wrath and anger and will enact vengeance on evil. I believe he is holy. My problem was not that God is or does any of these things. My problem was how I defined and understood these ideas, which shaped my view of God, people, and life in general.

So, what's the alternative? Is there one? Does God punish evil? If so, why?

| I Confess | I sought an answer to this question outside of God's being. |

I looked for some external reason for what would cause him to insist, demand, or want punishment for evil. That is, something in us or something we've brought to the table. Things like:

We deserve it.

We disobeyed his rules.

We hate him.

But I believe I missed the point of the question.

It seems obvious that God acts in a responsive way to events all the time. But when I ask, "What causes God to punish?", I believe only God can cause (by that I mean require or necessitate) God to do something. This is an *internal* reason.

To be clear – there is always in God the profound, unshakeable, unalterable goodness and love that is utterly opposed to sin, corruption, idolatry, abuse, pride – to any form of evil – as well as a willingness to do something about it. If God does not look at the sex trafficking of children with something analogous to anger, wouldn't we think something is terribly wrong about God?

However, I assumed that what God must and will do about evil is punish it.

So, here's what I'm really searching for: why is God angry about our sin? And why do we believe that anger motivates God to punish? What is it in him that necessitates punishment? What, in his nature, requires him to punish?

Indulge me as I play this out in an imaginary conversation as I question my younger self –

"What do you think would cause God to insist on or demand punishment for evil?"

I probably would have initially blown off the question, "Because he just does; he's God," I'd retort.

"You mean he just does it, because he feels like it? Or he just can't help himself? It's a control issue for him then? I'm afraid that won't do."

"No, none of that. It's because of his hatred of sin," I would have suggested.

"Maybe, but what does God hate about it? Or is he simply obsessed with moral perfection? Is it because we have broken his rules and laws? Does God love his rules so much that he would punish his children forever because they broke them? Does he love his laws, his righteousness, and himself more than he loves us?

"Why did he make rules or give us laws in the first place? Were they not, at least in part, to govern, teach, and help his children? Were they not for our good? Think of why you have established rules in your home. Is it because you love rules and you love to be obeyed, or are they designed to help your children? Are they for your sake or your children's sake? And when they break them, are you personally offended because they did something that defied you, maybe something you didn't like? Or does it upset you, because your child, in hurting others, has behaved in a way that is selfish and destructive, ultimately bringing hurt, ruin, and destruction to others and even themselves?"

"But we are flawed parents. We are not holy enough to see it as God sees it," I would have replied.

"*Exactly*. But you mean this differently than I do. I ask again, what is it about sin that God hates?"

"Sin is an affront to God. It offends him," I would have answered.

"That may be, and that should be considered, but what do you mean by offend? Surely you don't mean that God hates sin because it annoys or irritates him? I can't imagine God punishing people because he's annoyed or irritated. That thought seems unworthy of him. I assume that by using the word 'offend,' you mean that sin angers and displeases God. If so, I agree. But this brings us back to the same question. *Why* is God outraged with our sin? *Why* does he hate it?"

My emotions beginning to rise, I would have snapped, "He hates that we have defied, disobeyed, and rebelled against him."

"Again, the statement is true, but let's push a little further again. *Why* does God hate being disobeyed? *Why* does he hate it when we defy or rebel against him?"

Finally, my frustration would have boiled over. "Because he is more righteous than we are, so he hates *any* form of evil. We don't, because we're not as righteous or holy as him. And he, being God, deserves to be obeyed. He is the Creator. He is in charge. He is the authority. Therefore, he must be obeyed. And he hates it when we don't treat him like God, because that means something else has replaced him as God."

"Ahh… now we get to it!"

"I agree. He is righteous and holy, the Creator, and the authority, and he deserves to be obeyed. All these things are true. But if you think about it, the way you've framed these concepts, your answer essentially is: God hates to be disobeyed, because he *wants and deserves* to be obeyed. And you assume that reason is okay because of the previous things you said. He is God. What he wants is perfect. He should get what he wants. But here is where I believe things get a bit foggy. In your view, if he doesn't, then he punishes us for not giving him the obedience he wants and deserves. God punishes, because he doesn't get what he wants? Why would any of us assume that God's response for not getting what he wants is punishment? This sounds a lot like a performance driven relationship. I do this if you do that. It also sounds a lot like God is a very abusive father, a mean boss, or a tyrannical king. It sounds a lot like God is a bit self-centered.

"Does God love obedience more than he loves you? Does he love what he wants more than you? And what does he want? Does he want obedience, glory, or worship more than he wants you? Does he want you so that you will give him glory, obedience, and worship?

And is this desire so pure and intense that if he can't get it from us, he'll abandon us and punish us forever?"

"He is none of those things," I would have replied, "You just don't have a high view of holiness. He should love himself, for he is the loveliest and best thing in existence!"

"You are right; I do not have a high enough view of holiness. But neither do you. Who does?

"And this is the truest thing yet: he is the loveliest being in all of existence! And he does, in fact, love himself. But remember, 'himself' is *three* persons. His love has never been a solitary, narcissistic self-love. It has always been self-giving and other-centered."[22]

Incidentally, where is love in the opinions of my former view? Does it take a back seat to justice when God deals with evil? Does God compartmentalize his attributes so that love does not engage evil?

May I suggest a different reason why God hates sin? This was actually one of the first rays of light that broke into my darkroom and began to free me from my fear of the monster. It was the dawning of an understanding of what his justice is actually like. God hates sin because of what it is doing to his beloved. *It is causing ruin and destruction on the very ones he has set his love on* – and that includes everybody.

God does not hate sin because it offends his morality, holiness, or righteousness. He hates sin because of the destruction it brings to those he loves. And he loves everyone, including the oppressor.

I want to be very clear here. God hates sin, because it destroys all

---

22 All parts of this extended dialogue are things I actually said at one time. But I have also heard the opinions of my younger self echoed from students, teachers, and pastors so frequently that I would suggest this view is the dominant view in American evangelicalism of God and his justice.

that he has made, for it twists them, turning them away from the good. Our turning away is an attempt at relational independence, and he knows this is our death. I do not believe God created you, me, or any other person, only to abandon us to death at our first or millionth failure.

We *know* this to be true. For, if we are good parents who truly love our children, we would never abandon our children upon their first immoral choice or a lifetime of immoral choices. We hate the evil and sin our children do, not our children. If it were in our power, we would destroy that which is killing our children.

So, here is a question that haunted me for years…

Are we better parents than our true Father?

What God wants is for us to live in the love and light of the relationship he is and has within himself. He wants us to know him, for he is life. And God wants to share his life with us. The Father, Son, and Spirit want us to participate with them in their love and joy. The Trinity wants us to enter into their circle of love and light.

Nothing less will do.

CHAPTER 8

THE JUSTICE OF LOVE

*Jesus did not die to save us from punishment;
he was called Jesus because he should
save his people from their sins.*

— George MacDonald

    I imagine my journey out of the thing I called "justice" not unlike a scene from *The Two Towers*, the second book of J.R.R. Tolkien's trilogy, *The Lord of the Rings*.

    Good King Théoden sits aged before his time, gnarled and feeble from the blindness that enslaves him, only a shell of the man he once was. Gandalf and his three companions enter his court, and after a fierce struggle, Gandalf at last frees Théoden from Saruman's evil treachery. With compassion in his heart and wisdom in his words, he welcomes the king back into the light, "Breathe the free air once more, my friend."

    I kind of felt like that. So many questions... but *so* glad to be free!

    Yet the tenacity with which my version of justice held me was (and occasionally still is) disturbing. It is so entrenched; it is the default setting in my soul. Like a dog with a bone, it won't let go. If something happens that merely hints at unfairness or offends my sense of "right" or flat out hurts me, I want justice. And by "justice" I mean vengeance. I want the guilty party to pay some form of penalty for whatever they've done. I want them punished.

What actually is God's justice? What is it when confronted by evil?
What do we mean when we use the word "justice"?
Is it the "righting" of wrongs?
Is it cosmic karma being balanced by getting what we deserve?

I Confess	**I defined God's justice only in the context of sin, evil, or wrongdoing.**

I believed that when we spoke of God's justice, we were describing how he dealt with evil. Justice only had meaning if there was evil to be punished.

But how can this be? Does God become just when he must address something evil?

Wasn't God just *before* he created us?

Wasn't he just *before* sin became part of the reality of the universe?

Of course he was.

For the record, and there are tons of scriptures that say this truth plainly, God is just… and always has been.

Since justice exists in God before there is any evil to punish, the imposing of a penalty through some form of suffering can't be the primary idea of what it means to be just or to impart justice.

My point is this: if justice is part of God's nature, then it pre-exists evil. Therefore, our understanding and even our definition of justice must be larger and broader than simply how God responds to evil.

This was important for me as I reconsidered justice during the events with my sister. Finding justice with her wasn't about "getting even" with her financially, psychologically, or in any other way. Nor was it God doing it for me. It wasn't about hoping God would "punish" her. Finding justice was better than that. I began to suspect that it had to do with our relationship. And that would be *much* harder. That would require humility, communication, repentance, forgiveness, and a host of other things on both our parts. It seemed I really needed to rethink my view of justice.

So then, what is the justice of God before sin happens?

What does God's justice look like at the essential level of his being?

Maybe it looks like this: the Father, Son, and Spirit think, feel, and treat each other with *goodness* and *fairness*. There is no manipulation, deceit, selfishness, meanness, impatience, or favoritism in their relationship. They have integrity with one another and are always loving and truthful with each other. Their relationship is just.

If my description is even remotely close to the truth, this implies a rather huge idea. We must think of God's justice in *relational* terms and not as some abstract code of morality that must be fulfilled.

| I Confess | I did not think of justice as a relational quality. |

Aside from the fact that punishment appealed to something deep in me that was not good, I discovered another equally disturbing reason for defining justice as I did. I thought of justice as an abstract, moral idea. (Don't we commonly refer to it as "cold-hearted justice"?) Subconsciously, I had divorced justice from the righteous relationship of love that is God. I spoke of it almost as though God had to submit to justice, that he had to do this or that, because justice demanded it. So, in some bizarre way, God was beholden to justice.

This cannot be. No attribute of God is greater than him. That would be ludicrous.

Justice is a quality we believe resides in the nature of God's being. It's not merely an idea. It is personal and relational, because that is who he is.

My darkroom door just opened a wee bit more.

By thinking of justice in a relational way I recognized there was a far more fundamental concept to the nature of justice - something beyond just the way he deals with evil.

And what might that be? What is it in God that motivates him to be just? What is his goal in carrying out justice with his children's brokenness?

I Confess	I believed and taught that the thing justice *requires* is punishment.

It is obvious to even casual readers of the Bible (particularly the Old Testament) that it contains language of wrath and anger. Naturally, this raises a multitude of questions and the need for a rather lengthy conversation, which would extend far beyond the scope of this book. However, at the very least, I believe we can say this implies that God takes humanity's decisions and behavior seriously – whether good or bad. But should we then assume that if we see God's anger we will then see punishment on the pages of scripture? Do we believe that punishment is the only way by which God enacts justice? Is he required to punish in order to accomplish justice?

Growing up, my brother and I broke the house rules. When we got caught, the inevitable blame game started, attempting to avoid the certain punishment we assumed would follow. When my brother didn't get punished, I complained, "I can't believe you got away with that!" Never in a million years would I say he got justice. Luck maybe, but not justice.

Let's be honest, if we believe that justice requires punishment to be justice, then we are saying that for God to be just, he must inflict some degree of suffering upon evildoers. We cannot slip away from this idea by saying we bring punishment upon ourselves. Justice is not an abstract idea floating out there somewhere. It resides in God, and it is God who will exact justice throughout his cosmos. If justice requires punishment, then it is God who intentionally inflicts suffering to bring about justice. And if this is true, then I believe we have some serious problems on our hands.

Aside from the common yet erroneous belief that punishing the guilty somehow makes things right, could it be that this deep desire so many of us feel for God to punish really has more to do with our self-perceived need for the guilty to feel our pain?

This was certainly true with how I felt about my sister. Where does this come from? Why is this so important to us?

I think this may be a God-given desire. Yep, you heard me: a God-given desire.

Here's why. First, the desire for good and right relationship is part of being an image bearer. Second, the only way real reconciliation (that is, a return to right relationship) can occur, is if the guilty person can see, feel, and know the pain they have caused others, so that the victim's pain becomes their pain. Only then is true reconciliation possible.

The fall has twisted and distorted this in us, so we just want the offender to feel pain. We stop there, thinking this will suffice. It doesn't.

What we really want is reconciliation, and we mistakenly think punishment will achieve this. But punishment cannot atone or take away sin. Neither can it reconcile a relationship.

Still not convinced, my imaginary debate with my former self would continue something like this:

"Okay," I would have said, "God is sinless, so punishment isn't included in his definition of justice. But we are broken people. And because of our sin, God's justice must condemn and punish us, or he wouldn't be just! He can't let people get away with breaking his laws and commands. There must be a penalty for our evil, for us screwing up so badly. Besides, everyone knows we deserve punishment."

"First, God isn't going to let anyone get away with anything," I would reply. "He does condemn sin in us, but in this way, he judges it for what it is: evil. And he pronounces it unworthy of his kingdom and us as guilty for participating in it. He condemns it. But you have either made 'condemn' synonymous with 'punish,' or you have defined it in such a way that it must include punishment. Is it possible to condemn without punishment? Yes, it is.

"Second, does punishment turn the wrong into right? Does punishment redeem? Does punishment remove sin? Does it somehow, on God's cosmic justice scale, cancel the sin and restore balance to the universe?

"What if you stole your boss's car and totaled it in an accident? If he fired you, would that bring justice? If you apologized, would that bring justice? If you made restitution by buying him a new car, would that bring justice? What if you did all three?"

"Ah… now that would be justice," I would have replied.

"Even if we apologize and make restitution, can punishment undo/offset your wrong? Can punishment remove, undo, or heal the thing in you that caused you to steal the car to begin with? Can it reconcile you and your boss?

What about my sister? Would punishing her reconcile us? Not one bit. Would it untwist her wrong? Never. Would God punishing you reconcile you to him? Would God punishing Jesus, his eternally beloved Son, reconcile us to him?

This *frustrated* me. How can there be *no* penalty, *no* punishment to all the sick, evil things that happen on earth? Doesn't this just scream unfairness? Maybe we misunderstand. There is a penalty to be paid and something that requires it. But it is neither God nor his justice. It is *sin* that requires payment, and its payment is death. I was told this more times than I can count.

I grew up just outside of Philadelphia, and I attended college in south Florida. Over the course of four years, I made so many trips up and down I-95 in my 1968 VW Beetle that couldn't go faster than 52 miles per hour that I lost count. I felt like an interstate yo-yo. Every time I'd get to the Carolinas, I'd see this splashed across a billboard: "The wages of sin is death…" Right underneath that would be, "See Rock City." That usually brought a smile to my nearly comatose face.

However, consider this: a wage is a payment that has been earned for something you've done. Death is the wages of sin. It is sin's wage, *not God's*. Not even yours. The nature of what sin is requires that if you embrace her, you must pay what she demands for playing in her world: death.

Jesus came to save us from sin.

On the other hand, if punishment is required for justice to occur, and death was God's verdict of judgment in the event we rebelled, then the statement would be more accurate this way: Jesus came to save us from his Father's punishment, i.e., justice.

This can't be, because Jesus would be saving us from himself, for he is the same as the Father. But that is exactly where my version of

God left me.

One final thought about my former theory that justice requires punishment. I mentioned previously that as I matured through the ordeal with my sister, I no longer wanted her to be punished. However, if punishment is the thing God requires for him to be just and to exact justice on our evil, then I haven't really matured in my understanding of justice; I have regressed. Why? Because I no longer desire punishment, yet, according to my former belief system, he does and he will, in fact, punish my sister.

| I Confess | There was no room for mercy in my definition of justice.

For as long as I can remember I thought mercy and justice in God were opposites.

I taught that mercy proceeds out of God's love, and justice flows out of God's righteousness, as if God has a split personality. So, either he gives you justice (punishment) or mercy (withholds punishment). To do the one, show mercy, he sets aside the other, justice, and vice versa.

I assumed they resolved somehow in his being, but I thought it was obvious that they opposed each other in his actions. To my way of thinking, he couldn't be merciful and just at the same time. But wait a minute: does God ever act inconsistently with the nature of his being?

I am not alone in this view of justice and mercy. Not only have I heard this in countless sermons and classes, this theory also prevails even among those who have little or no belief in God.[23]

---

23 Consider the movie Noah, released in the spring of 2014. Not only did it portray God as primarily a judge bent on punishment (the flood), but justice was interpreted as synonymous with punishment. There was no mercy, except to Noah and his family. If you see the movie, or see it again, listen for how often the word "punish" is used.

But if justice requires punishment and forgiveness withholds it, then the moment God forgives, the moment he withholds what justice requires, he is no longer just, because he didn't do the very thing that, in my former definition of justice, makes justice... justice.

Simply, if God pardons sin, then he is not just. But God *does* pardon sin, right?

It's as if our sin puts God between a rock and a hard place. As if saving us created a dilemma or problem for him. Now, because of our sin, God must choose not only which way he will act – in mercy or punishment – but also who will receive his mercy and who will receive his punishment. If he pardons all of us, then he is not just. If he punishes all of us, then he is not merciful. I wonder if God has ever thought, "Shoot, if Adam just hadn't sinned…"

But this is only a dilemma IF God requires punishment to remain just.

Mercy and justice are both good and right – at least in God. Two goods cannot be opposed to each other. If God is merciful, then it must be a mercy that is just. And if God is just, then it must be a justice that is merciful.

God is not sometimes merciful and other times not. He is always merciful. Nor is he sometimes just and other times not. He is always just for all of his attributes are as infinite as himself. [24]

Today, I would say my thinking that mercy and justice are opposites is a false dichotomy.

A popular theory that I used to get around this dilemma was

---

24   I admitted earlier that I lean on George MacDonald heavily because he has been such a significant influence in shaping my thoughts regarding Justice. These two paragraphs are not a quote but the core of the explanation is his. See: George MacDonald, Creation in Christ: Unspoken Sermons (Vancouver, BC: Regent College Publishing, 2004) 68.

that God acted with mercy by withholding punishment from us and acted with justice by punishing Jesus. So, God got his pound of flesh and pardoned us at the same time. Does that work for you?

There are many who would say "yes, of course that works – that's the gospel". And, to be fair, they would qualify it. I am deeply aware that, at this point, we come to the summit of a holy mystery: the glory of the Incarnation itself. But no matter how eloquent we are in "qualifying" that God needs to be placated or appeased for him to justify, it is unavoidable that this says something about God's very nature. And what it says, in my view, is not good. Is it possible that for the last two thousand years we have been creating mythologies to whistle away our ignorance of this mystery? I know I have and probably will again. And if it is possible, why would we insist that our version is the only true or right version?

Let's take this a step further. What does God's justice look like for the oppressed? How about for the oppressor? Is the same true concerning his mercy?

This question is *critical*, because every single one of us, without exception, is both victim and victimizer.

What if God's justice heals the oppressed *and* the oppressor? Healing that reaches the depth of our soul, whether it be the wounds of the victim or the "untwisting" of evil in the victimizer, so that both come to love only the good?

Why would we believe God's justice to be less than this? Would justice that does less be justice?

Surely, God's justice offers more than just the external solution of reward and punishment, yes?

In his seminal work, *Against Heresies*, the great early church father, Irenaeus, developed a notion of justice as restoration. His word for it was *recapitulation*. Dr. Roger Newell describes Irenaeus's concept this way:

In this drama of divine justice, the eternal Son descends to space and time, and into our humanity, not to be an object of "divine wrath" so God lets us off the legal hook, but rather to reclaim the entire human journey from birth to death and beyond death, untwisting our disobedience by a healing obedience for the entire human journey, from Mary's womb to the ascension. So, God "defeats" evil not by ruthlessly punishing guilty parties but by faithfully untwisting every step of false response with true submission to the Father's will."[25]

T.F. Torrance says much the same:

"In the incarnate life of Jesus, and above all in his death, God does not execute his judgment on evil simply by smiting violently away by a stroke of his hand, but by entering into it from within, into the very heart of the blackest evil, and making its sorrow and guilt and suffering his own."[26]

Is it possible that mercy and justice come from the same wellspring in God's innermost being? That they are both expressions of something far deeper and more fundamental in God's nature?

| I Confess | I believed God's goal or purpose in punishing us was primarily *punitive*. |

I believed the purpose of his punishment was simply to inflict deserved suffering for the evil we have done. Before he creates, knowing we will fall, the goal of his justice was always to punish evil, because he has established that evil deserves and must be punished.

At best, this goal teaches us when we are wrong, and the wrong

---

25   I am indebted to Dr. Roger Newell for his insight into the understanding of justice. See *The Feeling Intellect: Reading the Bible with C. S. Lewis*, (Wipf and Stock, 2010), 32.
26   T.F. Torrance, *Incarnation*. (Grand Rapids: IVP Academic, 2015),150.

we do is not allowed in his universe. At worst, his punishment of our sin is purely vindictive.

I am not saying that punishment can never be part of the path to justice. Oftentimes it is. But it seems that punishment that is simply punitive can neither satisfy justice nor be called just at all. Let us be honest and call this "justice" what it is; it is nothing more than vindictiveness.

Even when I was in my twenties, I had the suspicion that punishment alone can't bring justice. But I didn't have a clue what I was missing. Frustrated, I remember hoping, *Justice has to be better than this!* That nagging doubt was the lightning rod that attracted me to this key question: "Why is God bound to punish sin?"

Can punishment undo, offset, atone, or make up for sin in any way?

Can punishment, regardless of the amount or its severity, change or untwist the wrong into right?

Can punishment change and heal the brokenness *in* me that wanted to do evil in the first place?

I'm suggesting punishment is powerless to do any of these things. And if I'm right, that punishment has no ability to amend, undo, or atone for evil, then why do we believe that punishment is required for justice to be justice?

Since his actions are always consistent with his nature, what in God's nature would cause him to punish for punishment's sake? What in God would be fulfilled or satisfied if he punished us?

When God exercises justice, does he abdicate his fatherhood and assume the role of Judge?

Does God set aside his love to judge?

When God judges, does he ever do it as a distant Judge, as though he has no relation to us?

Or is his judgment fulfilled through his fatherhood of humankind?

Is God's justice a competing notion with his love as Father, Son, and Spirit, or does his justice proceed out of this loving relationship? Let that simmer for a while.

I have found nothing within God's nature that would cause him to punish evil to accomplish justice. Neither have I found anything within Scripture that suggests the punishment of evil is, of itself, God's true justice. I would suggest that God's true nature looks far more like what George MacDonald so eloquently wrote, "God who loves righteousness and hates iniquity, does nothing he would not permit in His creature, demands nothing of His creature he would not do himself." [27]

Oh, I found plenty of books and sermons that listed God's attributes: holiness, righteousness, anger, wrath, vengeance, and, yes, his justice, were all cause for him to punish. These words are good words, true words. But they are defined through the framework of a fallen world that believes justice requires punishment. Is it possible that we read the Scriptures imprisoned by this paradigm and then throw our interpretations of the text back onto God? And then, with a bit of arrogance, pronounce, "Look! I told you I could prove to you what God was like."

That may sound harsh to you, almost judgmental. I suppose it is harsh, but it's not judgmental. I apologize, but I've thought about this a lot and for a long, long time. I do not know how to write my observation any better. No doubt, many of you will think of a way. But it's true. How do I know? Because this was true of me. I believed

---

27 George MacDonald, *Creation in Christ: Unspoken Sermons* (Vancouver, BC: Regent College Publishing, 2004) 69.

in and taught this version of justice most of my life.

How are you or I, or any other human being better off if God simply punishes us? How does this do anything to change us, not to mention reconcile us?

Is the world any better because evil has been punished? How does punishment accomplish the reconciling of the entire universe of which Scripture speaks? [28]

If justice holds the promise that all will be made right, will God have accomplished justice if, in some small corner of the universe, there remains the vast majority of the human race suffering punishment eternally yet defiant forever? Does this make the wrong right?

What good is it for God to punish me, to keep punishing me, yet allow me to continue to love evil?

My mind must change. My heart must change. My will must change. All of me must be made new. Isn't this exactly what he did? [29]

C. S. Lewis openly admits his dependency on George MacDonald for much of his understanding of God. This seems particularly true with regard to the subject of justice.

> "It seems Lewis would have us weigh competing forms of justice by the way he approaches this in The Lion, the Witch, and the Wardrobe. Almost immediately upon entering Narnia we meet someone that advocates an eye for an eye, a life for a life sense of justice. One that is primarily punitive. It is not Aslan. It is the white witch. Aslan's understanding is deeper and different." [30]

---

28 Colossians 1:20, "and through him to reconcile to himself all things, whether things on earth or things in heaven..."
29 2 Corinthians 5:14–18
30 Dr. Roger Newell, *The Feeling Intellect: Reading the Bible with C. S. Lewis* (Eugene, Oregon: Wipf and Stock, 2010), 30–31.

I think Lewis has given us a clue as to how he understands justice and atonement. Aslan submits to the white witch's version of justice by allowing her to punish him so that he ultimately dies. She thinks Aslan is her victim. She thinks she has used his justice to defeat him. But it is in his *submission* to this inferior version of justice that Aslan rejects and breaks this false version from which the white witch draws her power. Thus, he defeats her while simultaneously accomplishing Edmund's redemption.

So then, what is this deeper more fundamental basis to justice? What is this reservoir in God from where justice finds it source? What is the wellspring from which the pure waters of justice's purpose flow toward all creation?

I believe it is *relationship*. The reservoir is the relationship of Father, Son, and Spirit. And the most frequent word used in Scripture to refer to the way they relate is *love*.

The love the Father, Son, and Spirit have for each other birthed creation. They made us, so we could participate with them in their relationship. Participate in their justice, in their love. To participate with them as they are and have always been, long before sin entered their good creation.

Justice is, first and foremost, an expression of the way they treat and relate to each other. They act this way because they are this way. It seems, then, that justice is an expression of a broader concept: God's love.

God loves justice.[31] He cares infinitely more for the oppressed and oppressors than any of our rhetoric can ever describe. I repeat my earlier question, "Does God love justice more than the person he judges?" Think hard about it.

As a parent, when I discipline my children, do I do it simply because I'm angry at the evil they do? Or do I have a greater purpose

---

31 "For the Lord is righteous, he loves justice," Psalm 11:7

in mind? That is, to teach them their behavior hurts others and is also self-destructive. As a parent, *I know the difference in my heart.* My judgment (that is, the exercising of justice) with my family is an expression of love.

I judge my children (which may include punishment) to the best of my ability, because I love them. I want justice to have her way with my children, not just in their outward behavior but also in their innermost being. Anything less is not justice.

I was beginning to "glimpse the self-giving Father behind the legal robes of the divine Judge." [32]

Is God different in his love for his children?

Yes, only better. And if I truly love them, my love will want justice for and in them. I will never relent to the evil that grips them but will struggle all the harder to see my child's heart change and be free.

Again, I ask, are we better parents than our true Father in heaven?

Not a chance. Scripture is extremely clear on this:

"My son, do not despise the Lord's discipline and do not resent his rebuke, because the Lord disciplines those he loves, as a father the son he delights in" (Prov. 3:11–12).

This is even clearer in the New Testament. Consider the parable of the prodigal son in Luke 15:11–32.[33] Where is justice in this story? We miss it if we're looking for the father's threatening hammer of punitive justice to drop. The reason this story is so wonderful to us is because we don't see what we expect to see. There is no "hammer." What the son receives from his father is forgiveness – *before any con-*

---

[32] Dr. Roger Newell, *The Feeling Intellect: Reading the Bible with C. S. Lewis* (Eugene, Oregon: Wipf and Stock, 2010), 28.
[33] See Dr. C. Baxter Kruger, *The Parable of the Dancing God* (Grand Rapids: IVP, 2006).

fession or repentance.

This *so* scandalizes us that we refuse to call this justice. Instead, we call it mercy or grace, succumbing again to the fallacy that God cannot act with mercy and justice simultaneously.

Is it possible that what we really see in the parable is the beautiful, merciful justice of love?

If I am a good parent, my goal in exercising justice with my children is never punitive but rather restorative and redemptive. Always. When it is not, I know I am not being a good parent.

Maybe the goal of the Father's justice with broken children is reconciliation. Not just an external restitution of things, but an internal changing of my heart to bring me to the place where I love righteousness and hate iniquity. Maybe his purpose is to bring me to love justice – to love him.

It is here that the Father, through Mr. MacDonald, threw the door to the darkroom in my heart wide open, and Joy joined her cousin, Gladness. "Primarily, God is not bound to punish sin; he is bound to destroy sin. If he were not the Maker, he might not be bound to destroy sin – I do not know. But seeing he has created creatures who have sinned, and therefore sin has, by the creating act of God, come into the world, God is, in his own righteousness, bound to destroy sin."[34]

Can you see how this changes everything?

Only the destruction of sin can remove, cancel, and send sin away. The universe, the world, you and I and everyone ever born are better if, and only if God *destroys* sin.

Then justice will have its way. God's will shall be done on earth,

---

34 George MacDonald, *Creation in Christ: Unspoken Sermons* (Vancouver, BC: Regent College Publishing, 2004) 69.

as it is in heaven, for his children will have come to love righteousness and loathe evil.

Honestly, did we expect God to do any less?

So then, why does God punish sin? I have come to believe that if God is bound to punish sin, it is his own love that binds him. His purpose is to bring us to the place where the sin in us, which moved us to do evil in the first place, is destroyed. This is the healing of our souls - that we come to love and want the good thing.

"The only vengeance worth having on sin is to make the sinner himself its executioner," writes Mr. MacDonald. [35]

There is *no* refuge, *no* reprieve, and *no* place to hide from God's relentless love for us. This is what I have called "just-love."

When and how does God bring us to the point where we abhor sin? I don't know. But if punishment is involved, at least in part, it will be an instrument of love in his hand. His love is such that he will use whatever means necessary, including punishment, to deliver us from self-destruction.

Thus, it seems to me that the goal of God's justice is always reconciliation. A punitive goal birthed out of a moral reason is neither able to accomplish justice nor consistent with the Triune God's character.

Can justice have its way with us without violating our heart, mind, and will?

It *must*. If justice is to prevail and be like God's justice, if we are to participate in the divine circle of life, then our response must be freely given out of the depth of our being, reflecting who we are. In short, it must be our response, or we are not relating with others as God does.

---

[35] Ibid, 70

I have suggested that participation with God in relationship is what he designed us for. This is not just something the Father, Son, and Spirit do to us; it is something God does in us and with us.

I would like to say that I now walk in the warmth of light, having been freed from the isolation of my darkroom. But it is not always so. Old paradigms die hard. But God pursues…he always pursues.

I'd like to tell you of a happy ending, of reconciliation in the conflict between my sister and me, but I can't. However, as I was learning that God's justice proceeds from his love for us as our Father, it slowly began to change the kind of justice I wanted between us. I no longer wanted her punishment; I wanted her to walk in the love that refuses to give up on her and will not abandon her to the things that are killing her.

His fiery judgment burned me as well, by consuming sinful attitudes coming from within me. This is his relentless "just love" at work. And it's a good thing… always.

I am getting to the place where I can say that, for my part, I am reconciled to my sister. But this ebbs and flows as well. Emotions are not so quickly healed. Especially when, on her part, nothing has changed. But I have given up the god of movie justice. I have come to know that Jesus is far better.

The more I continue to grow in my understanding of God's righteousness – which flows out of the communion of love that is God – the more my heart sings. As I struggle for a way to articulate my description of it, the more the word justice is formed on my lips.

CHAPTER 9

RELENTLESS LOVE

Love sought is good, but given unsought is better.
— William Shakespeare

Over a half century ago, the Beatles wrote a song entitled "All You Need is Love." Regardless of what you think of them or whether you like their music, you have to admit, they weren't far off. Maybe their definition of love wasn't the best of definitions, and yeah, technically, we need food, water, and shelter to live, but I think those Brits were onto something.

As it turns out, they were, but this is nothing new. The idea wasn't original with the Fab Four. For millennia, the favorite subject of the human race has been love. In literature, music, stories, traditions… more has been written about love than probably any subject. We all know this. In fact, to deny it seems absurd.

Love is probably the strongest motivation we know. Love can do what power and money cannot. Some would argue that self-preservation is as strong or stronger, but isn't self-preservation really self-love's cousin?

When it comes to our thinking about God, is it because love is so important to us that we insist that the God we invent is perfect love? That his love is relentless, unconditional, and unilateral? Or is it the other way around? That God actually is love and, having made us in his image, love is the most important thing in life to us? We long for perfect love, because in him we know it is.

But as I think about it, it's amazing that we would believe that God loves us. Some would say that belief is nothing more than arrogance emboldened by our self-centered and inflated egos. Yet, as far back as I can remember, I have wanted to believe this. I think it had something to do with my mom. I never doubted for a moment that she loved me. So, when she told me as a young child that God loved me too, I believed it, because I believed *her*.

Therefore, for much of my life, I have believed. In fact, there are times when I've been deeply moved and humbled with wonder and awe as I thought of God's love. I would often compare it to myself loving just one of the trillions of grains of sand on the world's beaches. Though one of the big differences is I didn't create the sand. When we consider the vastness of the heavens, why would any of us matter to someone so incomprehensibly big as God?

And there is a bit of truth to this. A poem found in the Psalms says as much: "When I consider your heavens, the work of your fingers, the moon and the stars, which you have set in place, what is man that you are mindful of him, the son of man that you care for him?"[36]

Meditating on this truth can provide a healthy perspective, for it presents the opportunity to contemplate our smallness – which can check our arrogance – allowing us to avoid the ridiculous notion that we alone are "masters of our destiny".

On the other hand, there are also times that the same opportunity, when twisted by our brokenness, seems to expand the distance between us and God and we despair. When we consider our moral and relational failures we are pummeled with fears of unworthiness. It's like breathing doubt into our soul blurring our sight and clouding any vision of the stars, making it quite difficult to believe God actually cares.

---

36 Psalm 8:3,4

"Does God really love the world?" is a worthy question, but it was not this question that disturbed me. What persistently whispered in my ear was something different. And I think it's a great question, one I needed to pursue. That question is this: *Why* does God love us?

I assumed he didn't have to love us. I believed our failures gave him more than enough reasons not to love us. When I ponder this, I'm struck with the enormity of this seemingly impossible question. Not only am I asking what motivates an infinite being, I'm also trying to comprehend the incomprehensible. My Philly friends would quip, "Yeah, well, good luck with that."

I often spoke of my awe of God's love this way: "God loves me *despite my sin.*" I would say this wagging my head in disbelief, muttering incoherently something about how I'm unlovely, unworthy of his love because of what I've done. The point is, I knew my heart. I didn't need convincing that I was incapable of earning God's love.

It's true that I am a sinner. For me, there's no question. So, it seemed obvious that it wasn't my stellar conduct and behavior that won God over. If our performance was the way to God's affections, then I was up to my neck in quicksand and sinking fast. Hell, I couldn't win the affections of my high school crush, let alone the love of an infinite being, who has impossibly higher standards and knows everything!

I Confess	I thought God only loved morally righteous people.

Or at least he loved the good people more than the bad. Kinda like the great Santa Claus in the sky. I believed that God would have nothing to do with me until he cleaned me up. That he was so pure he couldn't even bear to look at me in my impurity. Essentially, God's love was imprisoned in a moral cage, and until something could be done to clean up my mess, his love was held captive by an insistence that we meet the demands of his moral perfection.

An implication of this belief was that God had objectified me because of my sin. In my sinfulness, I was nothing more to him than an object of wrath. Sure, God loved his creation. But when we sinned, that changed his thoughts and feelings about us. According to the Christian story I heard and then taught, wasn't this the reason Jesus came to our planet? Wasn't he born to suffer the Father's punishment that was meant for us? Isn't this how God cleanses us? Doesn't Jesus's sacrifice fulfill God's righteous justice and so free him from all moral obligations to punish us, so we can be with him?

Even though I have rejected this narrative, the tentacles of this imaginary god who treats his creation as commodities or objects, still reach into my soul. They choke any hope of a loving relationship because even now that I'm "saved" this imaginary god still wants to *use me*.

How often do we speak as though it is some sort of great privilege to be an object used by God? What child would love and honor a father who treated him as though his worth was only found in whatever usefulness his father found for him?

This was so ingrained in me it was how I defined service to God. In fact, I often prayed with earnestness and sincerity, "God, please use me in your service!" From this perspective, I reduced my relationship with God to little more than simply being an object for whatever task appeared on his eternal agenda.

Does that sound like love to you? Does it feel like love to you?

The other day, I was prompted by a friend to check out a preacher from a large church in the Midwest on YouTube. His video was professional. His presentation was educated and polished. The point of his sermon was that God's love is conditional and that God only loves those who respond to him. The climax of his talk was his declaration that the idea of unconditional love is *unbiblical*, which, for many, is the same thing as saying *untrue*.

Is God's love really conditional? Does he really treat us with love (or not) based upon what we believe or the way we act? Apparently, according to the Midwest preacher, he does.

This would seem to liken God's love to some sort of commodity that he possesses – like gasoline in a car that is slowly being consumed by our selfish acts of rejection, so that when his love runs out, his tank is empty, and all we are left with is righteous anger and fury. *Really?*

Why would anyone call this good news? What's so good about it?

So, I ask again, *why* does God love me? What is it in God that moves him to love?

I Confess | I had no idea why God loved me.

I was convinced there was nothing in me for God to love. My thoughts and behavior betrayed me. I couldn't control my passions. I was the one who had walked away. I wanted nothing to do with God. I had screwed up – badly. Not once or twice but pretty much every day. Multiple times a day… you get the point. I truly believed that I did not deserve God's love.

But was my immorality reason enough that God *wouldn't* love me?

I think it would be presumptuous and incredibly arrogant to think I deserve to be loved by God. I guess there are some who are so full of themselves that they actually believe their lifestyle puts God on notice that he should love them because they deserve it. But I think most of us are a lot more like I am; we don't need a lot of convincing to believe we are not very lovable. Yet, even while I felt this way, I believed and taught that God loved us unconditionally.

On one hand I believed God loves us because we give him a reason to love us. That somehow, we can make ourselves lovable to him.

That he has set up this thing called life in a way that I can attain enough value and worth through my behavior or faith to twist God's arm into loving me.

On the other hand I taught with conviction that God loves us unconditionally. And it was this incongruity that eventually exposed my lack of understanding and that I was paying lip service to unconditional love.

Have you ever seen the movie *Stripes* starring Bill Murray and Dan Akroyd? (one word: Netflix.) Anyway, I thought God was Sergeant Hulka on steroids – the divine, moral drill sergeant standing at the finish line of the obstacle course he created called "life," waiting for us to conquer and complete the test. Only then would we have earned his approval and love.

But wait a minute, does God love us because he finds the reason to love us in us? I mean, does he search our hearts and minds, looking for something in us that he can love? Does love find its reason to love in the worthiness of the person it loves?

Who came up with that idea?

Clearly, our response to his love must be involved somehow. It certainly matters. If we reject him and curse him, he would be angry with us for spurning his love, wouldn't he?

But what if our responses only change our experiences of his affection *not* his actual affection for us?

By the way, when did we start defining worthiness as something that is attained by moral righteousness? If that were true, wouldn't God only love himself, or at least love himself more than us, because only God is morally perfect? In that paradigm, once we've sinned, forget it. It's blown. No take backs.

One more thing, since when does God love because someone's behavior deserves it?

Do you love your children because they obey you? Do you really believe that attaining a certain level of moral perfection will sway God's opinion of us so that he pronounces us worthy to be loved by him? How could that be? I already knew I couldn't earn God's love or favor.

Think about it. What does "God loves us though we don't deserve it" imply?

First, if God does something he shouldn't do, then he's unjust and morally flawed.

Second, mercy is no longer. It just went bye-bye, vanishing into non-existence.

But what if you were absolutely perfect, like he is?

Does the Father love the Son and Spirit because they are morally perfect and thus deserve his love?

I'm going to be straightforward here, because I'd like to put this horrendous idea down for good. God doesn't love us because of who we are or what we have done. The Father, Son, and Spirit love us because that is the way they are. What we deserve or don't deserve has *nothing* to do with whether or not God loves us. Nor does it have any bearing on how much God loves us. (Are there degrees of love with God?) The concept of "deserve" doesn't even enter the equation – ever.

Here are some ideas that crept undetected into my thinking that I'd like to blow up so they don't sneak into yours…

God does not love me because he made me clean.

God does not refuse or cease to love me because I am unclean.

My moral cleanliness has *nothing* to do with whether he loves me or treats me with love in any way.

With Father, Son, and Spirit, there are no hoops to jump through to get them to love us. (Never mind that hoop jumping is impossible.) If God is like that, then that god isn't very loving.

Here's the good news, and *it really is good*. No bait and switch. We are loved more than we can imagine, and it's not because of something we do or the way we perform.

I'm not saying that we, as the human race, don't have value. We do. More than I think most of us believe. God gave us incredible worth when he made us. He proved this to us when he became flesh. We matter.

And I'm not saying that God doesn't love you in a unique way. He does. Each of us is utterly unique; and he loves the uniqueness that he designed in each and every one of us.

What I *am* saying is this: God's love for us is not, in any way, based in our value, whether we've "earned" it or it was given to us in the act of creation. God loved us before he made us. He loves the thought of us, even though he knew the mess we'd make. This shouldn't be that hard to accept. So, why is it?

Think about it. If you're a good parent, you loved your child before he or she was born. You loved the thought of your child while he or she was in the womb. You knew your child would make a mess, but that didn't change your love for your child one bit.

One last thing before moving on: please, please do not talk to me of a God who only loves some and not others. Or who loves in varying degrees. Or whose love embraces only those who trust him but doesn't embrace those that don't. This thought is unworthy of the Father, Son, and Spirit. I want nothing to do with that god. No, thank you. The world, myself included, is all too familiar with that kind of love. That god loves much like we do. That god throws all the responsibility on you and me to make sure we've done or believed the right thing to be loved. It makes God out to be a deity who loves with prejudice, favoritism, and partiality. And we know that is not love.

Do we love better than the Father of our souls?

Once and for all, God is not a conditional lover.

Yet, when I would bring up some of these questions and struggles, friends would inevitably attempt to encourage me with talk of grace. "It's true, John; we don't deserve it. But that's what so cool about grace! God gives you his love freely, not based on your performance." They were sincere, and they acted with kindness. I believe their counsel sprang from love. And so, for many years I would exalt in his grace, believing he loved me in spite of everything.

| I Confess | To me God seemed conflicted with how he felt about his creation. |

I'm not quite sure I believed this, but I know I suspected this about God, and it was a comet of doubt that made its way into my soul with every orbit of my heart. This doubt came from the deep place of my personal universe, and it made hundreds of assaults before it burned up in the light of his great love. It was not unlike my thought that justice and mercy were opposed to each other. I also considered love and wrath as opposites.

On the one hand, God loved me. On the other, he hated my sinfulness. Friends would suggest that God loved me but hated my sin. That made sense for a while; until it occurred to me that my sin doesn't get sent to hell. I do. So, it was nearly impossible for me to separate myself from my sin. As a result, "God loves me despite my sin" became a powerful "truth" for me.

It finally all came crashing down one day when I was having breakfast with a young man who had been attending a Bible study I led for about four years. As he was saying these very things that I just wrote, I asked a question. "That phrase, 'God loves me despite my sin,' why does that mean so much to you?"

Before he could respond, an answer entered my head with the subtlety of a lightning bolt. I think it was an epiphany of sorts. It was this: *Because he shouldn't love me.*

Right then and there, I realized I believed that God's love toward me seemed so amazing, because I assumed he shouldn't love me in the first place. I mean, him being God and me being me, you know?

As I understood it at the time, if I focused on God's holiness, righteousness, justice, or wrath, here's what I thought I deserved and what he should do with me.

I had condemned myself because of my sin. Therefore, he should judge me and punish me. And in my thinking, that meant hell. Abandonment, punishment, even torment was what I deserved. Wasn't judgment the right moral response for God to have against evildoers? And didn't justice require punishment?

So, when I focused on God's love with these thoughts in tow, I was convinced that when God loved me, he was doing something that his holiness and justice (as I understood them) dictated he *shouldn't* do.

This created a significant dilemma for me. And I had taught for enough years to know I wasn't alone. In fact, without question, it was one of the most common beliefs I encountered in my years of teaching Bible.

It's kind of like when your friend, who works at the movie theater, pulls you aside and, with his eyes darting in every direction, whispers, "I really shouldn't be doing this…" and proceeds to let you in the movie for free. You walk away thinking, *What a great friend. He must really like (love) me.*

Except in this scenario, it's God who lets you into heaven for free, even though you haven't paid, and then whispers in your ear, "I really shouldn't be doing this, because you don't belong here. But Jesus paid for your ticket, so I'm okay with you now." And you walk into heaven muttering, "I can't believe how much he loves me despite my sin."

So, it seemed at times like mercy and justice and love and wrath were fighting it out within God's being. But that was only half of it; I was beginning to realize something even more troubling in the midst of my epiphany.

> **I Confess** | **I believed the deepest truth in God's being was his moral perfection.**

The reason I believed God shouldn't love me was because I lived based out of an idea that there was a deeper truth than love in God's being. There was something that love bowed to, even in God. Something held love hostage. I believed what really was at the center of his being, the source from which all else flowed, was his undiluted moral perfection. The righteous thing for God to do was to pour out his vengeance and wrath against all that was evil – all that was opposed to his moral perfection. I was told that included me. This was at the core of why I believed God shouldn't love me and why I would talk about him loving me despite my sin.

Earlier I wrote about my journey to understand God as Trinity – my discovery that the fundamental, truth of God's nature is not moral perfection or his holiness or even his love. The deepest truth of his nature, his essence, his very being, is that the Father, Son, and Spirit are relationally *one being*.

But let's think again about this in light of "Why does God love me?"

Nothing is deeper than the three of them. And the word we use to describe this relationship is *love*.

Yes, it is morally perfect, but who describes the beauty of a perfect relationship as moral? We call it love. So does the Bible.

And yes, it is holy. It is completely and utterly unique. It is one of a kind. But who describes the beauty of a one-of-a-kind relationship as merely unique? We exclaim, "I've never seen love like that before!"

So, it is in the Trinity's relationship that we find the answer to our question, "Why does God love me?" It is because they are a communion of three persons who are forever in love with each other. God loves me, because it is simply who he is. He is not obligated to love me by anything other than his own nature. God loves in freedom, because *that is the way he is*. There is no other way of being for him.

God's love is the one constant, unchanging reality of everything. The essence of the Trinity's relationship is pure, self-giving, other-centered love. This is the way they are toward each other. They don't fake it. God's self-interest always involves two other "selves." Their relationship is the essence of their being.

If that is true, then their relationship of self-giving, other-centered love is what shapes God's character and all God does. Everything God does proceeds out of who he is as the loving community of Father, Son, and Spirit.

They loved what they were going to make before they made it. And though they knew we would fall and how bad it would be, they made us anyway. They had a solution in place before we ever turned away. They determined to untwist all that we would deform and redeem all that every single one of us would lose.

Our fall did not deter their love. When we fell in Adam, they did not stop loving us. They have never stopped loving us. To say they could have, is to say that something you or I do can change God's essence. And this cannot be. For God to stop loving would be like us to willingly stop the beating of our hearts – but even more so.

The Father, Son, and Spirit love us because God is love – "not despite" anything.

Some will protest that this kind of thinking will lead us to further sin. We may, in fact, do that; such is the corruptness of the fall. But even if we choose to act this way, God will continue to love us, for he will continue to be God.

| I Confess | I grew indifferent to love.

I heard the word all the time. In commercials, advertisements, songs, conversations… It became such an overused term that it lost all significance. Bombarded with cultural ideas of what love is, I almost became afraid to use the word. In the words of the band Pink Floyd, I became "comfortably numb" regarding God's love.

In the hugely successful TV show, Breaking Bad, the main character, Walter White, who was a high school chemistry teacher and a devoted husband and father of two, learns he has cancer. He knows his health insurance will not cover his treatments, which would consume their meager savings like my dog inhales his meal. What little benefits his family would receive from his career as a teacher would leave them destitute when the terminal disease finally claimed his life. The ensuing story chronicles his brilliant yet horrendous attempts to solve his financial crisis by becoming the largest producer of methamphetamine in the Southwestern United States.

I sat mesmerized, along with millions of others, as we watched the "breaking bad" of Walt, which included theft, lies, deceit, malice, arrogance, destruction of property, manipulation, and eventually multiple murders, all justified by his "love" for his family.

So, does God love me like Walt loved his family?

But don't blame the cheapening of love on just our culture. I sucked the meaning out of the word too.
I love the Spurs.
I love the salmon BLT with avocado at the Classic Diner.
I love Breaking Bad.
I love my wife. What? Like the Spurs? Like the sandwich? Like Walt? See what I mean?

I even did it with people.

Someone I barely knew, and I'm sure they didn't know me, would do me a favor, and I'd respond, "Thanks, man. You so bailed me out. You know I love ya for that."

So, I'd pray, "Thanks Father for bailing me out when I screwed up again. Love you for that."

I found myself slowly sinking into apathy about God's love. It was so difficult to conceive of God's love as a better love than anything I knew. I looked around my world, my community, to see if I could find an example, an anchor of sorts, to ground me, but there were few. I looked in Scripture, but I read it with the same theological baggage I'd always carried, so nothing changed there.

I read other Christian writers and theologians, and many of them were trapped in the same assumptions as I was. Nothing new there either.

But I eventually found something I thought might work to stem the tide of indifference poisoning my soul. I tried to think of myself as more unworthy than ever before. I figured I could accomplish this by focusing on my sins. I'd see myself as worse than before; then tomorrow even worse than the day before. Let shame and guilt widen the gulf between God and me. That way, God's love would seem even greater.

That's like a marriage counselor telling me that I can feel more in love with my wife if I exaggerate the distance between us. "John, if you'd just focus on the lack of intimacy and create greater distance between you and Terri, you'll feel more intimate."

Crazy, huh?

Here's an even crazier idea: I prayed. Many moons ago, I prayed.

"Father, since I am already being rooted and established in love, I pray that [I] may have the ability, together with all the saints, to *grasp how wide and long and high and deep is the love of Christ* and to know this love that is beyond knowing – that [I] may be filled to the measure of all the fullness of God."[37]

He is answering, and I am learning.

Joy has come… joy unspeakable. Because, how do I express something so wondrous, so beautiful, so stunning that even the whisper of it is almost more than my heart and mind can bear? My abilities are strained to their limit attempting to grasp just the fringe of a reality *so good* yet so vast it measures the universe as but a grain of sand. I am undone by the magnitude of what lies before us. I bow and point to God.

Words, pictures, stories… all are inadequate to the task. It seems our best are but grunts. Beautiful grunts to be sure but grunts nonetheless. God loves our grunts, because he knows they are the first steps toward talking.

Besides, I understand grunts. We all speak "grunt."

I wonder if the person who penned the following verse felt the same way –

Could we with ink the ocean fill,

And were the skies of parchment made,

Were every stalk on earth a quill,

And every man a scribe by trade;

To write the love of God above would drain the ocean dry;

Nor could the scroll contain the whole, though stretched from sky to sky.[38]

---

37   St Paul's prayer for the Ephesians 3:18ff
38   Verse three of the hymn, "The Love of God"

Talk about a grunt. Did you know that a man said to have been demented penciled this verse on the wall of a narrow room in an American insane asylum? The profound lines were discovered when they laid him in his coffin.

Eventually, I discovered some writers along the way who do far more than grunt. Their writing helped heal the callousness threatening to harden my heart. I'd like to share a couple of them with you. Admittedly, they are deep. So, I ask that you read them slowly, deliberately. Read them several times. Take your time with them. Let your heart and mind soak in them. Meditate upon what they are trying to convey.

> "Nothing is inexorable but love... For love loves unto purity. Love has ever in view the absolute loveliness of that which it beholds. Where loveliness is incomplete, and love cannot love its fill of loving, it spends itself to make more lovely, that it may love more. It strives for perfection, even that itself may be perfected – not in itself, but in the other.
>
> There is nothing eternal but that which loves and can be loved, and love is ever climbing towards the consummation when such shall be the universe, imperishable, divine.
>
> Therefore all that is not beautiful in the beloved, all that comes between and is not of love's kind, must be destroyed.
>
> And our God is a consuming fire."[39]

Here's another.

> "At this very hour, one from the hell of Adam's traumatizing mythology sits at the Father's right hand. He sees not

---

39 George MacDonald, *Creation in Christ: Unspoken Sermons* (Vancouver, BC: Regent College Publishing, 2004) 157-158.

through brokenness and baggage – he sees clearly, face to face with the Father himself.

And what does Jesus Christ see in the Father's eyes? What does he know? What does he feel? What does he experience?

Is it hopelessness? Is it fear? Is Jesus scared? Does Jesus feel that he sits beside a father who is cold, detached, and indifferent, whose disapproving heart watches his every move he makes? Is the fundamental truth of the Father's heart toward His Son that of a judge? Does Jesus hear "I am not acceptable, not important, not of any value," whispering through the halls of heaven?

...Think about it. Think about it long and hard. What does Jesus Christ experience at the Father's right hand? Are his knuckles white, grasping the spider's web as he dangles over the flames of hell? Is Jesus exhausted from hiding, from pretending, from keeping appearances up? Is he weary with the fear of it all, wondering if today the faceless, all-powerful potentate will finally leave him on the edge of the abyss, banished from his presence and abandoned forever?

Think of the incarnate Son right now, sitting at the Father's side. Can you not see how the Father loves His Son? Can you not see His sheer delight? Think of the Father's heart. Think of how he looks at His Son. What do you see in the Father's eyes? Think of how his words, his touch, his embrace, are filled with pride... What does Jesus know? What does Jesus experience in the Father's presence? Does the condemnation of the world carry weight at the Father's right hand?"[40]

---

40 Dr. C. Baxter Kruger, *Across All Worlds: Jesus Inside Our Darkness* (Jackson, Mississippi: Perichoresis Press, 2007), 39–40.

I've said it before, but it is worth repeating: the relationship within the Trinity is the most beautiful thing that exists. Are you not lost in wonder as you consider the love between the Father and the Son? Does your heart not quicken and your spirit soar as you imagine the love they have for each other?

Oh, but it gets *better*.

Like the proverbial fly on the wall, we get to listen to the most intimate of conversations between these two, so completely and totally in love with each other.

And here is what the Son says to his Father. "Father... May they be brought to complete unity to let the world know that you sent me and have loved them *just like* you have loved me... I have made you known to them, and will continue to make you known in order that *the love you have for me may be in them* and that I myself may be in them" (John 17:23, 26, italics mine).

Don't miss it because you've read it before. Don't rush over it in a wave of familiarity. *Think* with me.

Is it possible for the Father to ever stop loving the Son? Even for a nanosecond?

Is it possible for the Father to flinch in his affection for his Son? For any reason ever?

How sure is the love of the Father for the Son? Is it unalterable?

How long will the Father's love for his Son last? Will he ever tire or become bored with him?

Mark these words – the Father feels exactly the same way about you and me. *Exactly.*

This is the truth that rocked my world back when I was reading John those many years ago. I had come to holy ground… the unimaginable, staggering gift of the Trinity's love, which is this: *the Father, Son, and Spirit love us with the same love they have for each other.*

This is because their love is a communion of self-giving love. So, when they love us, it is exactly as they love themselves, because they are revealing and giving us themselves!

Could this be a hint at why God rescued us? Could it be that God's intention from the beginning was to bring us into the circle of their communion, to include you, me, the entire human race in their very being?

They don't love us one way and then love themselves better.

There are no settings of high, medium, or low on God's love.

They have one way to love – it's called perfect.

So, we have come to it. We have come to something that is impossible for God.

It is impossible for God to stop loving you, because he will not stop being himself – a communion of persons who are completely, unconditionally in love with each other.

How does the Father feel about you?

He loves you just like he loves Jesus.

How does the Father see you?

With the same unflinching gaze of love that he has for Jesus.

What is in the Father's heart toward you?

The same unwavering commitment and loyal love he has for Jesus.

Of all the ways that I used to believe the Father thought about me, so much of it was not true. Those things were lies and deceptions, mere illusions on my horizon.

But the truest thing that can be said about any of us is this: however the Father thinks and feels about Jesus, that is exactly how he thinks and feels about us.

It may look different to us in our brokenness and blindness, and that has certainly made this whole affair incredibly tragic. Nonetheless, all he does and feels toward us is no different than how he thinks and feels about the eternal Son.

This is the *heart* of the gospel. Jesus has revealed the Father to us and declares to us the good news of his Father's love. This is true regardless of how moral or immoral we are and regardless of whether we believe Jesus or not.

If it is not true, then neither is the love the Father has for Jesus. And this cannot be, for Jesus is of the same essence as his Father. They are one being, one nature.

Jesus declares a stunning fact: that every one of us is included in his life with his Father. And he offers a compelling invitation to everyone to act upon the truth of this good news of his Father's love. We are to trust him. Not so that we can be embraced by the Father but because *we already are*. By faith we can live out of that place where every man, woman, and child belongs and already is in our Father's everlasting heart.

"For I am convinced that neither death nor life, neither angels nor demons, neither the present nor the future, nor any powers, neither height nor depth, nor anything else in all creation, will be able to separate us from the love of God that is in Christ Jesus our Lord" (Romans 8:38–39).

CHAPTER 10

THE FATHER'S EMBRACE

*Good souls many, will one day be horrified
at the things they now believe of God.*

— George MacDonald

Sunday, June 15… Father's Day.

My thoughts this morning wandered to my three wonderful children and the incredible privilege I've had being their dad. Their lives have truly been a gift to me, and they have made fatherhood a long embrace of grace. I prayed this morning, asking God that he make his love known to them in ways I can't. Thankfulness fills my soul. They are alive and healthy; we talk and laugh with mutual respect; they are not religious; they love their mom and me; and they respond to their heavenly Father's love with sincere, trusting hearts. I couldn't ask for more. I am grateful.

Alas, my reflections are fleeting. In times like these, I can often evaluate my performance as a father. Such is the mind of a perfectionist, who listens to the whisper, *What you've done isn't good enough*. This exercise inevitably leaves me emotionally pummeled. I fixate on all the mistakes I've made: on what I could've done but didn't and for what I shouldn't have done but did.

For example, one of my favorite things in life is laughter. I also realize I'm not the funniest guy in the room. This is not negative self-talk; it's just a realistic observation of what I bring to a conversation in a room full of people. Nevertheless, I love to laugh, and my kids love to see me laugh. One of their favorite things to do with me is whatever involves laughter.

I smile in front of my computer screen as I reflect on this observation. And that's when the whisper returns (except it feels like a sharp jab to my head, rattling my brain with disappointment): *I'm too serious with these three; I haven't laughed enough with them.* I plan to change that.

Having spent too much time rummaging in the dumpster of my regrets, my thoughts return to the pure wonder of my children. Joy returns too. With my spirit quieted again, I turn my attention to my current project: this book. I have been cloistered away at a friend's house writing for a week, and today I inadvertently came to this chapter, which I had planned to write all along. What I didn't plan was that I would write this chapter on this day—Father's Day. In fact, I didn't even realize the connection until after I had been writing for some time. This coincidence is not lost on me. Often, it's in the little things that I hear love's song most clearly.

I met Randy when he was in tenth grade and I was a second-year college student – a *long* time ago. He is one of the funniest people I've ever seen, met, or heard. But, like many teenagers, he struggled with his family situation. Adding to the usual pressures of adolescence, his mom had recently divorced and remarried not long before we met. Let's just say her choice of a new husband wasn't Randy's choice.

What made matters particularly stressful for him was that his stepfather was super strict. I mean military strict. So strict it flirted with abusiveness. Randy thought his home life was an extended boot camp. He called his stepfather "Sergeant Dave." No joke.

Picture this sixteen-year-old with an amazing sense of humor, a creative laugh bursting the seams of his soul, and then imagine him being raised by an incredibly controlling man, who took the role of his father but didn't love him like a son. To say Randy walked on eggshells whenever his stepfather was home is an epic understatement. It's never easy to live in fear, and that's especially true as a teenager.

Randy discovered hope and peace when I told him about Jesus. After that, he became the "thing that wouldn't leave." No kidding, he was around all the time. And no wonder; he found freedom with my friends and me. In the simple act of laughing with Randy, we gave him permission to let the "funny man" out. He thrived in a community of people who loved him for the crazy kid he was.

He also had a genuine hunger to learn about God and the Bible. Rarely would he miss a weekly study I taught. Imagine the confusion that surely must have spun in Randy's head when I'd talk of a heavenly Father. He has since confided to me that when he tried to think of God as Father, his thoughts were conflicted, and he felt like he'd hit a wall. Trying to picture what a good father was like wasn't mere daydreaming for Randy, it was a hope for which he yearned.

Almost forty years later, Randy is as close to me as my family. We consider each other the best of friends. We laugh *a lot*. My kids love Randy not only for his kindness and involvement in their lives but also because he makes their dad laugh. Like I said, they love to see me laugh.

I can also vouch that he is as earnest in wanting to know God as anyone I've ever met. But it has taken Randy decades to deal with his father issues, to break free from allowing his dad and stepdad, instead of Jesus, to be the model that shaped his concept of "father." Even now, there are times this baggage returns to haunt him.

I wonder if we all don't struggle a bit with this issue. For some, maybe not as much as Randy; for others, far worse, for the scars of abuse run very deep. All our fathers are flawed, imperfect people. Far from a condemning, judgmental statement, I think it's an obvious observation. It's the human condition. But they were kids once, too

– climbing into their daddies' laps looking for reassurance that their fathers cared for them. They have baggage and carry scars from their dads as well.

I'm not trying to make this a gender thing. This tragedy isn't confined to dads and sons. It is true of mothers and daughters as well. As a man, I simply speak out of my experience as a dad and a son.

We – fathers, mothers, and children – come to God looking for someone to end the cycle. We know things can be different, and we know they should be. We come to religious leaders, teachers, pastors, and counselors, looking to them to tell us of a God who is better.

Randy came to me.

So, I offered Randy promises that tell us there is hope. God is a loving, perfect Father. And Randy bought in. In fact, so did I. So did a lot of us.

Simultaneously, I was being taught a narrative at Bible College that told me this Father would abandon me if I didn't meet his expectations. It was never said with that kind of directness, but, peel back the layers of many theologies, and that's pretty much what you get. Some would attempt to soften the story, claiming that God the Father did this reluctantly. But the truth was: I was being handed, and was eventually shaped by, a theology that stepped on our throats and crushed our hearts. It shredded our hopes and dreams of a better Father into a million pieces.

It was classic bait and switch.

Does that sound harsh? Does it sound like I'm judging again? That might be true except for the fact that I know this happens. Not only because it happened to me *but because I did it to Randy*. I taught him a theology that reinforced something that he naturally assumed, that God was a father who was no better than his stepfather. Maybe worse.

| I Confess | I taught Randy about a "god" who did things no good parent would ever do.

I claimed this god was the real God, the true God. I spoke mostly out of ignorance, because theology and parenting were disconnected for me. They shouldn't have been, considering my home life. But if you apply even a smidgen of scrutiny to the god I spoke about, which I finally did, you can't escape the conclusion that many are better parents than he is.

At first, my justification for this was fairly straightforward: God is not everyone's Father; he is only the Father of those who have accepted Jesus as their Savior – he becomes their Father when they believe and are born into his family. Consequently, he has no filial relationship with a person who does not believe. To be blunt, this means God treats non-believers differently because they are not in the family. Thus he has no obligation to them as if they were.

Sounds simple enough. But isn't that dark? I mean, how, in good conscience, could I ever say to someone who does not believe, "God loves you"? If I was being honest, the best I could offer was: "God really wants you in the family but…"

Does my explanation above create categories of people based in a metaphor for God? Had I believed this about God because it gave me a simple way to explain "us" and "them"? Or had I just believed this subconsciously to justify God's behavior toward the majority of his creation?

Maybe I was taking what I knew of human behavior and assuming it was true of God. I love my children more than other children – because they are mine. Did you love every baby in the nursery at the hospital like you loved your own child? My rationale was probably a combination of all these things.

Whatever my reasons, what I taught as the truth was that we

could do something that would cause God to become something different than who he eternally is. Simply, my belief could change God's fundamental relationship toward me, maybe even change something about his nature.

But this is impossible. How can I change God into something he already is? Stranger still is the notion that my belief can change God's fundamental essence. He is the Father; my beliefs or actions don't make it so. One of the persons of the Trinity is the Father. He is, has always been, and forever will be, the Father, the Eternal Father. He is the Father of my soul.

"But," I would protest, "What about John 1:12?" ("Yet to all who did receive him, to those who believed in his name, he gave the right to become children of God.") This was my proof text to demonstrate that only believers in Jesus can claim that God is their Father. (Never mind that I used the Bible as a proof text.)

I've studied the gospel of John a lot, and I freely admit that I don't have all the answers for the interpretive questions that arise from John 1:12. Though I've read many who think they have all the answers, I haven't read anybody who actually does. However, I'd like to share a few observations that may shed light on a different, but legitimate, way to understand this statement.

First, when I'm considering statements like this, it is helpful to keep in mind a distinction. Are we discussing the *truth* of our being (our ontological reality i.e., what the essence of our created being is) or the *way* of our being (our existential reality i.e., the experience of how we are actually living our lives)?

For example; how do we make sense of Jesus's statement in John 8:44, "You are of your father the devil"? Certainly, the devil fathered no one. So then, what does Jesus mean? This only seems to make sense if I understand Jesus's statement as a comment on the way of their being – *not* the truth of their being. Their *way* of living revealed that they gave the devil far more parental authority in their life than *the* Father. In effect, they chose to make the devil the parental figure to whom they submitted.

I would suggest the *truth* of our being is this: if we are human, God is our Father. But the *way* of our being can be, and often time is, very different. In other words, we don't act like God is our father. It seems the proverbial apple has fallen very far from the tree.

Second, John 1:12 is difficult to translate. The word that is usually translated into English as "authority" is *exousia*. This comes from two words, *ex* which is a prefix that means "out of," and *ousia*, which means "substance, essence, nature." So, the word literally means "out of one's essence or nature." You can see where the idea of authority comes from. Those who speak from the truth of their being know of what they speak, for they speak out of who they are. Thus, we say they speak with authority.

So, if you take the word a bit more literally, rather than our modern English meanings pertaining to rank, control, or having power over others, this is how it might read: "Yet to all those who receive him, that is, those that trust him, he gives them *through their trusting* the freedom to live *out of their nature*... that is, to live as the children of God they are" (emphasis mine). This is a very different thought from saying, "through belief they have the right to become children of God" (NIV), which, in the past, was the way I took the meaning of John's statement.

And whose nature is this? The next verse (1:13) says it's God's nature. Well, if we are living out of our nature as children of God, then we are already connected somehow to God's nature. John develops this idea later in his narrative, particularly in the upper room conversation of chapters 13–17, when he says we are *in* Jesus (see John 14:20).

I would suggest that maybe a better way to understand this statement is this – faith does not empower me to become a child; trust empowers me to live as the child I already am.

The truth of our being is that you and I and the entire human race are God's children. But the way of our being? Well, the vast majority of us are prodigals, and the rest of us are his older brother.

I think it's been this way from the beginning. When Luke traces Jesus' genealogy, he takes it all the way back to Adam. Of particular interest is how he writes the genealogy: "… the son of Seth, the son of Adam, the son of God." Luke believes Adam is a *son of God*. We are all descended from Adam, according to the biblical account, so what does that make us? Hmm…

Furthermore, in the Sermon on the Mount, probably Jesus' best-known speech, Matthew records Jesus referring to his Father as their Father at least fifteen times. He even instructs them how they should pray, "Our Father who is in heaven…" This crowd was made up of all sorts of people, not just his followers.

Was this just smoke and mirrors? Did Jesus mean to say, "Well, he's *not really* your Father. I'm just exaggerating a little bit, because it helps you if you think he's your Father"? Or did Matthew, the one who recorded this sermon, just get it wrong?

I'm not trying to belabor the point, but if we believe that Jesus is human and that he is also the creator of all, then he must be connected relationally at some level to every human being who comes into existence. Why was I trying to differentiate the level of his connection to me? Why do we need to come up with multiple levels, like some are his children and most are not?

I was father to my children the moment they were conceived—nine months before they took their first breath. When were we conceived in the mind of the Father, Son, and Spirit? How long was our gestation period in their being?

I accepted a narrative that bought into a belief that divided the human race into two categories: those who were children of God and those who were not. I think I did this partly because it provided a convenient way to categorize people as either in or out. It became part of my rationalization as to why God could treat some (family) with kindness, grace, and mercy and others (non-family) not so much.

Does this God sound like someone who is completely impartial or does he sound like he has favorites?

Does this God sound like he loves the world (everyone) equally or does he love some more than others?

Would a good parent show favoritism toward one of his children over the others?

Would a good parent love one of his children more than the others?

Though I would have never admitted it, I reasoned if God could show favoritism, why shouldn't I?

This presents some real problems for us as we consider God's nature (and my behavior). What I was saying is that God's relationship to human beings is different based on what they do. To those who believe, he treats them like family. To those who don't believe, he has no filial relationship whatsoever. If this is true, then not only is the universe a scary nightmare, it is also a hostile, inescapable prison, for the warden is neither fair nor good.

Some who see this as problematic offer the solution that our belief has nothing to do with how God feels about us, treats us, or brings us into his family. And I would agree with that. I see the same problem. But I disagree with their solution, which is that God chooses who he will bring into his family. It's not left to our choice; it's his. Which leaves anyone he hasn't chosen out of his family.

This may answer the problem that humans somehow determine how God will think and act, but it doesn't solve the question of God's nature. The question simply changes to, "Is God good?" Well, if he chooses a handful to inherit life and billions upon billions of others to inherit death, what do you think?

What kind of Father is that?

What kind of plan or purpose for creation is that?

A few years back I was at a small gathering. About thirty-five to forty of us were crammed into a room designed for half that many. We were waxing theological when a woman, from Mississippi I believe, offered a poignant parable.

Lisa prefaced her story by explaining she'd been married to a wonderful man who had been a pastor for twenty-nine years, yet she had heard for decades from others in the church that God chooses who will be his children and who won't. It had driven her to the brink of spiritual bankruptcy. Then she offered this story, which was her lifeline back from the edge –

Once upon a time, there was a father who had two young sons. Their mother had left to run some errands, so dad and the two boys sat down to enjoy lunch together. Their meal was interrupted with a phone call from the neighbor. When the dad hung up, he turned to the boys. "I need to go next door for a few minutes. Can I leave you here to finish your meal?" They both said yes, but their dad hesitated.

"The only thing I ask is that you promise me you won't go near the pool. If you finish lunch, you can play video games, watch TV, read, or whatever. I'll be right back. Just please, do not go in the pool." The boys nodded in agreement.

The father was gone for only a few moments, and when he returned, sure enough, the boys were in the pool. The problem was, neither of them knew how to swim. They were drowning. Dad didn't panic, but he was definitely upset. Frustrated with their disobedience, he bellowed, "I only left you one instruction: don't go in the pool! You promised you wouldn't. Did you not know my warning was for your good?"

But, being their dad, he loved them. So, he jumped in the pool and saved one of his sons, but he let the other one drown. Up on the pool deck, his son was shivering, coughing, and spitting water, almost in a state of shock. His father grabbed a towel and wrapped it around him and looked at him with loving yet stern eyes. "I love you, and I saved you even though you didn't deserve it. I warned you, but you disobeyed me. I hope you will never forget how much I love you."

We froze. The fan kept humming in the corner.

I could have heard others breathe, but I didn't, because we were all holding our breath.

I was stunned. She had just handed me my theology for lunch. And it didn't look very appetizing.

If I were to do that with my two girls, I'd be thrown in jail. There probably wouldn't even be a trial, so strong would be the consensus of opinion against me. It's just *wrong*. We wouldn't do this to anyone. What kind of monster would?

Like I said at the beginning, my theology was teaching me that I was a better father than God.

The Bible says that God is impartial – that he treats no one with favoritism. I believe it, because I see it in Jesus' life. Throughout the gospel stories Jesus continually displays a complete lack of prejudice on any level. Prejudice was a thought his mind never entertained. Favoritism didn't exist for him.

Consider the men he chose as disciples, which included a zealot and a tax collector. Different sides – same darkness.

Consider his interaction with the Samaritan woman. There is no racial, religious, or gender prejudice on Jesus's part. In fact, Jesus' actions were so unnerving to the woman that she essentially asked why he would have any dealing with her whatsoever, because she knew – according to the prevailing customs of her culture – he shouldn't be talking to her. Some prejudice had to sneak in there somewhere to put the brakes on that conversation, but it never showed up in Jesus.

Consider the story of the Good Samaritan. God-like love is blind to prejudice. It seeks only to help the neighbor in need.

Consider Jesus' friendship with Zacchaeus. Jesus simply liked this man and chose to have dinner with him at his home despite the fact that, as a tax collector, he had become wealthy by extorting his own countrymen and his neighbors.

I Confess	The stories of Jesus sang to me, but I remained prejudiced.

Jesus' freedom to live and act without bias of *any* kind is wonderful. It is compelling. Yet, prejudice was still very much alive in me some two thousand years later. And to my horror, I discovered that much of my prejudice found its roots in my theology – in a version of Jesus' story that had been handed to me all those years ago.

It goes something like this. God is holy (I am borrowing a rather common but twisted view of holiness here; that is, he is morally perfect), and his holiness not only prevents him from having a relationship with us but, also, causes him to look at us with disgust because of our utter sinfulness.

Furthermore, our sin affects the way he feels about us, treats us, and relates to us. His holiness is so profound and so pure that not only does he choose not to be with us; his holiness dictates he *cannot* be with us. I have in mind here the famous sermon by Jonathan Edwards, "Sinners in the Hands of an Angry God." I regret that there was a time I believed and taught about a god who closely resembled

Mr. Edwards' version.

However, I never realized that, if Mr. Edwards' vision of God in this sermon is true, then God is morally prejudiced toward his creation. If the way he feels and acts toward us is dictated by how moral (or immoral) we are, then there's no getting around it – God is prejudiced when it comes to morality. If we're good, he treats us well. If we're morally degenerate we disgust him and he treats us with anger and fury.

Wait a minute… would I feel the same way and treat my children like this if they did an immoral act?

Actually, if my children happen to do something immoral and I discipline them in anger and fury, don't I already know intuitively that it's my behavior that has derailed? That my immorality is at least as corrupt as theirs? Why would we posit this prejudice on a God who loves infinitely better than we do?

My way around God's moral prejudice was that we all are sinful so he treats us all the same. And this I believe to be true. But, then, to say everyone disgusts him? This simply will not do. Because I also taught that if I wasn't morally corrupt, then God would not have a problem with me. I believed that God would not be disgusted with you or me if we weren't so #!*##! depraved.

I think the first song I can remember singing at church went something like this:

Jesus loves the little children

All the children of the world

Red and yellow, black and white

They are precious in his sight

Jesus loves the little children of the world.

Simple, beautiful words aren't they? But, oh my, they are *profound!* Not a smidge of prejudice in them.

What happened? When and where did our theology stray from these powerful words?

Or maybe we believe children get a pass with God because of their innocence or ignorance?

I've asked myself many, many times: how did I live in this tension? On one hand, I believed that God had no prejudice toward anyone and that he never showed favoritism of any kind. On the other, I accepted a narrative that taught salvation was rooted in the assumption that God was morally prejudiced toward his creatures.

As I have reflected back, I think I just ignored it. I mean, I assumed I couldn't resolve this apparent discrepancy, so I didn't even try. But I also knew a host of people who believed the same thing. That at least gave me some comfort. Groupthink gives us some security, right?

The hypocritical part is that it gives me permission to rationalize or justify my prejudice toward others *in the name of God*. And that is really scary.

Ever hear of the game *Lifeboat*? For whatever reason, I had a couple of high school teachers who thought my class should discuss the scenario. They told us it was an exercise in values clarification. I think it was an exercise in revealing our prejudice. Here's an updated version.

A boat sinks in the middle of the Pacific. Nine people tumble into the water. They include: a lawyer guilty of embezzlement, a single mom with her infant son, an elderly couple in their late seventies, a gay high school history teacher who suspects he is HIV positive, a TV evangelist, a black gang member, and a Muslim from Syria. There's one lifeboat and it can only hold eight. Choose the eight who get in and the one who doesn't.

Then we discussed or argued over who deserved to live or die.

Life is not God playing lifeboat with the human race. Jesus doesn't play that game. Never will.

I do not believe the Father is morally prejudiced toward anyone. His feelings toward us, his treatment of us, his concern for us is not swayed by how moral we are or aren't. He loves everyone equally and treats us all in the same manner – with love. And any gospel that would tell me differently is no gospel at all.

But the greatest experience and true catalyst behind the evolution in my thinking regarding the Father was becoming a father myself. For me, fatherhood has brought light and clarity to this thing called life in ways that I never saw coming. It has done wonders for my theology. It certainly outdoes all my education, study, preparation, or teaching of any class. It has been a game changer for me.

And I'm pretty sure my wife Terri would concur. Even though we have been married for over twenty-five years and are deeply in love with each other, we would both say that parenthood, becoming a father and mother, has taught us as much about love as our marriage, maybe more.

Let me explain: I married Terri because in sharing life experiences with her I grew to know and love her, which convinced me to make the choice to live the rest of my life with her. This was mutual. Terri had grown to love me as well and made the same choice.

But the experience of romance – of falling in love with Terri – was just the beginning. It was kind of like "preparing the soil" of our souls so that a deeper, sustaining love could flourish. It began by uprooting the weeds of our egocentricity and planting the seeds of freedom to love another as myself. But there is an immaturity, a certain juvenile quality of romantic love, which eventually had to be put to death for our relationship to endure into marriage. Life in close quarters with another can be acutely painful and is just too messy to be held together by romance alone. The collective experiences of attending to another have been like light and moisture growing us to become increasingly free to deeply love each other. The more we taste the sun and rain the more we become free to love the other.

This freedom is not unlike a growing awareness emerging that I am no longer the center of my own attention in relationships. This has been incredibly liberating as I find myself mysteriously, inexorably engrossed for someone other than myself.

Not so with our children. It was different.

I remember when each of them was born. I was "all in" from the get go.

My love for each one was *instantaneous*. The moment I set eyes on them, I loved them with everything in my being. I would have stood in front of a freight train for any these three little lives that I had met just mere seconds before. I didn't grow to love them as I had with Terri.

My love was *unconditional*. There was nothing they needed to do to motivate me to love them – not a thing. They just had to be. Just their existence was all the reason I ever needed to love them forever. In fact, I loved them like this before they entered my world. Their birth just confirmed what was in my heart.

My love was *unilateral*. They didn't agree to love me in return. They had never had a conversation with me, they had never responded to me, they had never done *anything* for me, to me, or with me. I would love them regardless of whether they ever chose to love me in return.

My love for them was unlike any love I had ever known.

Terri loved them even more so. She carried them in her being. Not just a physical connection but, also, something on a much deeper and more profound level. The connection between mother and child is mystery in the truest sense. To say it is special seems almost trite. It is holy. The universe should lower its collective eyes in the deepest of respect when it sees a mother with child. George MacDonald wrote, "Love has ever in view the absolute loveliness of that which it beholds."[41] This truth never sings clearer than when we see a mother's love.

I believe our parental love reflects and echoes the logic of Trinitarian freedom.

What is in the heart of Father, Son, and Spirit?

Could their connection be less?

Could their love be inferior?

I do not believe so, for they are the source of motherhood and fatherhood.

Our love for our children has not diminished. Throughout their lives – despite the darkness that we as parents and children both have – we have not stopped loving them. Even though we get frustrated, angry, and impatient – we still love them. There is nothing they could do that would make us stop loving them. As our relationships have grown so has our love for them. Not in the sense that the volume of love has increased or that some previously undiscovered part of us loves them more; for we have loved them with our whole being their entire lives. But it has *deepened*.

Where does this love come from? Did we learn it? Is it merely psychological or physiological? Is there some kind of unseen genetic bond that creates this love within Terri or me for our kids? Do we honestly believe that our love for our children is a genetically

---

41   George MacDonald, *Creation in Christ: Unspoken Sermons* (Vancouver, BC: Regent College Publishing, 2004) 157

induced chemical reaction? Stranger still, do we really believe love originates in our own hearts?

I don't think so.

I would suggest that when I love another person, I am participating in the only source of love that exists in the universe: the love of the Father, Son, and Spirit.

Love does not originate with me; it originates in them. I believe that when I love my children as I previously described, it is because that is the way God loves. I am only joining the Father, Son, and Spirit in the love they have for every single human being who has ever lived – including my children.

So if I am (as a flawed, fractured father) capable of a love that is –
– Unconditional
– Unilateral
– Without prejudice or favoritism
– Without a loving response in return

How much more does my Father in heaven love like this?

How could we have conceived of a theology that results in me being a better father to my children than the Father is to us? Why would I want to? What strange thinking is this?

Don't you find it a bit preposterous to think that God created persons in his image and yet chose not to love them as much as other persons? Is it supposedly because some have become his children so that he is now responsible to love them? Such thoughts of the Father seem so unworthy of him.

I don't know what to do with that… other than to reject it.

I love my children even when they don't reciprocate my love.

Does God?

I do not withhold my embrace from my children because they have disobeyed me or not trusted me.

Does God?

I love my children as I love myself.

Does God?

I loved my children before they ever responded to me.

Does God?

I love my children when they don't respond to me in like kind.

Does God?

I love my children more than any virtue I possess.

Does God?

So, what about that "father god" I taught to Randy?

I have rejected that god. I no longer believe or teach that father exists.

Others may want to love, worship, and learn about that father. I can't.

My rejection of that god is not a claim of omniscience. The truth is, I have more questions than answers. But I am sure of this: no matter how real that god may seem to us, I know he isn't, because I know I am not a better father than the Father.

I believe after all our theories of theology have been played out and all the interpretations of scripture have been debated, we will still be mere infants in knowing our Father. I am certain he will be better than any of us have ever imagined.

Let me conclude with some more words from George MacDonald – "Of him not a thought, not a joy, not a hope of one of his creatures can pass unseen… The perfection of His relation to us swallows up all our imperfections, all our defects, all our evils; for our childhood is born of His fatherhood."[42]

Jesus, help us receive your knowledge of the Father.

---

42 2 George MacDonald, *Creation in Christ: Unspoken Sermons* (Vancouver, BC: Regent College Publishing, 2004) 35.

CHAPTER 11

INTO DARKNESS –
THE HEALING OF OUR SOULS

> *Love is the only force capable of
> transforming an enemy into a friend.*
> — Martin Luther King, Jr.

All humanity has been stumbling around in a darkness that is so pervasive it seems to be almost inextricably woven into our lives. While we may not be consciously aware of the sheer depth of our darkness and the futility it manifests in our lives, we ache for what we do not know. Could it be that we yearn with an unquenchable thirst for something better? Not just some *thing*, but for *us* to actually *be* better?

I believe this dull ache in our hearts is evidence that what we long for is the healing of our souls. The thing in me that lusts for evil this is what needs to be removed or destroyed. This does not happen through behavior modification, the power of positive thinking, or following carefully crafted spiritual disciplines.

Throughout this book I have been writing with the assumption that God actually wants to heal us; that the Father, Son, and Spirit really do want to save us from the destruction of our self-induced alienation and free us from the clutches of our self-imposed prisons. I believe I have good reason to assume this – namely, the nature of this triune God revealed in the birth, life, death, resurrection, and ascension of Jesus, the Incarnate Savior of the world.

The Triune God who spoke the cosmos into being loves all that he has made. He does not continue to sustain its existence only to destroy it later. God wants to save it and us in it: especially us – for we are the ones who caused the ruin and destruction. God is working to renew, rebuild, and reconcile all things. His goodness exceeds our theology.

Two thousand years ago at the birth of the Christ, Joseph was instructed by the angel to name the baby Jesus, for "he will save his people from their sins." Over the subsequent two millennia, followers of Jesus have believed he is the One who secures the reconciliation of all things. He is the Savior. And on this all of the Christian faith agrees.

However, a continuous wrestling match with *how* Jesus heals or saves us has marked our history. These differing thoughts have been formulated over time into various atonement theories. Sadly, this conversation ceased being a conversation when we turned our theories into dogma. "Doctrinal debate" then escalated to the point of argument, division, separation, and even violence.

Aside from our fallen humanity, another reason we have grappled so long with this is that we are constantly attempting to peer into a mystery that is supremely good yet, ultimately, eludes even our greatest minds. Fortunately, the silver lining of God's kindness helps offset our folly for the mystery reveals our ongoing participation with him.

The Triune God's likeness was woven into our nature so that we bear their image. Too often I have trivialized this as merely an external resemblance to God when I behave and act like he would. For us religious types, what we really mean by that is usually just obedience to some kind of moral code. But we are far more than that. We desire to know and be known. We want to understand the relationship of all things. How do birds fly? What makes a car engine run? Why did she start crying when I said that? Why am I here? Even though it may be impossibly difficult, we forge ahead, studying and exploring, driven by this desire to know.

Eventually, we collide into an immovable object called mystery. But the pride of our brokenness has twisted our desire to know to the extent that we have approached mystery as something to be conquered or controlled. But the truth is, we only truly learn, understand, and grow when we are subdued by mystery's wisdom.

All too often it seems that mystery is dangled like the proverbial carrot in front of our eyes – just out of reach. It entices us but then refuses our advances. However, this is not a tease, for mystery guards its secrets so that we learn its wisdom – that *trust cannot be separated from knowing*.

Even in our brokenness, God's likeness in our nature still manages to radiate with brilliance when we are transfixed by wonder and beauty. This seems especially true when things that are beyond us confront us. We are fascinated, almost mesmerized, by what we cannot comprehend. Like moths drawn to light, we seek connection to that which we perceive is good even though we don't understand. Indeed, when what occupies our attention is so thoroughly perceived as good, a certain wholeness and health embraces us in our contemplation. And yet, when mystery is perceived as possibly bad or evil, we can be gripped with fear so paralyzing that we try to erase it from our minds and avoid its word on our lips.

This explains why my thoughts of God produced an unrivaled tension within me. To hear of love, acceptance, and belonging not just from another human being but from my Creator was a mystery that invited wonder, awe, and trust, even worship. But to hear in that *same narrative* of the hoops that I needed to jump through to earn his love along with the impending eternal punishment if I failed to make it through the hoops – well, this produced confusion and fear that strangled my soul. Here again was the monster under my bed.

"Atonement" is a word that is commonly used as a comprehensive term almost synonymous to our salvation. But don't let that fool you. It is a beautiful word that describes a mystery of the most profound sort. It, too, has produced a seeming infinite string of debate. This debate is not something this book seeks to address. So, for now, I will simply offer this: to think of the atonement is to think "at-one-ment." It is the process by which the Father, Son, and Spirit unite the human race to themselves to deliver or rescue us from our complete and total brokenness (i.e., to save us from our sins). Here is how I often think of what is going on when we speak of Jesus "saving" or atoning for our sins…

I grew up just outside of Philadelphia, one of the few cities where the US Navy has a working naval base and shipyard. As it happens, my granddad was a career Navy man. Though he had actually retired in Lexington, Kentucky (Go Wildcats!) he would come to visit us pretty much every year. And whenever he came he would always make a trip to the base.

In my early years he would occasionally take my brother and me with him. These were family excursions we absolutely loved because it meant we'd get to go down on the docks and walk alongside the enormous ships that happened to be in port. Mostly there were destroyers and cruisers. These were so big to my young boy eyes that they became my benchmark of what "big" meant. I remember one particular time when there happened to be an aircraft carrier in dry dock being repaired. I had never seen anything that large – at least nothing else was as big that moved – which instantly made it the coolest thing ever! The bow rose from the water like a giant and incredibly steep, precipitous cliff; dwarfing not only me, but every other ship tied at the docks! Giant numbers painted in white, ten times longer than I was tall, hung like the sun in the metallic grey sky. It's one thing to see them from a distance out on the water, but imagine a six-year-old boy standing a mere thirty feet from the hull of this floating city…

My experience with these great naval ships had a lasting influence on me. Years later when I did a presentation in school for my year-end project I chose to do a report on a book titled "The Sinking of the Bismarck", primarily because it was about the largest battleship ever constructed. No doubt my childhood trips to the navy yard were the unconscious influence behind my choice.

However, as an older man, it isn't the ships that I remember best when I first think of these special visits with my granddad. Strangely, I immediately recall the gigantic ropes that were used as mooring lines to tie the ships to the dock. I think part of the reason I have that lasting impression is that I expected the ships to be big. My mind knew they were, so their enormity wowed me but didn't surprise me. But the ropes were a different matter. Ropes were something I knew, something I held in my hand and used. I just couldn't get over seeing and touching ropes that so wildly staggered my perceptions. To this small boy, the massive ropes were so fantastic; they seemed unreal, even while I was actually touching them.

These ropes were made of thousands upon thousands of individual strands twisted together. Not very impressive when taken individually, but, when twisted together, they were so strong they could secure ships that weighed up to a hundred thousand tons! Imagine what it would take to untwist every strand, one by one, until the rope was no more.

These ropes remind me of our inner worlds as a result of the fall.

Our lives are twisted beyond our ability to even know where to begin. So if untwisting the enormous ropes that held these mighty ships boggles our imaginations what would it take to untwist the brokenness of our lives?

Atonement is the means by which the Triune God is untwisting every evil desire, every wrong step, every thought or motive that ever entered our hearts and minds – *one strand at a time* – so that not one thing is left bent, broken or twisted.

Nothing is left unhealed.

Anything less would not be justice.
Anything less would not be mercy.
Anything less would not be salvation.

If we carry the metaphor further, it's not just one rope that atonement is untwisting – it's billions of ropes. And they aren't all laid out in perfect order. All these billions of ropes are entangled with each other because none of us lives in a vacuum – we are all connected.

So it seems very weird to me that when we engage in conversation about Jesus's atonement it usually revolves only around the external realities of his death. Oh my! It must be so much more.

Nevertheless, his death really is incredibly important. So then, why did Jesus die? To many in the Christian religion, this is the foundational question of their faith, because they believe their salvation centers exclusively on this event. So much so that most will answer the question as though they are on theological autopilot reciting an answer for a catechism class.

It was this way for me. Had you asked me that question after seven years of college and graduate theological education, I probably would have shrugged, cocked my head sideways, and stared at you with a puzzled, scrunched-up face and thought, *What cave have you been hiding in?* I mean, this is America; doesn't everybody know why Jesus died? He died for our sins. It's plastered on billboards all across our nation's interstate highway system.

Thankfully, I have grown and I have changed. My understanding of the atonement has evolved. And this is, I believe, because our knowledge of the atonement is in direct proportion to our understanding of the Incarnation. By that, I mean that the supreme question of the atonement and our ability to grasp at the fringes of this mystery is best attempted by not addressing a "why" question but rather a "who" question: "Who is Jesus?"[43] In practical terms, though Jesus's person and work are not separate, priority should be given to understanding Jesus the person, so we can better understand what he did. Unlike Batman, Jesus is not defined primarily by his actions. But let's put this on hold for just a bit. I will explore this in detail in the chapters that follow; I promise.

In the current religious climate of the evangelical West many frame the story of our atonement as though the Father does not want to heal us. The meaning of Jesus's death has then been delivered to the vast majority of us in a narrative that features a god who, because of his holiness, is angry. And he will no longer tolerate the proliferation of our immorality, whether it be our indiscretions or undiluted evil. Thus, the consequence of our sin is that we will receive a punishment from God. His justice demands that we pay for the mess we've made.

Furthermore, his holiness, justice, and wrath can only be propitiated, satisfied, or fulfilled when the guilty have been punished. Simply, our atonement requires punishment. He will cause us to suffer at least to the degree that we have caused suffering. Though it may not happen in this life, we can be certain it will happen in the next. His ultimate justice will be served and his holiness satisfied by a second death, which is withdrawing his good presence from us and abandoning us to hell for time without end.

From this perspective the gospel message is: atonement has been accomplished because Jesus took our place. He was our substitute. In fact, the primary reason he became flesh was to be the focal point of God's wrath toward our sin instead of us. He suffered, died, and was abandoned by the Father for us. Now that the Father's holiness and justice have been satisfied in Jesus, he is free to be merciful and

---

43 *This point is made repeatedly throughout the writings of T.F. Torrance.*

gracious to us and thereby save us.

So then, in this narrative the suffering servant's excruciating death was nothing less than a horrible, cruel punishment administered by God for sins the human race committed. He bears the punishment from God that we deserved and that was intended for us.

The "good news" is that God's anger has been appeased, so there is no longer any need for him to punish us for our sins, because they have been punished in Jesus, the substitute.

Or is there?

According to my former version of atonement, if a person rejects Jesus and will not trust him for salvation, that person will experience a punishment in hell for time without end. So, is there still a punishment coming or not?

There are many assumptions that have shaped this narrative. Here are a few:

1. This assumes there is something in the nature of God that is capable of cruelty and torture.

2. This assumes God is capable of punishment that is punitive, retributive, and a bit vindictive.

3. This assumes God's holiness is only a moral quality, which is the motivation for him to punish.

4. This assumes that God requires punishment for justice and atonement to occur.

Do you believe this about God?

I Confess | I grew up with this narrative.

This was the story handed to me. In my church background, it was called the doctrine of penal substitution. It wasn't given as just another theory trying to explain how Jesus saves us. It was dogma.

It was the "truth".

For years I accepted this theory of atonement as if it were not a theory but the gospel itself. I believed and taught others that Jesus came to rescue me from his Father's wrath.

I was so convinced that this narrative was the true gospel and the biblical and correct way to understand the meaning of Jesus's death, I would admonish my students with passion that any message that deviated from this version was heretical and should be accursed.

What madness is this that the Father could think and feel differently than the Son?

This grieves me deeply. I am ashamed that I could have ever thought such a thing, let alone teach it. I understand how I got there, but it doesn't lessen the regret I feel for the things I believed and taught about the Father.

Maybe you have been handed the same narrative. Maybe you find it difficult to trust a god who says he loves you, but when push comes to shove, he actually loves himself and his moral perfection more than he loves you. If you find this troublesome, bordering on the absurd, then I have great news! God is not like that; he is far better.

I have been told that my explanation of the penal substitution theory is an exaggeration, a half-truth, a gross caricature.

It's not. Really… it's not. My explanation is *not* a straw man.

I know, for I have heard this version of the gospel more times than I can recall in meetings and churches all over the world. In fact, I am absolutely certain it's not a caricature or an exaggeration, because this was the message I taught.

I do not judge why people teach this; I assume it is because they believe it. I certainly did. Do all who believe or teach the penal substitution theory think so negatively of God? No, they do not. In fact, there are many pastors and teachers who would be extremely uncomfortable, reluctant even, to speak as I have.

But I did.

I have heard and taught things about God that made him out to be much like a monster. And along my journey, I have met hundreds of others who believe and teach as I did. But, to be fair, there are now some more nuanced versions that tone down the rhetoric of "God's wrath needs to be appeased through violent divine punishment." But regardless of how they say it, if you follow their logic to its conclusion, you arrive at the same place; namely, something in God's nature requires him to punish anyone who falls short of him.

Looking back, the sheer enormity of my confusion was so astonishing it is hard to believe, for I would speak of God's love for the world out of a sincere, believing heart while simultaneously issuing the sternest of warnings that God will punish us by abandoning us forever if we reject his love.

Would love actually do this? Can love actually do this? Would you do this? Would God?

I believe love will punish, but not because some other thing requires it, and certainly not because love can only be appeased with our punishment. If love punishes, the only goal is to destroy that which is destroying its beloved. It is only for restoration that love will punish.

Maybe an even better question is this: would God, as revealed in Jesus, do this? Time and time again in the Bible, Jesus has the opportunity to punish, and he *never* does.

The woman at the well...

The woman caught in adultery...

Judas, who betrays him...

The Pharisees who want to stone him...

Oh, he judges, to be sure, and he even condemns evil as evil wherever he confronts it.

But he does not punish.

Instead, his judgment is revealed in an act of utterly staggering love – he willingly, lovingly *submitted to our punishment of him!* He submitted to our evil by bearing our hatred and scorn so that he might heal the darkness that grips us.[44]

But where is the justice in this? This is not fair, is it? Yes, it is. It is fair and far beyond it.

It is justice that is merciful.

Jesus didn't come to deliver us from a penalty he and his Father imposed on us for not playing according to their rules. That would mean he came to save us from himself!

But wait, Jesus died on the cross for our sins, didn't he?

Yes, yes he did! It is our sin – our hatred, our contempt, our self-righteousness – that ridicules, punishes, and tortures him. Aren't we the murderers here? Isn't his death at our hands our ultimate punishment on him? Maybe a better way to think of this is that Jesus died *because* of our sins.

If Jesus didn't die to appease the Father's holy, just wrath toward our sin, why did he die?

---

44 "What marks out God above all false gods is that they are not capable and ready for this. In their otherworldliness and supernaturalness and otherness, etc., the gods are a reflection of the human pride, which will not unbend, which will not stoop to that which is beneath it. God is not proud. In His high majesty he is humble. It is in this high humility that he speaks and acts as the God who reconciles the world to himself. It is under this aspect first that we must consider the history of the atonement." Karl Barth, Church Dogmatics, IV.1, (Peabody, MA: Hendrickson Publishers, 2010), 159.

He died because to reach the depth of our perversion, he had to go all the way. He had to meet us at our worst, in our hatred and murder of the very One who loved us into being.

It is the only way to heal the depths of our brokenness. By taking his union with us into the depths of our depravity, he is now able to heal us from the inside. By taking his union with us down into death he broke death's power over us from within and thereby completely destroyed death's grip on us.

God does not simply wave some magic wand over us pronouncing forgiveness. Nor does he merely execute an external transaction to satisfy some need for punishment. T.F. Torrance states, "We must understand the Cross as the act of God Almighty taking all that abominable evil upon himself... not by way of some kind of external transaction but by entering into it and dealing with it from within its entrenchment in the depths of perverted human existence."[45]

And again, "In all that, Christ was on the one hand so one with God that what he did, God did, for he was none other than God himself acting thus in our humanity. And therefore, there is no other God for us than this God, and no other action of God toward us than this action in which he stood in our place and acted on our behalf. On the other hand, he was so one with us that when he died we died, for he did not die for himself but for us, and he did not die alone, but we died in him as those whom he had bound inseparably by his incarnation. Therefore, when he rose again we rose in him and with him, and when he presented himself before the face of the Father, he presented us also before God, so that we are already accepted of God in him once and for all."[46]

Today, I have a very different view of the atonement. I hold this

---

45 T.F. Torrance, *The Mediation of Christ*, American ed. (Wm. B. Eerdmans, Grand Rapids, MI 1984) 51.
46 T.F. Torrance, *Atonement: The Person and Work of Christ*, (Downers Grove, IL Inter Varsity Press, 2008) 154

viewpoint passionately, but I also hold it loosely, knowing that my understanding of it will continue to evolve. As I said earlier, when we speak of atonement, we enter the sacred space of mystery.

However, here are a few ways my view has changed: First, I believe the moral and legal theories trying to explain what is happening on the cross fall woefully short. Second, our salvation is not accomplished in just one thing Jesus did, not even his death on the cross. Rather, atoning reconciliation comes to us through the entirety of the birth, life, death, resurrection, and ascension of Jesus. Third, an event, even the monumental event of the cross, does not save us. Jesus, the person, saves us. Fourth, he saves us primarily by uniting himself to us, not by simply doing something for us that we cannot do. I am not denying the importance of what Jesus has done, nor do I think salvation is something that we can work out in and of ourselves. But his union with humanity *precedes* and is the means by which we have all been forgiven, justified, redeemed, and reconciled.

But, probably the most important idea that has changed in my understanding of the atonement and the one that I feel the most strongly about is this: the atonement that results in our reconciliation cannot be attained by punishment. No amount of punishment can ever turn an enemy into a friend. Only love can do that. "And God was in Christ and reconciled the world to himself…" (2 Cor. 5:19).

Late one evening, a dear friend of mine arrived at my house. I stood at the door waiting to welcome her. She was hunched over, walking slowly, as if in great pain. As she got closer, I saw her eyes were red from long sessions of tears. In fact, as she lifted her gaze toward me, she began to cry again. I rushed off the porch with my arms extended to embrace her. She fell into my arms, sobbing uncontrollably.

I had no idea what was wrong. I just held her tightly as she continued to groan, sobbing all the more, great heaves of emotion convulsing like waves breaking onto the shore.

With her face buried in my shoulder, she tried to speak through shudders and gasps for breath, "David... left... me ..." I held her all the more tightly as tears welled up in my eyes too.

And then the most amazing thing happened.

As I embraced her, I began to share in her pain and feel her anguish. Even more remarkably, she began to share in my strength and feel my comfort and peace. The tiniest seed of healing was beginning to take root in both of us. This was a small fraction, merely a glimpse into a window, of what union and relational participation is like. For even though what she and I experienced was authentic and beautiful it only came primarily through a physical embrace.

Jesus' union with us is *far* more than a physical embrace. It is ontological. He unites himself to the deepest, darkest places of our being, and he embraces us there. This is the way to the healing of our souls.

I refer to T.F. Torrance once again – In the profound interaction between incarnation and atonement in Jesus, the blessed exchange it involved between the divine-human life of Jesus and mankind has the effect of finalizing and sealing the ontological relations between every man and Jesus Christ.[47]

A friend of mine told me a fascinating story about one of his classmates from graduate school. His name was Peter. Peter's son became deeply involved with a cult. Eventually, he moved in to their commune. Peter's response was to move in too. He didn't move in to debate, shame, or police his son. He didn't plan their escape route. He entered his son's mess. Without buying the lies his son believed, he lived there, just to be near him and with him. And relentlessly, day after day, he loved him. He stayed there for over a year. Finally,

---

47   T.F. Torrance, The Trinitarian Faith, (T. & T. CLARK LTD Edinburgh) 182.

his son came to his senses, and they both left.

Hmm… a son who was lost in his blindness had become an enemy to his father, and his father's response was to dwell with him in his mess and love him into reconciliation and freedom.

Sound familiar?

CHAPTER 12

THE ECLIPSE OF JESUS

Is there a god behind the back of Jesus?

- T.F. Torrance

I hate phoning airlines. Or credit card companies. Or any customer service that I have to call to resolve problems, questions, disputes, or conflicts. Not the way I'd like to spend my Sunday afternoon. On the bright side, at least there's a person to whom I can talk. We won't go into automated or online customer service. Makes me want to pull my hair out and curse. But I'm rapidly losing my hair, so I just curse a lot.

It doesn't matter which company; they all seem to follow the same protocol. If you have a problem of any kind, the rep is trained to give you a scripted answer. And no matter how many times you try to explain that your situation is different, you get stonewalled. It's not the customer service representatives' fault. They are simply doing what they've been trained to do. It goes like this:

"Hello, thank you for calling Acme Credit Card Services," the cheery voice chirps. "May I have the number of your account?"

"Hi," I reply in my deadpan voice, and then give my number.

"Thank you," says the blue jay on the other end of my phone. "And what is the name on the account?"

"John MacMurray."

After a few other obligatory questions for identification, the real conversation begins.

"How can I help you?"

"Well, I purchased a new DVD player three months ago, and I returned it less than a week after I bought it. Never took it out of the box. They examined it at your store. They said they would refund the total purchase on my card. But for the past few months, you continue to charge interest on a balance that I do not owe. Would you please refund the purchase and reverse the interest that has accrued?" I explain this in my nicest, most polite, "Can I have another piece of your cake, please?" voice.

"I'm sorry, Mr. MacMurray, you have not made any payments on your card, so this has gone to a collection agency. There is nothing I can do about this."

"I understand that it has gone to a collection agency; that's why I'm calling. It should never have gone there. I haven't paid, because I don't have the product. It was returned unused and in perfect condition. The box had never even been opened."

"I'm sorry, Mr. MacMurray. There's nothing I can do about this."

This verbal ping-pong goes on for another five minutes or so, until I say the magic words…

"May I speak to your supervisor?"

At this point, they're probably thrilled to get off the phone with me. Why don't I begin by simply asking for the supervisor when I get on the phone? Seems like it would save a lot of time. Probably lower my blood pressure too.

My point is this: I ask for the supervisor, because I know there is someone with authority behind the customer representative who probably knows more and definitely has the power to do what the representative on the phone cannot.

THE ECLIPSE OF JESUS

I Confess | In the past, a discussion regarding the deity of Jesus was a conversation that usually exposed a nerve for me.

Though I believed and taught Jesus was God, equal with the Father, I had this nagging feeling that the Father was bigger that Jesus. Though Jesus was deity, there was a god behind his back who really called the shots – and it was his Father.

This belief wasn't part of my theology. It wasn't even an idea with which I'd ever agree. It was more like a pinched nerve in my back that I tried to ignore. Never seen but always felt.

In a real sense, I felt Jesus was like the customer service representative, and the Father was the supervisor. Simply put – they just weren't equal.

On several occasions, I heard the idea that creation and salvation were the Father's plan. The Father sent Jesus on a mission to carry out that plan. The Holy Spirit was the guarantee that the plan worked and was successful. Unaware of the effect this kind of hierarchal language can imply, I bought in to the notion that the Father is the boss. He's in charge, and he has the final word. Because I never admitted to this private struggle, I assumed I was alone, a freak of nature within the evangelical subculture.

I Confess | When doubt chipped away at my convictions, my knee-jerk reaction was to emphasize Jesus's deity in my lectures with increasing passion.

In reality, it was nothing more than theological self-talk. My "passion" was a disguise for dogmatism, and my dogmatism was a poorly constructed tourniquet for my soul – to stop the hemorrhaging of my faith.

The first hint I was not alone occurred one evening a few years after I stepped down from teaching at a bible college. A former student called me on the phone…

"Hey, John, it's Hayes."

"Hayes! Great to hear you! How ya doing?"

"Good."

We caught up, mostly small talk; but after a few minutes, it was obvious something was on Hayes's mind.

"What's up?" I asked. "I know you didn't call to get a report on the Portland weather."

Silence. Long enough that it became uncomfortable.

"Something wrong Hayes?"

"Well, not really. At least I don't think so. But I think you will."

"I will what?"

"Think something is wrong."

'Okay," I said, waiting.

"I've decided to become a Jehovah's Witness," he finally blurted.

Now there was silence on my end.

I gathered my thoughts. "Why?"

"Well, the truth is, I never really thought Jesus and God were equal. He was always a little less than God, you know? And that's what the JWs believe. I guess I'm finally being honest with myself, so I decided to join them, because that's what I've always kind of believed."

I don't remember how long we talked, but it was a long conversation. Hours I'm sure. I tried to assure him that he was still my friend, but much of the conversation was an emotional debate attempting to convince Hayes that Jesus was God.

It was half-hearted on my part. Hayes had just admitted out loud what I felt in secret.

You may be wondering why I didn't admit my tension and doubts to Hayes. Good question. First, on an intellectual level, I thought the Scriptures were far more convincing in favor of Jesus's deity than against it. Still do. Second, I thought history came down on my side as well. And I still do, more than ever. Third, how does a teacher in the mainstream Christian tradition admit that he's not sure if Jesus is really equal to God the Father? If word got out about my struggle, I would be blacklisted faster than Bugs Bunny can say, "What's up, Doc?" It would have been no small thing to sabotage my own career.

Obviously, a glaring difference existed between Hayes and me. Though we both felt the same way, his belief agreed with his feelings. Mine did not. I was trying to conquer my feelings with my beliefs. He resolved the tension by changing his beliefs. I would not. So, I continued to live with the tension, which is fine for a season. But a conflict of this magnitude can't be ignored forever. Eventually, I knew something had to give.

However, something unexpected came from that troublesome conversation that was good, even healthy. Now I knew I was not alone in my struggle. Surprisingly, this gave me some measure of relief, because it gave me permission to live in the tension and pursue a solution in a more honest fashion.

During this time, I also realized that doubt was not an enemy to be feared but a valuable, though somewhat uncomfortable, companion on my journey to learn and grow.

Even more important, my struggle was not purely intellectual. Though that was certainly a part, I realized I couldn't resolve my tension merely by accumulating more Bible information and theology. My struggle was a personal one; a struggle of my heart. God was calling me further in. I needed to engage *him*, not just information about him.

I know this again begs the question, "Who is Jesus?", and we'll get to that more in the next chapter. But first, I want to tell you about a couple of other ideas that had stolen their way into my heart and mind, hiding subconsciously in my theology.

I Confess	**I was working from the assumption that truth should make sense – not breed confusion.**

As I confessed in an earlier chapter, intellectual certainty was my "holy grail" of biblical and theological study. However, mystery was quite the opposite. It was vague, inconclusive, almost ghost-like and should be avoided at all costs. Is it any wonder that mystery became something I thought should be eliminated?

So, to think that God became man, that humanity was united to deity? That was like embedding a lethal virus into my data search. My brain froze, the little colored circle swirling endlessly until my entire theological system crashed.

Ignorance was the tool I used to sweep the virus off my grid. Like so many, I chose to ignore what I couldn't grasp. Maybe it was simply intellectual self-preservation.

But shouldn't we expect this? The idea of God becoming human is antimony for us. It violates the law of non-contradiction. I mean, our very definition of deity excludes humanity.

I also realized that it was impossible for me to find balance in figuring this out. For when I pondered Jesus's deity, I lost his true humanity. And when I considered his humanity, it diminished his deity.

But what if I had encountered the Word himself instead of merely an idea of who he was; would I have fared better? Today, I believe I would have.

I am aware that many people, myself included, have encountered the Living Word through the written word of the Bible. And this is good. But there were two critical mistakes I made. One was equating understanding a text as an encounter with Jesus, thinking they were one and the same. They are not. Two, my mistake went beyond ordinary confusion for I thought of the Bible as the exclusive revelation of God – that it was the only way someone could encounter Jesus. It is not.

Anyway, I struggled with what I believe many others have also struggled – the thought that when people looked at a human being they were really looking at the Creator of the universe. But I also stumbled over his humanity too. Sure, I believed Jesus was a real authentic human but I felt like Jesus cheated at life. I mean, he felt the frailties and limitations of a human body, but whenever life got too hard, he'd just rely on his divine power to find a solution and resolve any difficulties.

This, too, was not something I admitted, nor do I remember being taught this explicitly. Nevertheless, I felt this way, even though I may have had no good reason. Don't get me wrong; I had some reasons, but they were about as good as walking into a swordfight with a toothpick.

Here's one: only God can do miracles. So, when Jesus performed a miracle, it was the "God" part of him that bestowed the gift.

Here's another: in some biblical stories, Jesus appears to be omniscient, which is a divine attribute. So, whenever Jesus dispensed divine knowledge, it was the God part that spoke through the vocal chords and lips of the human part.

Or maybe, for a moment, Jesus stopped living in the limitations of being human and acted as God. Not unlike Clark Kent, rushing into a phone booth to throw off his clothes to reveal the large red "S" on his chest. No longer Clark Kent, he became Superman.

Can you picture Jesus throwing off his humanity to reveal the large red "G" on his chest? It must have been exhausting for him, all that changing at the speed of thought – back and forth, back and forth, deity to humanity, humanity to deity – a million times a day.

Seriously, I had a real problem holding these two truths together.

What I didn't know at the time was the reason why. These misconceptions created a tension in me because they had developed out of a basic misunderstanding of the Incarnation. I thought when God "took on flesh" that meant he united himself to a human body. Like pouring water into a glass, God "poured himself" into a body. The human part of Jesus was simply the body that God chose to inhabit. That sounds an awful lot like the Incarnation was really the "Invasion of the Body Snatcher." Creepy, huh?

But the mystery of the Incarnation isn't that God united himself to a human body – the mystery is infinitely more profound – God united himself to a human *being* without ceasing to be the divine being he eternally has been.

My solution? Instead of embracing the mystery of the Incarnation, I reverted back to the only way I knew to deal with it – I ignored it. This set me on a trajectory that has taken years for me to recover.

Today, I am content to embrace the tension and paradox of this wondrous mystery. And the craziest thing is happening: I find my love and faith growing. I am grateful I've come to experience freedom to learn and be amazed. What an extraordinary gift!

Another factor contributed to my eclipse of Jesus. Believe it or not, it was the cross.

I Confess	The cross became so central to me that it virtually eclipsed who died on it.

I had a theological and psychological fixation with the cross. It was such a dominant part of my rationale that I carelessly shoved the entire Incarnation to the margins of theology and life.[48] It was almost like Jesus' death was so important that everything else about him seemed secondary. Have we not been told the reason God became human was to die? That atonement for sins was achieved only

---

48   *I spoke of this at length in chapter 6.*

in his death? Why else do we say the way to heaven is to believe Jesus died for our sins? Look no further than the Apostles' Creed.

> I believe in Jesus Christ, his only Son, our Lord,
> who was conceived by the Holy Spirit
> and born of the virgin Mary.
> He suffered under Pontius Pilate…

The creed goes from Jesus' birth immediately to his death. What happened to his life? Doesn't that seem a bit odd to you, a bit disproportionate? Is it possible that there might be just a smidge of imbalance with this?

My problem was far greater than just a bit of imbalance in my perspective. I missed the truth of who Jesus actually is. This disparity dulled my perception, choked my trust, and stifled my worship of Jesus. Jesus' real identity was lost – another piece that brought an unconscious, nagging feeling there was a god behind Jesus' back.

I am acutely aware that whenever anyone within the Christian community calls into question something to do with the cross, they are skating on dangerous religious ice. I know how the ice is – it's thin where I'm skating. You would think that such a question could bring down all the woes found in the Bible – and there are a lot of woes.

Sarcasm, aside, my intent is not to belittle the importance of what happened the day God died. It is incredibly important. It would be difficult to overstate the significance of the cross, but I fear we have. And that's my point.

So, instead of immediately writing me off, please consider there may be people who believe as I did, and they've lost any vision or passion for the One who died because of our sins. My hope is that we can return to some sense of balance in this conversation, so that we fall more in love with Jesus our Savior rather than with the tree on which he died.

/

CHAPTER

13

THE INCARNATION – THE BEAUTIFUL MYSTERY

And the Word became flesh.

— St. John

Have you ever become so familiar or accustomed with something that you forget it even exists? Say, for example, your teeth. Barely give them a thought… until you have a toothache or cavity. On a more serious note, think about how we take our loved ones for granted, until they are no longer with us.

When I first moved to Portland as a young man, it was late summer, and the Northwest was experiencing the weather that gives everyone a reason to endure eight months of cloudy, rainy skies. Bright sunshine, clear blue skies, no humidity, eighty degrees, fifteen-hour days. Ahh… the bliss!

If you are ever fortunate enough to visit our quirky, lovable city, you will discover one of its unique and charming features: from almost anywhere you happen to be, you will probably be treated to a view of our most recognizable natural landmark, Mount Hood. At 11,250 feet, adorned in a perpetual white robe of creamy snow, its sharp, triangular features dominate our eastern horizon. Portlanders usually just refer to it as "the mountain."

Being freshly transplanted into this Shangri-La, I was like a little puppy who first discovers mud. Every time I was outside, I strained my neck to find the mountain. Didn't matter what I was doing –

driving, walking, or running to the grocery store – I wanted to see Mt. Hood. I was captivated by its beauty and majesty. And I didn't want to just see it, I wanted to stare at it, take it in, absorb it. I wanted the image beamed like a laser into my consciousness, because it might not be there the next moment. I'm surprised I never got a tattoo.

But even that wasn't enough for me. I'd pull out a camera wherever I saw it – in a parking lot, at the movies, as my friend drove east on the Banfield Freeway, *anywhere*. And this was *way* before digital cameras and cell phones. Locals thought I was nuts.

One year I wanted a picture of Mt. Hood from a specific location. I went there *every day* from November 1 until Thanksgiving, twenty-five days straight. Never got that image… never even saw it.

About ten months after I moved to Oregon, I went to a barbeque at a home that had a particularly beautiful view of the mountain. I could barely concentrate on the food or the conversation. I was like a crack addict. I just kept staring at it. I couldn't get enough, I loved looking at the mountain. My friend, who lived at the house, shook his head at me and said, "You'll get used to it, dude."

Familiarity has bred contempt in many Portlanders. I fear they have come to take the stunning beauty of where they live for granted. This is sad. But thankfully, if you ask them to stop what they're doing and take a long unrushed look at the majesty of this dramatic peak, usually their senses revive, and beauty stirs once again in their soul. They remember why they live here.

I Confess	Magnify this phenomenon a hundredfold, and, to my embarrassment, this is what I had done with Jesus – taken him for granted.

Just like a stagnant pool of water breeds mosquitoes, my familiarity with whom I *thought* Jesus to be produced apathy when I read his name. My grasp of who he is had no more effect on me than seeing a glossy perfume ad in a fashion magazine. I just flipped the page. My former lens or way of seeing had only proved to blur who Jesus really is by "reducing the Incarnation to nothing more than a footnote to Adam".[49]

Like a Portlander who needs to see Mt. Hood from a visitor's perspective, I needed a new lens or, better yet, new eyes to see the wonder of Jesus again. Thankfully, the eyes of my heart have begun to heal. Indifference is fading, and my spirit is being revived. My understanding is growing, and a new perspective is emerging as beauty charms my soul once again.

So, who is Jesus, really? Our calendar revolves around his life. We curse just about everything under the sun with his name. We've seen his picture a million times. Or have we?

Over the last two millennia, millions have died for him. To humanity's shame, maybe even more have been killed in his name. It would be foolish to ignore him.

What do we do with him? Do we trust him? Maybe a more important question – since our belief stands on theirs – did those who knew him trust him? They knew him better than we do, yes?

Most were martyred for their trust. Who did they believe him to be? I think their answer would be: Jesus is the Incarnation of God. Not just any god but the Creator God. They affirmed this by using the phrase, "Jesus is Lord."

By that creedal statement, they did *not* mean "Lord," as in God is like a great king dispensing punishment and reward from some grand throne, fascinated with his greatness and obsessed with his glory.

There was a time when this caricature wasn't too far removed

---

[49] *This is one of Dr. C. Baxter Kruger's favorite phrases, which my friend generously allowed me to borrow.*

from what I believed of God. He seemed almost schizophrenic to me; for there were times he seemed to act with unimaginable love (like Jesus did) and yet, other times he acted more like Jupiter and Zeus, deities who do whatever they want, because they are gods. Divine prerogative, you know?

My justification was that humans reasoning about what is right or wrong are not the same as God's – that his ways are higher than our ways. This was my defense for God acting in ways that we would call cruel, prejudicial, or sociopathic in humans. It's difficult to trust someone who seems to change so arbitrarily.

As I have been wrestling, trying to understand the Incarnation, it has wrecked me. It has exposed the skewed thinking in my perceptions of God by revealing the overwhelming beauty, the mind-boggling genius, the staggering love and humility, and the sheer enormity of his goodness. It has brought my theology to its knees. And this has been a good thing – a very good thing.

From what I can tell, the apostles and the early church understood that Jesus is the final, best, and ultimate revelation of God. So, whatever we think God to be like, if he isn't like Jesus, then we've been fooled.

So, what is the Incarnation? And why is it so important?

Religions and mythologies abound with stories of God (or the gods) assuming human form. Many predate Jesus so the idea of incarnation is neither new nor original with Jesus and the Bible. But Jesus' claim and story are unique from those of all the gods of any and every religion. Maybe considering what it's not will help us better grasp what it is.

The incarnation or "en-flesh-ment" of God is not some feeble attempt by the Creator to communicate with his creatures. Nor is it anything like the mythological Zeus calling down fire on our stupidity or secretly visiting the planet cloaked in the shell of a human body to provide aid or thwart the endeavors of his children. Neither is it a fulfillment of some external, moral, or legal obligation that God meets for his creatures, because they couldn't.

The Incarnation is not a perfect representation of God, like a reflection we see in a mirror, painting, or photograph that only resembles the divine but falls pathetically short of God's substance. Nor is it a mere man who was so in tune with the spiritual consciousness of the divine in him that he lived in a perfectly god-like way. Nor is it a myth – some sort of fairy tale to cover up God's "ugly side" in the Old Testament.

The Incarnation is not a temporary event God orchestrated, like a coat he put on and eventually took off, a kind of cosmic, deistic bait and switch, where he appears to be one way to win us over, only to reveal afterward that his real nature is one of power and dominance, commanding us to fall at his feet and worship him. That would never do. I may as well worship at the feet of Caesar.

The truth is, we may act with hidden agendas in our pockets and behave in ways not consistent with our nature to get what we want, but that's called hypocrisy. God is not like that.

Whoever tells you he is or comes up with an interpretation from some religious book that makes him out to be like this, run from that dogma and person as fast as you can. Seriously.

| I Confess | Today, I have taken my place alongside the Nicene fathers in declaring that Jesus is God in the flesh. |

Jesus is "*homousion ton patri*," of the same being or substance as the Father. He is the union of the divine with human.[50] He became completely man while still remaining completely God. And without either his divineness or humanness diminished in any way or the two merging into a new sort of hybrid, he remains 100 percent God and 100 percent human simultaneously in his one Person. Or, as T.F. Torrance stated, "He is God of the nature of God, and man of the nature of man, in one and the same Person."[51]

It is not God alone, but God and humanity together that comprises or fills out the meaning of "the Word of God." Jesus *is* the Word of God.[52] He is God's best word. He is God's final word. He is God's ultimate word. For he is the One and Only Lord of the universe, and all creation resides in Him.

And in the moment of a sentence and the breath of a word, we have entered into mystery.

This mystery is first and foremost a manifestation of the eternal, tenacious, and unyielding love of the Father, Son, and Spirit to stop our free fall into darkness and gather up all of creation into the everlasting goodness of their Triune life. It is nothing less than the divine community we call God stooping to meet us face to face by becoming one of us. Not merely like us but one *with* us. It is about *union*.

---

50 "The creative and sustaining Source of all human being has come himself to us as a particular human being, yet without ceasing to be the divine Being he eternally is." T.F. Torrance, The Mediation of Christ, American ed. (Wm. B. Eerdmans, Grand Rapids, MI 1984) 67.

51 T.F. Torrance, The Mediation of Christ, American ed. (Wm. B. Eerdmans, Grand Rapids, MI 1984) 66.

52 This profound thought is a major theme throughout the writings of Karl Barth.

THE INCARNATION – THE BEAUTIFUL MYSTERY

Without ever ceasing to be who he is, the eternal Son – one with the eternal Father – becomes bone of our bone and flesh of our flesh – i.e., absolutely, completely, and fully human in every way.

This means that there is now in Jesus Christ not only a physical, tangible revelation of what God is like but also a human life that embodies all that God intended for humanity from the beginning. He is not simply an example for us to follow from a distance; he is so much more than that.

Jesus of Nazareth is the pivotal point of human history. Indeed, he is the focal point of all cosmic history. He is not just God in man but rather God *as* man. From birth to ascension, his life is the Triune God's heart laid open for all to see. It is heaven's great revolt against evil and its violence. It is the Father, Son, and Spirit acting in such complete oneness to utterly destroy all that is destroying his precious ones. For the Incarnate One becomes the arena where the final conflict between light and darkness will wage war. The stakes are eternal. Our world hangs in the balance of this extraordinary moment. It is the moment in time when the One who is beyond time and space invades and penetrates our world of darkness in a profound and entirely astonishing way to realize the eternal dream of these Three that are One. It is the "fullness of time."

Incredibly, this mystery deepens; for, how does the Changeless One "become"? It is the very One who is Light, in whom no darkness dwells, that has become flesh. This "becoming" is not a changing where God alters his nature in any way. Rather, it is a changing more in the sense of taking on or assuming a new or different form of existence.

The mystery continues deeper still, for when he enters our world, the Eternal Word doesn't simply become human; he becomes *flesh*. In Jesus Christ, God himself came as a man into our broken world and united our sinful human nature to his divine nature.[53]

This was necessary, for, if the entire person is to be healed, then the entire person has to be assumed by Christ; for the un-assumed is unhealed, or that which God has not taken up in Christ is not saved.[54]

And so, he immersed himself into our fallen nature *without being fallen in it*, for the Light, though united with humanity, will forever remain the Light – clear, pure, and true.

The mystery penetrates even deeper, for the Incarnation is not an event that happens outside of the Trinitarian life, like a magic trick he spins into existence apart from himself. If the Father/Son relationship is the essence of who God *is*, then the Incarnation takes place in *God's very being*. When Jesus reveals the Father to us, he does not reveal something different from himself; his revelation of God is a *self-revelation*. Jesus does not speak for God; he speaks *as* God. This implies that in our knowing Jesus we begin to know the

---

53 "The paradox at the heart of Christianity is that the Son of God entered into fallen Adamic existence without ceasing to be the Son of God . . . The life of the Trinity intersected the brokenness of fallen human existence. How is this possible? How could the fellowship of the Trinity penetrate Adam's hiding? The answer is that it is not possible—something has to give, something has to change. Either the fellowship of the Father, Son, and Spirit grinds to an eternal halt, or Adamic existence is fundamentally reordered. Either the love of the Triune God is broken, or Adamic flesh is converted to God. There has to be a conversion, a fundamental restructuring either in the being and character of God, or in the being and character of Adam." C. Baxter Kruger, *Jesus and the Undoing of Adam*, (Jackson, MS: Perichoresis Press, 2003), 34.

54 "The Incarnation was the coming of God to save us in the heart of our fallen and depraved humanity, where humanity is at its wickedest and in its enmity and violence against the reconciling love of God. That is to say, the Incarnation is to be understood as the coming of God to take upon himself our fallen human nature, our actual human existence laden with sin and guilt, our humanity diseased in mind and soul in its estrangement or alienation from the Creator." T.F. Torrance, *The Mediation of Christ*, American ed. (Wm. B. Eerdmans, Grand Rapids, MI 1984) 48.

unknowable. We participate in knowledge that God has of himself within himself.

This staggers the imagination! How can this be? How can we participate in knowledge that God has of himself *within* himself? But this is precisely what the Incarnation does. In Jesus, we come to know God in a real way, for he shares his knowledge of the Father with us. *And to know God is eternal life.*

The mystery explodes everything we have assumed to be true. For it is the Creator and Sustainer of all things, the One who upholds all things by the word of his power, that comes to dwell in and among us. The Eternal Son didn't become flesh to connect himself to us as though he isn't already related to us. He didn't come because he was absent and now in flesh he becomes present. How could this be? He is the Creator. Wouldn't we simply cease to exist if Jesus withdrew his connection to us?

The Triune God has held and sustained us and therefore been inseparably joined to us from the moment he conceived us and brought us into existence. The amazing and startling thing of God becoming flesh is this: his union with us penetrates and spreads *even inside* the darkness of our fallen minds and hearts, establishing his *already existing* relationship with us in a way that it previously had not existed.

The mystery stretches into the very *heart* of the Living God. For at the heart of the Incarnation is God's *humility*. The framework in which the entire story of our redemption finds itself is a love so profound, so self-giving that only humility can contain its sheer majesty.[55]

The advent of the One who holds the worlds in place is the irrefutable revelation of the true nature of God's power. He rejects all notions of intimidation, retaliation, manipulation or control, dismissing and redefining our understanding of authority. The power that ignited a trillion galaxies, *genuine* power, comes to us in person, as this particular person, Mary's son.

What do we make of the fact that God was in a Nazarene neighborhood for thirty years and almost no one noticed? Not only does this obliterate our dualistic categories of sacred and secular, it forever dignified all that is human. The sheer anonymity of this is staggering. He needs no applause, no "thank you," and no recognition. This is not an isolated incident in which God condescends out of some sense of pity to meet us. This is the truth and the way of his being. Love, not pity, comes to us and becomes part of the very fabric of the community, engaging in the humanity of it all.

The Source of all living things stoops before and beneath his creatures, not to earn our respect or praise but out of sheer love for us. God's love is inexpressibly pure and undiluted, moving the Father, Son, and Spirit to always act with a humility never before imagined by the gods of men.

The One True God never acts differently from what he is. If Jesus washes our feet, he does it because that is the way the Father and Spirit are. Jesus is not revealing something different from God's true

---

55 "In being gracious to man in Jesus Christ, God acknowledges man; He accepts responsibility for his being and nature. He remains Himself. He does not cease to be God. But he does not hold aloof. In being gracious to man in Jesus Christ, He also goes into the far country, into the evil society of this being which is not God and against God. He does not shrink from him. He does not pass him by as did the priest and the Levite the man who had fallen among thieves. He does not leave him to his own devices. He makes his situation His own. He does not forfeit anything by doing this . . . God shows Himself to be the great and true God in the fact that He can and will let His grace bear this cost, that He is capable and willing and ready for this condescension, this act of extravagance, this far journey." Karl Barth, Church Dogmatics, IV.1, (Peabody, MA: Hendrickson Publishers, 2010), 158–159.

nature. He and the Father are one. The Incarnation is not the pitch of some divine used-car salesman trying to manipulate us to buy in to a wonderful plan.

Could there ever be clearer proof that humility is the essence of God's being than the death he died on the hill of Golgotha? How else are we to understand his statement, "No one takes my life, I lay it down," if that is not God *submitting* to us? We didn't take his life; he laid it down for us to take.

The true nature of divine power is revealed once and for all in that moment when Jesus *gave us power over him*. Jesus' death was his confrontation of our twisted darkness as he actively surrendered to our murder. This is the way of the cross, the way of suffering, the way of Jesus. Our king bears our scorn and hatred, culminating in his death and our salvation.

He submitted to minds he designed that, in their scheming hatred, premeditated a way to kill him.

He submitted to hands that he knit together, which beat and tortured him.

He submitted to hearts he formed that screamed with a blood lust that could only be appeased with his murder.

He submitted to wills he fashioned that manipulated both laws and people to shame him and get what their hearts wanted.

The Creator yielded to the blindness and brokenness of humanity, to us at our worst, so he could heal the very hands, minds, hearts, and wills that were trying to end his life.

In Jesus, the utter darkness of the human condition is bound to the immeasurable glory of the divine. The mystery reaches to the ultimate depth of human existence – for in Jesus, God has united himself to us *forever*. There now stands within the very circle of relationship that is the divine triune life a human being and, vicariously, all of humanity with him. This is not pop theory or a pie-in-the-sky promise. What has happened to Jesus has happened to the entire human race.

Dietrich Bonhoeffer said it this way – "Jesus is not *a* man. He is man. What happens to him happens to human beings. It happens to all and therefore to us. The name of Jesus embraces in itself the whole of humanity and the whole of God."[56]

The mystery of the Incarnation is unfathomable, far beyond all human understanding. What these words are trying to express is infinitely more beautiful than our description of it. It is impossibly and utterly staggering to our senses when we unplug from whatever technology has captivated us and meditate in these thoughts. And when we do, the eyes of our heart are enlightened, and we behold his incomparable beauty. It may be that we see "through a glass darkly," but that glimpse is enough to satisfy our deepest longings and sustain us through our darkest days. For even the briefest glance will take our breath away as we hear the Spirit call to our spirit, saying, "We are your home."

---

56 Dietrich Bonhoeffer, *Dietrich Bonhoeffer Works Vol. 6- Ethics*, (Fortress Press, Minneapolis, MN 2009) 84–85.

CHAPTER 14

JESUS – THE ONE AND ONLY

*Our longing desires can no more exhaust
the fullness of the treasures of the Godhead,
than our imagination can touch their measure.*

— George MacDonald

Every culture has its idols. Many who studied during my era gathered at the feet of the god called Reason. Education was our road to salvation. As we bowed ever lower to rationality, avoiding any attempts to consider matters of the heart, our minds were crushed by what only our hearts could carry. Our relationships withered, suffering such tragedy that we, as a society, became increasingly distant and detached from one another, leaving us with scorched lives and an unfulfilled thirst for meaning and significance. Many mistakenly blame technology. It is not the cause of our ever-increasing dilemma; it has only exacerbated it.

Sadly, faith and spirituality became irrelevant, in a polite sort of way, as even our theology was seduced to follow only Reason as a god worthy of our devotion. Our imagination was crippled as our understanding of who God is was trapped in a logjam of previously assumed metaphysical categories.

Considering the soil where my thoughts took root, it is no surprise that my spiritual journey started as an intellectual one. But as old categories fell like dominoes I began to hear freedom's song and I willingly submitted to its enchanting melody. I found not an escape from reason but the submission of it to Jesus.

The journey you've been reading about has led me to here, and what follows is from my heart. My understanding of Jesus has gripped me, unlike before, in ways I struggle to articulate. Though my words are inadequate, I gladly yield to the Spirit's embrace and follow her into a wonder beyond wonder – the staggering beauty of the Incarnation of the Eternal Word.

Immanuel – God with Us

The cosmic drama of the Incarnation began when a middle-eastern teen-age girl consented to bear in her body the One who is above all things.

The God who transcends all time and space, who cannot be contained in the highest of heavens, willingly limited himself within the boundaries of time and space to abide in the womb of this inconspicuous and unassuming adolescent.

In an instant, the Giver of Life became utterly dependent on a life he created, the life of this trembling peasant girl. And for nine months, she carried and sustained the One who carries and sustains the universe.

It was the Eternal Son who descended to miraculously take up residence within Mary's womb – the One who handcrafted men and women from the earth and lovingly bestowed his breath into our lifeless humanity – *this* One was now as helpless and frail as every one of us.

What could possibly motivate the mind and heart of God that he would willingly submit to the helplessness of humanity, growing as a fetus within a womb?

As a newborn infant, God's descent continued; for the One who is the Word that spoke all things into being made himself speechless.

Mary And Her Baby

All drawings in this chapter by Scott Poole

Wrapped in modest, peasant cloth by hands he knit and held together he lay in a feed box bewildered and astonished by the world outside the warmth and safety of his mother's womb. His infant cooing was abbreviated only by gulping for air that he created.

This descent was not merely that of the Creator taking on the temporal and spatial limitations of his creatures, as if that isn't baffling enough; it is infinitely more mystifying in its absurdity.

The One who exists in unrestrained joy and freedom became a creature subject to necessity, subject to the very laws he designed to order the universe – gravity, hunger, breath, movement.

But that is not all. In becoming fully human, God, in whom there is no darkness, stood at the bottom of our abyss, becoming subject to the evil that those who bear his image do – slander, jealousy, violence, betrayal, murder.

The One whose glory graces the farthest end of the galaxy needed no recognition or status to authenticate his coming. Instead, he arrived in anonymity. Other than Mary and Joseph and maybe a small group of strangers gathered in a humble room, he had no family, no relatives, no friends, and no celebration to welcome him into our midst.

The entire universe watched in stunned silence, transfixed by humility, astonished by love.

What has humanity done with this extraordinary, inconceivable series of events? Some acknowledge this birth with routine indifference, like what a horse may give to a passing barnyard fly. Many have bastardized his birthday as an opportunity to turn a profit, not unlike a time two thousand years ago when merchants profaned his temple. Still others, sensing something remarkable has happened, turn to what is meaningful and celebrate family and relationships. But even this falls short – reducing his birth to merely the romanticized sentiment of a good life. And then there are some who cherish this sacred season with wonder and awe along with a deep, profound sense of joy celebrating the day God visited this planet and became one of us. And we all call it Christmas.

This past December, our little tribe attended a Christmas Eve event at church, and we sang some familiar and obligatory Christmas songs. The predictability of the event lured me into the quicksand of apathy. However, we ended by singing "O Holy Night," and we repeated the first verse a cappella. It was beautiful. When we sang together, we recited words that strained to touch the heavens. Words that – ever so faintly – begin to encounter this amazing and stunning reality.

> O Holy night, the stars are brightly shining
>
> It is the night of our dear Savior's birth
>
> Long lay the world in sin and error pining
>
> Till he appeared and the soul felt its worth.

On that most beautiful and holy of nights a gift was given beyond our comprehension for the question of human worth was settled forever. The value of you, me, and every person since the beginning of time was emphatically declared to the farthest reaches of the universe. On this glorious day, the Creator became one of us and dignified all that it means to be human. And if that were all he did, this would be a remarkable gift.

But the truth goes far deeper than this. More than an act of profound affinity toward humankind, more than a radical identification with all that it means to be human, more than simply becoming one *of* us; in the Incarnation of the divine Son, God became one *with* us.

Our Creator took on flesh and bone and united himself to his creation. And by "us" I mean *everyone*. Every part of every one of us, every person ever conceived, all have been united to God in the Incarnation – *forever*.

This is beyond great. This is beyond any superlative we can use. Words cannot express the depth and width and height of such love.

I am astounded by the purity of such humility. I am silent before such unstoppable love. I am undone.

In the coming of this One, life as we know it is forever changed.

Life will never be the same.

The cosmos will never be the same.

God will never be the same.

All has been turned right side up, as it were, and we live not as mere spectators of this remarkable miracle but as participants, experiencing the stunning truth that our Creator has traversed the cosmos and all that is in it to fulfill the day when he would whisper love in our hearts and worth into our souls.

The beginning of the revelation of God is the birth of the eternal Word become flesh.

The Power of His Life

As he descended into the black hole of our darkness this newborn God, who owns everything, entered this world not in privilege or wealth but in poverty and would soon be marginalized, as his parents became immigrants seeking refuge from political tyranny.

Our hearts and minds reel at the impossible irony laid before us as the One who fashioned what human *is* absorbs all the complexities of being human as he *learns* from his creatures how to live as a creature.

As a child, the Word who speaks life into being learned speech.

His young mother wiped tears from the face of the One who shepherds her soul.

Walking On Water

The One whose being *is* relationship learned how to relate as one of us.

The Designer and Sustainer of every cell of our bodies learned personal hygiene.

This seeming absurdity continued, for, without condemnation, rebellion, or any trace of selfishness, he continued to learn – culture, carpentry, fishing, how to build a fire…

He learned to navigate his emotions through rejection, ridicule, affirmation, and love.

He learned from his friends and siblings, who believed they were right, what is and what should never be, even learning obedience from loving parents who often failed to obey his Father.

The One who knows the deepest secrets of quantum physics and infinitely more, toiled and strained with earthly elements whose very atoms he holds together, working with wood, hammer, nail, and saw.

As the Incarnate Son lived out his divine sonship as a man, he grew in wisdom and stature, filling out what it means to be truly and fully human. And the conflict with our darkness intensified…

Despite the growing awareness of his mission here in his world, he patiently listened to the rabbis, who, in their arrogant blindness, misjudged his Father and said all manner of evil about him.

How often was he misunderstood, judged, and scoffed at by his neighbors and all those he held dear as he lovingly explained, that he must "be about his Father's business"?

As an adult, the One who is Light advanced into the darkness and illuminated the emptiness of our broken lives.

"God did not send his Son into the world to condemn it."

"Come to me, and I will give you rest."

"I am the Bread of Life."

"The Kingdom of God is here."

And the conflict escalated further with every miracle, every speech, every healing, every conversation.

The young rabbi who never entertained prejudice chose men who embraced prejudice as a way of life. These young brash men joined him on a journey that their wildest imaginations couldn't begin to grasp, and he smiled and entrusted them to his Father for their good.

A towel around his waist and a basin of water in his hands, the One whose power is measureless shunned all displays of coercive force by coming to us as a servant, revealing the true nature of power and strength.

Like a mother who tenderly holds the head of her sick child convulsing in violent spasms, he patiently, lovingly suffered the vomit that even his own followers spewed on his Father.

He instructed with clarity and virtue, out of the pureness of his being – and they wanted another meal.

He healed – some wondered, most scoffed.

He taught – some thirsted for more, most argued.

He revealed – some were amazed, many claimed he had a demon.

Love came to town, but his beloved was preoccupied, oblivious to his presence and bereft of anticipation, let alone a welcoming or loving embrace. Yet, his expectancy was always kind, true, and compassionate.

Some locked eyes with him and knew at that moment they were truer, healthier, and more whole than at any other moment of their lives, and they adored him.

With unwavering commitment to both his Father and us, the Son of Man descended steadily into the darkness that his creatures both love and fear. For over thirty years, he endured our pettiness, our rivalries, and our prejudices without ever partaking in them. But the darkness took his children's minds where minds were never meant to go – into deceit, abuse, torture, murder.

They schemed to blot his life from theirs, supposing they could free themselves from the One who is forever bound to them in inseparable union, even to the deepest part of their being.

They plotted to kill God.

The Day God Died

Without a word, *the* Word who speaks everything into being suffered treachery and betrayal of the worst kind – and called him *friend*.

And the entire cosmos shuddered at what was about to happen.

The perfect storm gathered under the blood-red sky. Perversion and corruption, torture and contempt, loathing and disgust joined together to unleash hell with violence so savage in its brutality that the cosmos recoiled in horror.

And the Lamb suffered in silence...

But the unbridled rage witnessed by the heavens served only to expose the desperation of the darkness to overcome the Light.

With every cruel punch, every vicious lash, the Light penetrated deeper into our twisted blindness and darkened nightmares, finalizing and sealing the union between God and the human race – even including his torturers.

Love moved inexorably forward conquering the darkness and

Crucifixion

healing a broken universe…

a twisted race…

Adam and Eve hiding in the bushes…

you and me trapped in our fear.

Drenched in his own blood and crushed beyond recognition, the ruthless scourging having ripped the flesh from his back, the Ancient of Days saw this coming long before we were ever made. And with each insult, each punch, each thorn, each lash of his Beloved Son, he applied the balm of his healing love deeper into our wounds.

And the Son descended even deeper…

Scandalized and seething with malevolence, the frenzied mob screamed for his blood, even while the One who is Love saw the absolute loveliness of the very ones who lusted for his death.

In fact, so loyal is his love for humanity it delivered a severity of wrath ferocious in its resolve to destroy all that was destroying his cherished children. And he gave his life to make it so.

The excruciating, gratuitous torture the Son of Man endured that day unmistakably and conclusively revealed that the God above all submitted to the most heinous evil his loved ones could imagine to inflict upon him.

The wounded God was nailed to a tree.

Gripped in unbearable agony, his body seized involuntarily, as wave upon wave of unrestrained hatred erupted out of hearts he treasures… that beat by his command. In mock sympathy, they violated the Bridegroom by offering him the bitter gall of his Beloved's infidelity.

And his heart and body were broken for us.

Sneering with contempt and hissing venom in their taunts, they mocked the One who is before all things, "Save yourself! If you are the Son of God, come down from the cross."

So other-centered is his love that even while bearing the scorn of his little ones, his heart broke, as did his silent suffering. Bordering on suffocation, the One who breathed life into everything, gasped for air and lovingly prayed, "Father, forgive them, for they do not know what they are doing."

And the Father already had.

The nails driven into his flesh banished any and all religious thought that would have us believe the God who creates and upholds the cosmos by love is in some other part of himself one who destroys. [57]

The divine community of self-giving love was neither surprised nor conflicted about what was happening.

We may be, but they were not.

Death was trying to kill Life.

Darkness was trying to extinguish the Light.

But the One who dreamed of our creation and spoke it into being did not falter.

The Eternal Three-in-One do not seek to merely pardon us; they *long to save us.*

The only thing God cares to destroy is sin.

Then the darkness, like a great tidal wave, gathered in one final

---

57 I borrowed this sentence, with his permission and blessing, from my friend, Kenneth Tanner.

attempt to overcome and extinguish the Light, and the Anointed One lurched with a cry so visceral the ground shuddered and swayed in horror.

Heartbreaking anguish surged from the depths of the Man of Sorrows as he arrived at the very bottom of our alienated human existence, confronting the full force of our hatred, suffering the despair of humankind's tortured blindness. The sky cracked open, and the heavens peeled away in shame as he cried, "My God, my God, why have you forsaken me?"

Darkness had unleashed its most terrifying weapon upon him, but the Light did not fail before the doubt. This was not the cry of a helpless victim overcome by fear for, immediately he trusts, "Father, into your hands I commit my spirit."

And with his last breath, Love was surrounding him and breathing the same air.

And it was *right there*, in his union with us at our worst, the Lover of our souls healed the souls that he loves. [58]

Our premeditated execution of the only true Innocent One is the shocking and definitive revelation of not only how horrendous our fallen chaos is but also how far his union has penetrated into the depths of our broken and twisted lives.

The disturbing nature and appalling extent of our darkness is surpassed only by the uncompromising determination of his relentless love. For he has graciously gone from deep to deeper, plummeting to the depths of the darkest spaces in our souls, where, in our complete blindness, we struck out in fury, pounding nails into his flesh and murdering the very One who is life and light to us.

---

58 "Then the disciples understood the passion of Christ, not as something for the holy but precisely for the sinner. It was their sin, their betrayal, their shame, their unworthiness, which became in the inexplicable love of God the material he laid hold of and turned into the bond that bound them to the crucified Messiah, to the salvation and love of God forever." T.F. Torrance, The Mediation of Christ, American ed. (Wm. B. Eerdmans, Grand Rapids, MI 1984) 43.

What kind of metaphysical juggling is it to frame the Incarnation – this staggering spectacle of love – into some mere cosmic judicial balancing of the scales? Does God command us to not murder and then murder his one and only beloved Son?

Nothing in the heart of the Living God needs to be appeased. Nothing.

But where is wrath and vengeance in this?

It is here – With determined, relentless love the Beloved Son overcomes our evil with his good by absorbing the hammer blows of our malice and draining the cup of our wrath utterly refusing to let darkness destroy us.

What did he do with our mutiny of rage and madness when he bore it in his body hanging on this tree?

Your friend has submitted to it, judged it, condemned it, and forgiven us – the ones who brought it to the table and gloried in such insanity.

Even more, and this is outrageously astonishing, he has used our very darkness as the means to bind us to himself forever.

Every... single... one of us.

This is the scandal of the Incarnation.

The Time Without Hope—Our Darkest Hour

Only the undying love of a mother and the duty of the one charged with her care would stay to witness the humiliation and final halting breaths of the Lord of heaven and earth.

If life is a song written with the melodies and harmonies of our relationships, his song was over...

Was there a chord still being played in the heart of Nicodemus (the one who requested a secret conversation with a young rabbi under the cover of night) that sang compassion or courage so that, now, he would prepare and lay to rest Jesus' body in Joseph of Arimathea's private tomb?

What notes were left in the hearts of his disciples? After spending years by his side witnessing miracles, hearing words of life, and experiencing a love so compelling they left everything to follow him, these men who knew him best had abandoned their teacher and friend in his greatest hour of need.

Their entire world had been devastated – their lives had been shattered – for all their hopes and dreams died with him. And now they hide in shame, besieged with fear.

Has anything changed since Adam?

What was going through their minds? Had they forgotten his words, which burned in their hearts when he spoke with them? What of the meal they shared just a few nights earlier?

Did they think the One who raised the dead could be destroyed by it?

Some tried in vain to return to their lives before they met him, but it wasn't the same.

Nothing would ever be the same.

Imagine the crushing weight of their shame and the overwhelming burden of their guilt.

Can you hear the insults from neighbors and relatives as they mocked these eleven foolish men?

Do you feel their humiliation? – The One who was their rabbi, friend, and Lord was betrayed by one of *them*.

Do you feel their anger? – The religious elite conspired against him. The Romans ruthlessly tortured and executed him. The people – who just a few days earlier had laid down palm branches with shouts of adoration adorning his entry into their city – they turned on him with vengeance, screaming for his death.

Do you feel the pain of their sadness and grief? – They feared they would never hear his laugh again. Never see his smile again. Never hear his words breathe life again. Oh, his words! Words like music that captured their hearts, that sang affirmation, "You belong to me." They would never see his gaze of love again. Oh, his eyes! Eyes of light that penetrated into their very souls and whispered, "You are safe with me."

Do you feel their bitterness? – Their teacher taught that death does not have the last word – he does.

But that day, death mocked them... their teacher was dead.

Do you feel their fear and hopelessness? – They disappeared behind closed doors. Religion won. The Romans won. Death won.

What saved these men and women?

Resurrection

Ever since the Garden of Eden, death has cast its shadow of terror across the hopes and dreams of a crippled race, enslaving humanity in a fear and bondage infinitely greater than the Romans. Like a contagious, incurable disease whose corruption is inescapable, death has spread from us to every living thing. For too long, we have endured in this shadow world of fear, where even our best and greatest are reduced to futility, as death always proclaims the end of all things.

But not that day.

For the men and women who followed this carpenter-be-

Resurrection

come-rabbi, the trauma of the last forty-eight hours left them hiding in misery, shocked and overwhelmed.

He was more than their teacher. He was their *friend*. He was their *Lord*.

Like a ferocious punch to the stomach, the unexpected abruptness of his death ripped their breath away, leaving them stunned and gasping for meaning. Muted desperation was thinly veiled behind closed doors and anxious questions.

How did this happen?

Why didn't anyone step forward to defend him?

Why didn't we?

For three women in particular, the wounds inflicted on their hearts by his death were too fresh for time to begin its mending. Their exhausted minds were still in triage; emotional numbness was their morphine. Life had lost its color, dissolving into a desolate, unearthly world of dull grey, where every effort to move was tedious, and the ashes of hopelessness darkened the air, permeating and choking everything. Days seemed like weeks as ever-present pain reminded them that fear lurked just beyond the next moment, threatening to capture and imprison their souls.

Supposing they could deaden the sting of their anguish, they looked for routine to replace the joy stolen by the cruelty of their Lord's death, wishing desperately that somehow a return to "normal" would distract them from their sorrow and the crushing weight of their grief. Routine might have come easily, normalcy… not so much.

So, they began the day like every other day, with a routine walk. But it was far from normal.

Preoccupied with the burden of loss they carried, they moved silently and slowly, more out of necessity than joy. Gone was the spring in their step. Their walk ended in the garden where the One who held all their hopes lay buried. They intended to add fresh spices for his body and maybe find solace lingering there.

How could they have possibly known this day would be unlike any day in the history of the human race? How could they have known that *everything* was about to change?

After the cataclysmic devastation of Adam's disobedience in the garden, how fitting that God would stage the coronation of love and life in *another garden*!

The dew was glistening like rare jewels on the garden landscape announcing the dawn of a new day.
The stillness hinted of peace approaching the eastern horizon.
As first light filtered through the morning air, the long shadows danced, celebrating the retreat of darkness.
Air that was fragrant with life gently stirred as birds joined the renewed chords singing to the rising of the Son.

His song wasn't over.

In *this* garden, fear and shame were banished. Hope was restored. Anger and bitterness, humiliation and pain were healed.

For the Son of Man had gone down into death, even allowing death to seize him, but it could not hold him. And through this very act he has shattered its grip on all things and has overthrown its dominion forever. Stripped of its power, death will never twist or steal the dreams of his beloved again.

The crucified God has risen!

Do you see those who knew him best now?

What happened to their shame and fear? Do you feel their courage? Who removed their humiliation and anger? Do you feel their strength?

Who healed their pain, grief, and bitterness? Do you feel their joy?

Who restored their courage and hope? Do you feel their love and passion?

The answer rests in the Risen One. They may have forsaken him, but he *had not forsaken them.*

He has, does, and always will see them in their absolute loveliness, for this is the nature of divine love.

Yet now when they beheld him, they began to see with the eyes of their heart, and slowly realized the truth of who he really is and *the truth of who they really are.*

After encountering their risen Lord, this band of broken and devastated brothers and sisters became a transformed and emboldened people. Like an unstoppable juggernaut, they bore witness to the One who rendered death powerless with such courage and conviction that it was said of them, "they turned the world upside down." Nothing less than the supernatural could cause such a radical change in these defeated men and women.

The resurrection of Jesus of Nazareth is not a hoax or the scheme of desperate men. It is no mere magic trick or grand illusion designed to deceive people. It is the decisive proof to the cosmos that the dream of the beautiful Three-in-One will not be denied. It proclaims emphatically that God's answer to the human dilemma is infinitely greater than our failures. It is the conclusive, irrefutable word that darkness can *never* overcome the Light.

Jesus's return from death is the declaration of our freedom. No longer imprisoned, cowering under the tyranny of death's shadow, we emerge from our sleep as one who awakes from a tortuous nightmare, never again to be subject to death's cruelty. For the resurrection announces that all of God's promises are indeed true and has established forever that the Word can be trusted.

No matter who accuses us, his resurrection is the indisputable witness that the message of the good news – "nothing can separate us from the love of God" – is unequivocally true for all. It dismisses all notions that there is any person beyond the reach of God's reconciling love.

When we sentenced God to death, the Ever-Gracious One pardoned us to immortality. All things are being made new through the power of his life, for in his resurrection we have been born anew into *his* life. This carpenter from Galilee has conquered our greatest fear and secured hope for every one of us by vanquishing death once and for all. Death is no more! Life is greater than death.

The real illusion is that we would believe this not to be so.

The Reunion

We have no record of what happened to Jesus after he ascended. We are told that after the resurrection he spent nearly six weeks with his disciples, teaching them about the kingdom of God, and then he departed. So, it shouldn't come as a surprise that it is often ignored as nothing more than an asterisk to the Incarnation. When was the last time you heard a sermon on the ascension?

But the ascension of Jesus is not some imaginary event tacked on at the end of the story to explain his disappearance from our planet. It is absolutely crucial for God and even more so to us.

From the beginning, the singular, unceasing constant of the cosmos has been and will always be *God*. And the wonder that reaches beyond wonder is this: God is entirely good and altogether lovely!

The Father, Son, and Spirit embody a perfection that staggers the imagination, a relationship of eternal, never-ending purity, passion,

Ascension

and integrity. The truth is, they are a continuous, eternal relationship of love one for the other. Their stunning beauty is immeasurably beyond the best descriptions of our greatest poets. All the best of what we aspire to be is what they are – and infinitely more.

But there was a moment (if we can speak like this) in which this unchangeable bond of being *became* something that from time eternal they were not. The Son willingly became flesh, and something of the Triune God's existence *changed*. Though the Son's relationship with the Father and Spirit never ceased to be, we read of his longing to return to be with Father and Spirit, as he had from the time before time. Yet, when he ascended, he "returned" different than when he left – for he is now and will forever remain the Incarnate God. This is a wonder that is simply beyond us… there is now and for all ages to come a man, fully human, in the circle of relationship that God is.

Our minds and hearts reel with the attempt to grasp at this utterly staggering and incomprehensible possibility that confronts us. And though it is difficult – even impossible – it is regrettably to *our loss* and probably our shame that we have all but erased the profound importance of this event from most of our conversations. His "home-going" is the decisive refutation of the notion that the mess of this world is the collateral damage to a divine plan gone bad.

This "reunion" of Father, Son, and Spirit; what do you think it was like?

Do you think the Father and Spirit were so preoccupied with the duties of deity that they barely noticed his return? Were they glad to be reunited but eager to get back to whatever "stuff" it is that God does?

No, I don't believe it.

I imagine his return was a joy inconceivable in its spectacle, far beyond anything any creature has ever witnessed. The breathtaking beauty and intimacy that were revealed must have been astonishing, staggering the imagination of all who dwell in heaven.

But most of all, the outpouring of undiluted love between these three may have been the most unique and precious exchange ever to have emerged from the beginning.

If there ever was a party, this was it, yes?

Why? Why would I imagine this?

Because this was the homecoming of the eternal Son who had gone into the "far country."[59]

It is the celebration of the Lamb, the Lion from the tribe of Judah, who returns to "take his place again" in the circle of the community we call God. It is the reunion of triumphant joy that declares to all of heaven and earth that Jesus "did all that the Father gave me to do"[60] and "he has reconciled all things in heaven and earth"[61] and has "made (the Father) known to them and will continue to make him known."[62]

The ascension is the conclusive act of the Word become flesh, finalizing all that Jesus accomplished in the reconciling of the cosmos. His seat at the right hand of the Father proves it to be true.[63]

And what gifts did he bring back from his journey into the far country?

He brought a reconciled cosmos – you, me, and everyone he created – back to his Father and Spirit.

His place at the Father's side is the steadfast, unwavering, unquestionable guarantee that we are included in the revelation of Love

---

59   See previous footnote 44. This is a phrase repeatedly used and applied most brilliantly to the Incarnation by Karl Barth.
60   John 17:4
61   Colossians 1:20
62   John 17:26
63   I would suggest this is the basis for the writer of Hebrews line of reasoning throughout his entire epistle.

that is the Incarnate One. He is seated in the place of honor, face to face with the Father he adores, in the Spirit. And we are right there with him.

So, if deity is united to humanity in the person of Jesus, how much of the human race is united?

Some? Many? Most? All?

Interestingly, I have never met a student of the Bible who doesn't believe that Adam's fall was passed on to *everyone*. Just ask them if they believe everyone has sinned.

If the fall of the human race is universal in Adam, and by this I mean that through one man, all humanity inherits Adam's status as a sinful person, then what is true of the human race in Jesus, the Incarnate Word of God? How much greater is humanity's union with Jesus than with Adam?[64]

The fascinating, even perplexing, irony of all my studies is that, for most of my life, I gave greater credibility and significance to our relationship to Adam, a mere man, than to Jesus, the God-man.

Furthermore, if the entire human race is united to Jesus, then we are where he is.

And where is he? He is in the circle of relationship that is God.

If so, where do you think every single human being is?

When he died, we all died.

When he rose, we all rose.

When he ascended to the right hand of the Father, we all ascended to the right hand of the Father.

---

64 I have in mind here a layered meaning in Paul's discussion found in his letter to the Romans, chapter 5:12–19. If the entire human race fell into ruin in Adam (a mere man), then how much more is the entire human race justified by the God-man Jesus?

This is not the privilege of a select few or the reward for a group of folks who jumped through the requisite religious hoops the correct way.

Jesus is the man for all humanity. What happened to him happened to us, and what became of him has become of us. His fate is our fate too.

This, my friends, is the *good news*.

How we respond to this is another question altogether. And it is an eternally essential question – for our response will determine our experience of what is real.

"Through his penetration into the perverted structures of human existence he reversed the process of corruption and more than made good what had been destroyed, for he has now anchored human nature in his own crucified and risen being, freely giving it participation in the fullness of God's grace and blessing embodied in him. Since he is the eternal Word of God by whom and through whom all things that are made are made, and in whom the whole universe of visible and invisible realities coheres and hangs together, and since in him divine and human natures are inseparably united, then the secret of every man, whether he believes or not, is bound up with Jesus for it is in him that human contingent existence has been grounded and secured."[65]

---

65 T.F. Torrance, The Trinitarian Faith (T. & T. CLARK LTD Edinburgh, 1988), 182–183.

CHAPTER 15

THIS PILGRIM'S PROGRESS

> *There is no fear in love. But perfect love drives out fear, because fear has to do with punishment.*
>
> — St. John

Recently, I was having some late night tacos at the Matador in Portland with Michael, a young friend of mine. I actually got to know Michael through his older brother Eric, who currently lives with his family in South Africa. Nearly every summer, when I was in the early stages of my career as a landscape nature photographer, Eric and I would backpack into some incredible wilderness destination somewhere in the western U.S. or Canada. I remember with fondness the amazing adventures we shared.

Of course, on trips like these you are completely "unplugged" from any and all technology, which provides plenty of time for conversation – a *lot* of conversation. Our talks would often revolve around the amazing landscape we were experiencing and so, quite naturally, the conversation would eventually segue to the God we both believed had made all the beauty that we found ourselves in. Those were good times.

However, over the past four or five years it has been Michael, not Eric, who has engaged me in numerous conversations. Many of these have been strangely similar to my talks with his older brother, except my responses to him have been vastly different from those I gave Eric decades earlier.

Well, as we were feasting on our delicious tacos, Michael shared that he and Eric had a long conversation about the changes Michael has undergone in his thinking and believing…

I stopped eating momentarily, "So how did Eric respond?" I asked.

"Well, he basically just said, '*so what?*' He wasn't being belligerent or anything like that. It was more like, what difference does it make? What difference has it made in my life?"

"Good question", I said and I went back to my tacos.

And it is – it's a *really* good question.

Much of this book has often focused on the questions I asked during my journey because they were crucial; not only in the direction my journey took, but also in how I would evolve in the journey itself. And besides that, it seems I've always been driven by the "why" question.

Even though Eric's question isn't a "why" question, it, too, is essential. It may be nice that we think or believe differently about something or that we've learned something we didn't previously know, but if we haven't changed for the better then "so what?" Consequently, I'm not surprised that I get this question. But the frequency of the question has been unexpected. Maybe it's because most of us long for the "divine" in our lives – and we want it to *transform* us. I know I do.

So – how has this new perspective transformed me?

Years ago, early in my evolutionary process I was on a day trip driving to central Oregon with a friend. Kristin was on staff at the church I attended and we were looking to rent some homes for a "school of theology" I was putting together. It was late spring, I believe, and it had turned into a lovely day. Like one of those "I'm just grateful to be alive" sort of days, you know? Our morning had started in Portland where the weather was the usual overcast of dreary drizzle. More than occasionally, but less than typically, when you cross the mountains of the Cascade divide you break out of the monotone grey of western Oregon into the bright sunshine and blue skies of the rest of the state. This happened to be one of those days. By the time we cleared the dense forest of the western slope the skies had cleared and Mr. Sun greeted us with a warm "hello". It seemed fitting to listen to Jim Morrison's distinctive, visceral screams on "Break on Through (to the Other Side)" but I couldn't find the CD.

We had been steadily talking for ninety minutes about a variety of things when she asked me,

"John, how would you describe the changes you are going through"? She paused, "I mean, I know you are thinking differently but how has this affected *you*"?

Always one with a quick answer, I had nothing. I knew I was changing but I had never really tried to articulate it because no one had ever asked.

Stymied, I mumbled, "I'm thinking Kristin… not sure how to answer".

We both sat frozen in the moment, just gazing out the window at the beautiful landscape speeding by.

Seconds seemed like hours before I hesitantly offered, "Well, I really don't know if this is the right word Kristin, but it's the one that popped into my head and won't go away. The best word I can come up with is *freedom*. I feel free, which is weird because if you had asked me if I felt free a year ago I would have said 'yes'". I turned and smiled, "But this is definitely different. This is a freedom that is solid, unclouded, and… I just don't know how to describe it but it sure is *good*. I wouldn't give it up for anything in the world".

She smiled back, "I can tell".

Today, more than a decade later, if I were asked this question again I would still use the same word to describe my spiritual evolution. But as I have continued in this journey I have begun to identify and articulate with a little better clarity what I struggled to say to Kristin so long ago.

I'm not talking about financial freedom, political freedom, or freedom to choose how I live my life. Nor am I simply referring to freedom from oppression, injustice, or slavery. These are all freedoms, which for the most part, I currently enjoy. And I am profoundly grateful for all of them. But, I'm really not referring to any type of behavioral freedom at all.

I have more in mind – an *inner* freedom, one that is not controlled by external circumstances.

But to clarify further, I don't mean a freedom to live with authenticity or to simply "be myself". The problem with "being myself" is that "self" can be – well, candidly, not a very nice person. It is possible to be authentically mean or selfish, right? Often times my cry for freedom is simply an excuse to do whatever I want regardless of it's consequences or it's effects on others. That's really a freedom of ego, or what some might call the "false self". However, if what we mean by "myself" is referring to the *true me*, the one created by and in the image and likeness of the Father, Son, and Spirit, then freedom to "be myself" is very close to what I am trying to say.

The freedom I am referring to is freedom from *fear*.

Here's a simple, but I believe, revealing exercise to try sometime; take a day and keep track of what motivates you to be the way you are in relationships. For example, what influences me to make the choices I do? When I actually thought about this question I found that a staggering amount of my decisions were motivated by fear.

The fear of being misunderstood.
The fear of being left out.
The fear of not being liked or loved.
The fear of uncertainty.
And on and on they go…

Imagine – no longer living intimidated by the whispers of –
I am not good enough.
I am not loved.
I am not wanted.
I am not successful.
I am not smart.
I am not significant.
Etc. etc. etc… I think you get the point. [66]

Imagine living free from the fear of –
Death.
Eternity.
Punishment.
Shame.
Failure.
Suffering.
Rejection.
Betrayal.
Expectations.
Being abandoned.
Regret.
God.

---

[66] I would encourage you to listen to Dr. Baxter Kruger speak about the "I am nots". If you ever get the chance to hear him in person around this topic it is worth its weight in gold. If not, there is a free post that briefly touches on the subject entitled, Freedom To Be (Feb 2010) available at his website: www.perichoresis.org

Imagine living free from being a slave to questions like –
Will people like me if... ?
Will I be successful if... ?
Will I be accepted if... ?
Will my life matter if... ?
Will I go to heaven if... ?

Imagine living free of all your fears – living free to be who you really are.

On the other hand, I find it intriguing, almost enlightening, that when I think or do something I know is wrong I immediately find myself trapped again by the unholy trinity of fear, guilt, and shame.
Fear of getting caught.
Fear of being found out.
Fear of consequences.
Fear of judgment.
Is it any wonder we have invented a million ways to medicate in order to deaden our senses? Maybe what we're really trying to do is just turn the fear, pain, and shame *off*.

Why do we wrongly assume that callousness can protect us from fear? Do you really think it can?

Curiously, freedom from fear was not a completely foreign concept to me. There were many times I would experience small "tastes" of this freedom when I would be backpacking and photographing in the wilderness. For me, there was a joy and freedom being in the beauty of Nature that was intoxicating. It was as if the beauty of his artwork in creation had somehow unlocked a freedom within me that my theology was never able to touch. When this grandeur would confront me my theological perspectives would shrink, losing their voice to the overwhelming sense of Presence I experienced in the beauty that surrounded me. So much so, it made my life of theology seem like shackles that hobbled and imprisoned me. Beauty was *life* to me.

In fact, it was this love and delight of the beauty I found there that initially compelled me to leave teaching the Bible as a vocation and become a nature photographer. Years later I now know it was this beauty that allowed me to survive the decades of toxic food I regularly ate; meals of what I would now call bad theology. My experience in Nature kept the hope alive (which my theology would have surely killed) that communion with God was not only beautiful and real; it was actually possible. Today, I realize that nature photography was a lifeline that God in his kindness gave me – a lifeline that never let me go and eventually led me to discover the incomparable beauty of their Triune relationship.

In Paul Young's novel *The Shack* the character of Papa shares a profound truth with Mack using a bird as his object lesson. The punch line comes with loving authority as she gently explains, "Mack, pain has a way of clipping our wings and keeping us from being able to fly. And if left unresolved for very long, you can almost forget that you were ever created to fly in the first place."[67]

Fear clipped my wings.

And it was left unresolved long enough that I forgot my experiences in the wilderness – I forgot I was loved – I forgot who I was – I forgot I was meant to be free.

Jesus made this incredibly bold statement:
"You shall know the truth and the truth shall make you free".[68]

It's a rather well known statement that has been quoted by teachers, philosophers, authors, revolutionaries, emancipators, screenwriters, politicians, preachers, lawyers… pretty much everyone. Though

---

67 William P. Young, The Shack (Windblown Media, Newberry Park, CA, 2007), 97.
68 John 8:32

the statement is common, what we mean by it has as many possibilities as there are stars in the sky.

What do you think Jesus meant?

Well, I think there is a lot to that. Probably a multi layered answer for sure. Here are a couple of layers that occur to me.

Let's start with some things he *didn't* mean.

First, when Jesus said, "know the truth" I don't believe he was referring to knowing the correct information. Neither was he referring to knowing all the information. In fact, I don't believe he was referring to information at all.

I believe he was speaking of relational knowledge, that is knowing a person. I am aware that in the preceding sentence Jesus was talking about learners who follow his teachings. But what did he teach? Later in the same story he states that he is the truth and he is the life. And even later in the story we learn that knowing a person, specifically him and his Father, is eternal life. So I take this statement as a relational reality.

Second, don't think of this as something you need to do (get to know Jesus) and then Jesus will do something for you (set you free). Getting to know Jesus is not a task, goal, or hurdle you must jump in order to experience freedom. Relationship with God is not based in our performance.

Think of it more like this; it is actually in the process itself. As we are doing this – coming to know Jesus – we experience freedom. *The knowing is the freeing.*

Jesus lives in complete freedom. What does he fear? The nature of his life is freedom for this is the nature of the love relationship he is along with the Father and the Spirit. Their communion is the actual, personal, intimate, blessed experience of their union. For they are *in* one another, they are *one*.

Furthermore, since he is related to us[69] and we are related to him, there exists the real possibility that we can experience his life of freedom in our normal, everyday lives. Through the knowing of him we become increasingly aware of our participation in their communion so that it becomes our communion as well.

As I said earlier, this "knowing" is not an accumulation of information about him; it is a knowing in a relational sense so that his freedom becomes our freedom.

This is a mystery of the grandest kind. This is the mystery of how our union becomes communion or fellowship. We scarcely can comprehend it, much less explain it.

But whatever you do – don't fear it.

However, as wonderful and beautiful as freedom from fear is; it is only the result or fruit of something even greater.

Many would say that knowledge overcomes fear. But I wonder if we haven't short-circuited the truism of the proverb by stopping short of a greater reality. If we are speaking of knowledge as possessing accurate information, I'm afraid that won't fly. Oh, we all could recite stories of courage and bravery and point to examples of how knowledge has overcome fear and it would all be true.

But the best that information can do is only to *control* our fears. No amount of knowledge, even if it is completely accurate, has the power to destroy our fears; only love can do that.

God does not destroy our fears with his omniscience.

He destroys our fears for he met us in the flesh face to face. He came to win our love back.

He came so that we might know, really know in the deepest part of us, that we are loved and embraced – and we always will be.

---

69   ". . .in him we move and have our being." Acts 17:28 – This is a statement by St. Paul from his famous conversation with the Greek philosophers of Athens.

"There is no fear in love. But perfect love drives out fear."[70]
The community we call God is perfect love.
Perfect love breeds freedom.
Therefore, there is no fear in them.
Their life – the life of the Father, Son, and Spirit is the relationship in which we have been included.

And this, my friends, brings us back full-circle to where this story of my journey began.

My greatest fear, the one that was really like a foundation to so many others, was the fear of a god who appeared to me to be far more like a monster rather than the Father in whom no darkness dwells.

It was this fear that drove me to try and control my world.

Theology was my tool of choice. And like the plumber who tries to fix a faucet with a crowbar, controlling my life with theology was a complete disaster. I ended up making my problem even more of a mess. How did I do that? Simply – I twisted the pursuit of knowing God into learning information about God.

But meditating on the stunning mystery of the Incarnation is changing that.

For he is…

The light that gives sight to our blindness.
The peace that conquers our fears.
The joy that untwists our madness and insanity.
The kindness that transforms our hatred.
The forgiveness that reconciles an enemy into a friend.
The unceasing goodness that will never do less than his unwavering best for us.

---

[70] 1 John 4:18

The compassion that eradicates our prejudice.
The justice that will make all things right.
The balm that heals our hurt, pain, and abuse.
The wrath that says NO to our self-destruction.
The promise that never abandons.
The strength that never tires.
The parent that will never be impatient.
He is all these things, utterly and completely, for he is perfect love.

He is the truth that sets us free.

So, back to Eric's question of "so what – what difference has this made in my life?" I would respond that it has made all the difference in the world for me. The universe is no longer a scary place. I no longer live feeling like I've got to control all my outcomes or that I need to be right about all my beliefs. I have come to know the Lord of this Cosmos – and he is *good*. This isn't just information for me. I've actually experienced him and his goodness in my life.

This awareness is tethered to a real relationship with the Father, Son, and Spirit, who love us just the way we are but also love us too much to leave us there. To be grasped by this truth (which is to be grasped by them) has set in motion within me a freedom to respond to others that is healing my life. Coming to terms with the staggering, other-centered love of God expressed in the Incarnation and experiencing God as the *Triune* God, the God who acts in freedom for the other because he is love – this is Trinitarian freedom. It is this journey that has freed me from my fear of the monster.

And the freedom has stuck.

Obviously, there's an ongoing learning curve in being freed from self-preoccupation. But this process is continuing to grow with every passing day. I am learning to live in the embrace of their relationship and they are destroying my fears and healing the apathy and coldness of my heart. I can't tell you how *good* that is – it is beyond wonderful! Knowing I am one with them, even if I don't always feel like it, has brought me into a deeper, richer, and more consistent awareness of having communion with them. It is freeing me to love, to delight, to accept others, to be at peace, to be secure, to be a better husband and father, to work and play – freeing me to be all the Father, Son, and Spirit dreamed for me to be.

Not long ago a young man I mentor asked me what my spiritual goals were. The question caught me off guard. I've never been much of a "goal setter" and even less so now. It seems so task oriented. But in an effort to speak his language I thought about it for a bit and I gave him this:

My goal is to be completely free of fear so that every day, in every decision, life flows from a place within me where fear has no say in any of it.

This isn't just a goal for me – it's far more than that. It's a strong, intense desire, a response really, that seems to have no intention of leaving. It was initiated and shared with me, planted deep inside me by the tenacious, relentless love of the Spirit and frankly, I don't ever want to give up on it – for they will never give up on me.

I'd like to think that it is possible to live every day in such a way that my life really does authentically flow out of the truth of who I really am.

I suspect you do too.

AFTERWORD

by Brad Jersak

George Costanza: "God would never let me be successful. He'd kill me first. He'd never let me be happy."
Therapist: "I thought you didn't believe in God."
George: "I do for the bad things."

As fellow readers, we've just experienced John MacMurray's great pilgrimage. It's also likely that we've shared common waypoints along the path, bothered by similar niggling questions and invited to more generous vistas – viewpoints of a more gracious God and a more beautiful gospel.

Along the way, I would argue that with eloquence and precision, John has rightly diagnosed a persistent and pernicious disease that has infected the heart of Christian faith – indeed; it can be found tormenting those of any faith in every age. At key points, he rightly named this malicious malignancy for what it is: "the monster under my bed." That is, toxic images of God that not only haunt us from childhood, but as primal fears, end up driving us as individuals and societies.

Fr. Kenneth Tanner writes,

"*When we read the Bible with the church we learn that not every line of Scripture has equal weight in answering the question, "Who is God and what is God like?"*

We would have a very odd schizophrenic God if we took every line in the Bible as a literal revelation of the character and nature of God.

Athanasius wrote a work denouncing the projections and false images of God that ancient pagans worshipped. We need a new Athanasius to denounce the many idols of God that Christians worship when our God is divorced from God's self-revelation in the flesh of Jesus.[1]

When I read Fr. Tanner's challenge, I think of John MacMurray and the growing company of men and women arising in the spirit and power of St Athanasius.

In recent years, Pastor Brian Zahnd has challenged the popular Evangelical vision of God as wrathful and retributive (along with its wrath-appeasement views of the Cross) in his "Monster God" debates and articles. In an article titled "God is not a monster," Zahnd says,

"*There are monsters in this world, but the God who is Father, Son, and Holy Spirit is not one of them... The good news is that the God revealed in Christ does not belong to the category of Mars and Moloch, of Ares and Zeus. These are the false gods of our frightened and shame-laden imaginations. The Creator God, the One True God, is not vengeful and retributive like those gods of the primitive pantheon. In his triumph Jesus put these petty and vindictive gods out of business. It's only their fading ghosts that haunt us today.*"[2]

---

[1] Fr. Kenneth Tanner, "Read the Bible from Its Measure, the Word made Flesh," Clarion-Journal.com, Jan 20, 2018.
[2] Brian Zahnd, "God is Not a Monster," BrianZahnd.com, Oct 26, 2015.

A key moment in my evolution occurred when I first met Archbishop Lazar Puhalo at his Monastery in Dewdney, British Columbia. I remember expressing my doubts about the atonement theory I had inherited, confusing it with the gospel itself. I had learned it, taught it, preached it and wrote about it in my MA thesis, "The Nature of Christ's Suffering and Substitution." Abbot Lazar summarized my account something like this –

> "What you're telling me is that God is not simply free to forgive sin. For God to forgive us, He must first appease the demands of his own wrath by punishing his only Son in a child sacrifice. And to all who cannot accept this as true, God will consign them to the fires of hell for all eternity."

"Something like that," I replied. It sounded crass, but if I was honest, that about sums it up.

"I see your problem," the old sage said, looking eerily like Gandalf. "You don't worship Yahweh – you worship Molech."

Oddly, I didn't feel condemned at all. I felt liberated, because now I could in good conscience abandon the monster under my own bed. It's not that I literally worshiped Molech, but alongside my authentic love for Jesus Christ, I feared his Father truly was like Molech, demanding a child sacrifice and/or causing billions of others to "pass through the flames."

Intuitively, I knew God couldn't be like that, but if I were to reject the retributive caricature I had laminated onto Triune Love, I knew I'd be dismissed as one of those "Liberals." But here was hierarch in the Eastern Orthodox Church, a steward of early Christian dogma – of those saints who gave us the doctrines of the Trinity, the deity of Christ and who gathered the New Testament for us – assuring me that my intuitions, far from liberal, reflected faithfulness to the historic Christian vision of the Trinitarian God.

We call these foundational theologians "the church fathers and mothers." Their rejection of paganized images of God as perverse echoes through the centuries. For example, St. John Cassian warns,

And so as without horrible profanity these things cannot be understood literally of Him who is declared by the authority of Holy Scripture to be invisible, ineffable, incomprehensible, inestimable, simple, and uncompounded, so neither can the passion of anger and wrath be attributed to that unchangeable nature without monstrous blasphemy.[3]

He regards human projections of "avenging wrath" – a sin in Cassian's view – onto God as unworthy of God's nature (namely, immutable goodness) and indicative rather of one's own stricken conscience, tormented by fear of punishment. Cassian proposes that those who expect judgment will read God's justice, "with whatever kindness and gentleness it may be conducted, … to be the most savage wrath and vehement anger." He regards this fear – John's former fear and mine – as pathological.

So when we read in Scripture that God is angry, the fathers urge us to understand such expressions as metaphors describing the consequences of sin – and not to be understood as literal descriptions of God's disposition towards us. St. Ambrose of Milan explains it this way:

We read that the Lord was angry… These things are written that we may know the bitterness of our sins, whereby we have earned the Divine wrath. To such a degree had iniquity grown that God, Who by His nature cannot be moved by anger, or hatred, or any passion whatsoever, is represented as provoked to anger.[4]

---

3 *St. John Cassian, Institutes*, ch. 3.
4 *St Ambrose, From the Book upon Noah's Ark*, ch. 4.

In other words, "anger" is used to denote the outrageousness of sin, and not in fact the outrage of God. To mix up the two is understandable, but when attributed literally to God, also formally heretical.

We need to press this point, because the malignancy runs deep. St. John of Damascus, in a tome featuring the intimidating title, Exact Exposition of Orthodox Doctrine, claims that when it comes to the mystery of deity, not all things are understandable or "utterable."

Many of the things relating to God, therefore, that are dimly understood cannot be put into fitting terms, but on things above us we cannot do else than express ourselves according to our limited capacity; as, for instance, when we speak of God we use the terms sleep, and wrath, and regardlessness, hands, too, and feet, and such like expressions.[5]

Did you notice that? To his list of anthropomorphisms that cannot be imposed on a transcendent, divine and eternal Spirit – hands, feet and sleep – the Damascene adds wrath! In other words, God can no more be "wrathful" than he can fall asleep!

"But it's in the Bible!" Indeed, but then let us join the biblical authors in their cries to God – not only that he calm down, but that the One who neither slumbers nor sleeps should also wake up!

No, God cannot actually be aroused, neither from sleep nor to wrath, because he is immutable. That is, God is infinite and unwavering love.

"Every good and perfect gift [and only good and perfect gifts] is from above, and comes down from the Father of lights, with whom is no variableness, neither shadow nor turning," (James 1"17). Like Father, like Son, for Jesus Christ is "the same yesterday, today and

---

[5] St John of Damascus, *Exact Exposition of Orthodox Doctrine*, book 1, ch. 2.

forever" (Hebrews 13:8). This is the New Testament declaration of immutability.⁶

But since "God is love," this immutability has little in common with Arisototle's "unmoved mover" who made such an impression on the late scholastics of Catholicism – but only a millennium later. Rather, our heavenly Father is known by a "mercy that endures forever" and his "lovingkindness is everlasting."

Immutable love is a non-negotiable dogma of the Christian faith, because in his infinite love, our God is not fickle like Homer's pantheon of gods who might feign to love you, then turn on you at any moment, manipulate your death or sleep with your wife. And he's not like the monstrosity of Calvin's double-predestination, governing evil and foreordaining damnation "to his good pleasure," or Zwingli's God who inspires and causes sinners to sin, yet without sin in himself for doing so!

No! Simply, NO. Our God is always good, always for us, always toward us. Did not Christ say that the Father makes the sun rise and shine on the evil and on the good, and sends rain on the just and on the unjust" (Matt. 5:45), without discrimination. He is gracious, compassionate and merciful – "he is kind to the ungrateful and wicked" (Matt. 6:35).

Jesus said that. And so too, have the best of his theologians – including St Anthony the Great and John MacMurray of Portland. You've already read the insights of the latter. The former adds his "Amen," asserting that "to say God turns away from the wicked is the same as

---

6 For Open Theists who worry about so-called Greek thinking behind the doctrine, note that the doctrine appears most assertively in the two most "Jewish" letters of the New Testament. I think we see the influence of Philo of Alexandria here, who had already integrated Greek and Jewish thought beautifully prior to the writing of the New Testament.

to say that the sun hides itself from those who lose their sight."[7]

We ought then to ask, "But if God doesn't literally get angry or lash out in wrath and vengeance, does this mean he doesn't 'chastise' or 'judge' or 'correct'? Does grace mean anything goes?"

Of course not. But if this objection doesn't come up, then we've not preached the gospel of grace found in Paul's preaching and writing. Grace must be so radical and God must be so good that opponents must ask, "What then? Shall we go on sinning that grace may abound?" Paul of Tarsus and John of Oregon and St Isaac of Nineveh all respond, "May it never be! Don't be obtuse!" Readers can review Romans 6 for themselves, but allow me to offer you St Isaac's perspective here. He assures us that divine Love obviously chastises, but:

> God chastises with love, not for the sake of revenge – far be it! – but seeking to make whole His image. And He does not harbour wrath until a time when correction is no longer possible, for He does not seek vengeance for Himself. This is the aim of love. Love's chastisement is for correction, but it does not aim at retribution... The man who chooses to consider God as avenger, presuming that in this manner he bears witness to His justice, the same accuses Him as being bereft of goodness. Far be it that vengeance could ever be found in that Fountain of love and Ocean brimming with goodness!'[8]

For faithful biblicists who don't pay Isaac much heed, we recall the author of Hebrews 12:4-6 affirming the very same truth. The Father's corrections are restorative and proof of our sonship and daughterhood –

---

[7] St Anthony the Great, Philokalia, cited in s on Texts of the Saintly Life, 150.
[8] St Isaac of Nineveh, The Spiritual World of St Isaac the Syrian. <http://www.syriacstudies.com/2013/12/04/st-isaac-the-syrian-a-theologian-of-love-and-mercy-bishop-hilarion-alfeyev>.

In your struggle against sin, you have not yet resisted to the point of shedding your blood. And have you completely forgotten this word of encouragement that addresses you as a father addresses his son? It says,

"My son, do not make light of the Lord's discipline, and do not lose heart when he rebukes you, because the Lord disciplines the one he loves, and he chastens everyone he accepts as his son.

Endure hardship as discipline; God is treating you as his children. For what children are not disciplined by their father?"

The question strikes me – why would he write this? It was because Hebrew Christians of the diaspora had experienced great pressure. In assuming their trials proved God was either a vindictive judge or a parent who abandoned them, they were tempted to give up and turn back. They needed to know that neither was the case: God is not punishing you and God hasn't left you. Whatever is going on, look for God's love at work – not causing the trials, but redeeming them for your good.

And this, it seems to me, is the pastoral destination of John MacMurray's amazing journey and his fatherly theology. God is a loving father – not a legalistic judge, not an avenging warrior, not a childhood night terror. Fathers discipline, monsters avenge. Fathers correct, monsters destroy. Jesus' God (and Jesus-as-God) is about restoration versus retribution, forgiveness versus vengeance.

Readers who've walked (or crawled) through dark valleys, shadowed by death's curse – those who've experienced tragedy and affliction and unthinkable loss – know how the Hebrews must have felt. When it hit the fan, where was God? If he's absent, then he's no better than a deadbeat dad, unreliable and unseen when we needed him most. Or worse, if he's present, he did this to me and he's a monster to be despised. Maybe he even came out from under the bed to devour all that I most loved.

Ken Tanner again –

"*Apostasy can be a good thing. To hear the gospel we first need to abandon the false gospels we were taught. Unlike the ancients, who had to unlearn their worship of idols, contemporary persons must reject the distorted projections of Christ with which we were raised.*"

To those who've felt these feelings or thought these thoughts – as the Psalmists so often do – the apostles, the fathers and John MacMurray all testify, No, God is good and all he does is goodness. "God is love" and love alone. "God is light and in him there is no darkness at all" (1 John 1:5). Through whatever we endure, God poured himself out into the world to co-suffer with us, to rescue us from them and/or redeem us through them. Christ came to reveal the Father as mercy alone and to become the means by which mercy has the final word. I appreciate how Fr. Richard Rohr sees this –

God walks with crucified people and thus reveals and "redeems" their plight as God's own. For them, God is not observing human suffering from a distance but is somehow in human suffering with us and for us. Such a God includes our suffering in the co-redemption of the world, as "all creation groans in one great act of giving birth" (Romans 8:22).[9]

If it is true that "mercy triumphs over judgment," (James 2:13) then the God who triumphs is forever mercy and not finally judgment. The sacrificial love of Christ did not triumph over the wrath of God the Father. Rather, the Incarnate image of the triune God – infinite love himself – has triumphed over every blasphemous image of the monster god… once and for all.

I'm grateful for John MacMurray's pilgrimage to this revelation and for his commitment to leading us there.

---

9 Fr Richard Rohr, "The Mystery of Suffering," Daily Meditations, Jan. 24, 2018

ACKNOWLEDGEMENTS

There is a movement happening, an ongoing conversation really, regarding a renewed vision of the Triune God seen in the face of Jesus of Nazareth. Just the other day a friend let me borrow *Sinners in the Hands of a Loving God* by Brian Zahnd. Within minutes I was reading a story that was eerily parallel to mine. Phrases I have said, thoughts I have pondered were splashed across the pages. Yet, I have never met Brian. I have never heard any of his sermons or talks. I have never seen him on YouTube. I have never read any of his books. But what has happened in his heart happened in mine. There *is* a movement happening…

A Spiritual Evolution is my contribution to the conversation – of which I am thrilled to be a part. It is obviously an autobiography of sorts. So it's no surprise that my individual journey has been the focus of this offering. After all, it's *my* story. Yet my story did not take place in a vacuum. We all are defined by our relationships and I am no different. I wish to express my gratitude to those who have contributed significantly to the book you now hold in your hands. Many did so sacrificially; all did so out of love for the message and me.

There are so many… how could there not be? Doesn't everyone you know have a hand in shaping who you are – even a little bit? It is difficult to know where to begin – and I will no doubt forget to thank somebody who probably deserves far more than just a mention of gratitude in the back of a book. Call it a premonition or just old age, but it will happen. So I offer a preemptive apology for any who may be hurt by my forgetfulness. It was not intentional.

To Robbie Foster and George Eischen, who gave me lodging free of distractions and provided me with a place of solitude so that I might get some writing done – thank you!

A hearty 'thank you' to my original "guinea pigs" – the M&M class – they were willing to hear me out in the beginning stages of my evolution. I hope you will continue to hear me. To my friends in Slovenia – you influenced me in the early years toward relationship. *Hvala*! To our small group that read through George MacDonald's *Unspoken Sermons* for about three years – Patrick, Emily, Torie, Jason, Julie, Brandon, Jenna, Zach, Erica, Dean, Tabitha, and Jesse – those were great and formative times! It was delightful.

To the students that have attended NW School of Theology – thank you for your listening hearts and inquisitive minds. To all those that have attended the Open Table Conferences – thank you for joining me in my journey. May we continue to explore in the years to come! To our little community that meets on Sunday evenings – thank you for continuing to travel together with me. I hope our lives are richer for it, I know mine is. To all those that have participated in the Gospel of John class that I teach year after year where I hammered out so many of these thoughts. Thank you. Your reception speaks to the power of this Good News.

I also want to thank those that contributed to the actual production of this book. To Kevin Miller, who at a considerable discount first edited the manuscript. To Don Woodward – who bugged me with the tenacity of a pesky mosquito to write this book. But he didn't just pester me; he did all the graphic design and layout so the book could actually be printed. *And* he introduced me to Mitch Frey, who did the cover art – which I think is killer! The famous Dutch artist MC Escher may have inspired him, but the work is his and it is original. To Scott Poole, whose incredible illustrations grace the chapter on the Incarnation. They are stunning! To my daughter Elle, who illustrated the Introduction and sketched me – making me look better than I really am. You (and the art) are amazing! To Jennifer Treadwell, who gave me a plan that made self-publishing less daunting and made me think it was actually possible.

Special thanks to Donald Miller, who was one of, if not the first person, to read the original drafts of the beginning chapters and offer this encouraging advice, "tell more stories John – more stories." I did. To Kenneth Tanner, who inspired me to write better. To Phil Carnuccio, who continues to hammer out with me the implications of a better view of Jesus. To Terry Jackson, who walked with me through much of the writing process – your consistent encouragement and willingness to talk and read with me, even though you didn't always agree, was the way I wish all conversations would go. You became my prototype "target audience". To Randy Thompson, my life long friend who is almost as excited about this book as me – Eyahr! Thanks for making me laugh and always having my back. Your thirst to know humbles me.

To those that have taught at School of Theology – Rick McKinley, Shaun Garman, Paul Metzger, Brad Harper, Donald Miller, Tony Kriz, Katie Skurja, Geordie Zeigler, and Roger Newell. You all have influenced my thinking in profound ways, especially Dr. Zeigler and Dr. Newell. Geordie's enthusiasm and comments along with Roger's encouragement and insightful questions to make this book better were a gift.

Sir Isaac Newton said, "If I have seen further than others, it is by standing upon the shoulders of giants." This is particularly true for me. Of those I never met but only read, several stand out beyond the rest – Athanasius, the brothers T.F. and J.B. Torrance, Karl Barth, John Sailhamer, C.S. Lewis, Robert Farrar Capon, and last but certainly not least, George MacDonald. Their writings sang to me with beauty and intelligence and beckoned me to know and be transformed.

There are three to whom I can quite literally say, "this book would never have come to exist without your influence and friendship." They have my deepest respect, steadfast love, and eternal gratitude. One wrote the Foreword, another wrote the Afterword, and the third I quote and reference in the book more than anyone else – even more than TF Torrance!

Paul and Baxter – I see you fingerprints all over this book. No doubt, others who know you will too. But more importantly I see your fingerprints on my life. Paul, from the day we first met in McMenamins and Baxter, from the evening I walked up the driveway to your crawfish boil in MS – I have treasured our friendship.

For over a decade we have heard each other speak, engaged in conversations, taught in conferences, seminars, and classrooms, exchanged emails, called and texted with each other so many times it seems like there are moments we think as one. We all can pretty much predict how the other will respond to a given question. I love doing life with you. May it continue as long as we have breath.

Brad – you were last to this particular fellowship, but the ease with which you immediately engaged us was amazing. But really, this is not a surprise. Your scholarship, kindness, and love for people washed over us like a cool breeze on a hot, humid day. I found in you a friend – an instant kindred spirit. You literally said to me standing in front of my garage, "You need to get you butt in gear and finish this book!" It was the proverbial weight that finally tipped the scales to get it done. Thank you.

I am a fortunate person, blessed in so many ways. Not the least are my three children.

Chris, you are the poet – you think deeply and feel strongly. I love that you want your life to bless others. I don't think I could ever be prouder of you, but then you do or say something and I discover that I am!

Elle, you are the artist – creativity and kindness merge in you – blessing any that know you. I love your sense of humor. You are precious beyond imagination!

Cassy, you are the explorer – determination and affection merge in you and you will shape the lives of many. I love your love of life. It is irresistibly contagious. You are a treasure that enriches my every moment.

I have no greater hope than this: May all three of you continue to know, for yourselves and your future children, the beauty and relentless love of the Father, Son, and Spirit.

And to my wife and best friend Terri – you are everything to me. This is yours as much as it is mine. I love you! Thank you from the bottom of my socks!

John MacMurray
April, 2018

THE AUTHOR, JOHN MACMURRAY

by Elle MacMurray

ABOUT THE AUTHOR

John MacMurray is the founder and director of the Northwest School of Theology and the Open Table Conferences. For more than a decade John served as an adjunct professor of Bible Literature at Multnomah University in Portland, Oregon. He has also taught Bible, Theology, and Photography for various schools and organizations internationally.

John is a landscape nature photographer who uses a large format camera and still shoots film. His images have appeared in *Sierra Club*, *National Geographic*, *Audubon*, and several other prestigious nature publications. He is the author and illustrator of *By Chance?* and *The Call of Creation*. John also co-authored a book, with best selling writer Donald Miller, entitled *To Own a Dragon* – now under the title *Father Fiction*.

John is married to Terri and they have 3 incredible children. They make their home just outside of Portland, Oregon.

www.johnmacmurray.com

Twitter: @john_macmurray

Open Table Conference

Open Table is a unique conference that provides space for authentic dialogue to explore questions about God, life, and spirituality. It is part of a relational movement – a growing awareness – that bows at wonder and mystery and delights in love and freedom. Hidden agendas do not fuel our conversation; rather it is the relentless love of God, like living waters filling the deepest spaces of our stories that we seek to engage.

www.opentableconference.com

Northwest School of Theology

A week together within a safe community of kindred learners is set amidst spectacular natural surroundings, offering the opportunity to explore questions of life and faith with a depth that is hard to match in the rhythms of daily life. Group size is limited to twenty participants and provides an environment that encourages genuine spiritual dialogue so that we are stimulated to think critically and act humbly.

Nationally recognized writers, speakers, and teachers join and lead us to examine familiar paradigms and integrate different perspectives. Personal access to these men and women is unparalleled.

For more information and how to enroll go to:

www.opentableconference.com

You can purchase A Spiritual Evolution here:
www.aspiritualevolution.com